Law and Society in Contemporary Cuba

Second Edition

Debra Evenson

KLUWER LAW INTERNATIONAL
THE HAGUE / LONDON / NEW YORK

Published by:
Kluwer Law International,
P.O. Box 85889, 2508 CN The Hague, The Netherlands
sales@kluwerlaw.com
http://www.kluwerlaw.com

Sold and distributed in North, Central and South America by:
Aspen Publishers, Inc.
7201 McKinney Circle, Frederick, MD 21704, USA

Sold and distributed in all other countries by:
Turpin Distribution Services Limited
Blackhorse Road, Letchworth, Herts.,
SG6 1HN, United Kingdom

A C.I.P Catalogue record for this book is available from the Library of Congress.

Printed on acid-free paper

ISBN 90-411-2165-X

Printed and bound by Antony Rowe Ltd, Eastbourne

For my mother

CONTENTS

PREFACE TO THE SECOND EDITION

Without doubt a significant transition has taken place in Cuba since the first edition of this book was published in 1994, but not a transition to a multi-party, free market system as many outsiders predicted. Internal reforms are converting the centralized economic model patterned after that of the former Soviet bloc to one that maintains national government control of macro economic policy while introducing decentralized decision-making and management at the macro or enterprise level. These measures and others that employ some market mechanisms are not moving Cuba towards a free market economy based on private enterprise. To the contrary, the unaltered objective has been to preserve the fundamental principles of socialism and to create a new model suitable to Cuba. To underscore that commitment, in June 2002, the Cuban Constitution was amended to make its socialist system irrevocable.

Although some measures have introduced new private actors into the economy, the primary emphasis has been on reforming internal economic structures and mechanisms. State enterprises, reorganized and stripped of subsidies, are compelled to become self-managing and made self-financing. Greater decentralization of management has had repercussions for management/labor relations. The banking system has been restructured, and a tax system introduced for the first time since the revolution. In the "private" sphere, the 1995 Foreign Investment Law expanded the areas of foreign investment and created new forms of foreign participation. Moreover, the government has broken up large state owned farms and formed new cooperatives, distributed many small parcels to individual farmers and expanded the area of self-employment and other private economic activity.

Reform of Cuban socialism has meant a constant flow of new legislation and regulations, particularly in the area of economic and commercial law. The task has not been easy. While economists have worked overtime to draft plans for a sustainable socialist economy, lawyers and legal academics have raced to learn new areas of law and to develop the knowledge and skills needed for Cuba's insertion into the global economy. Much has been accomplished since 1994; yet, much remains to be done. The present edition of *Law and Society in Contemporary Cuba* includes substantial new material on the legal developments supporting economic reforms through 2002, and explores the process of retooling of the legal profession to confront the changed circumstances.

Moreover, the economic crisis and the measures taken to bring about recovery have had a dramatic impact on Cuban society. Although no single legal measure caused or could remedy each consequence, new laws and regulations have had both negative and positive aspects. For example, the introduction of a parallel dollar economy to provide critically needed hard currency has forced Cubans to accept the social consequences of a certain degree of economic inequality not present prior to 1993. In addition, criminal activity, particularly thefts, increased significantly and new forms of delinquent behavior reappeared that had been virtually eradicated decades earlier, such as prostitution, drug trafficking and various types of "white collar" crime. In response, both substantive and procedural laws have been amended to confront new kinds of crime and to modernize the criminal justice system.

Not every reform has had to do with adjustments to the economic crisis and the new international context in which Cuba finds itself. A new environmental law was adopted in 1977. Important reforms of the judicial system and intellectual property laws simply emerged as part of the ongoing process of modernization and improvement begun in the 1980s. Indeed, every area of Cuban law has been the subject of analysis and reform, including the role of law itself. Important new laws are being drafted as this book goes to press including a new labor code and a new code of civil procedure.

As it has for over 40 years, United States maintains an aggressively hostile policy towards Cuba that distorts the island's economic, social and political development. Discussion of the embargo is beyond the scope of this book, but it significantly impedes Cuba's economic recovery, even if it is not a definitive factor. Similarly, implementation of programs that supply material support to internal dissidents for the purpose of undermining the socialist system have provoked protective measures in Cuba. As long as United States policy persists in having as its objective the undermining of the Cuban socialist system and the destabilization of the Cuban government, it will continue to circumscribe developments.

The question that continues to weigh on everyone's mind is what will happen in Cuba when Fidel Castro is no longer the Commander in Chief. This book does not attempt to make any predictions. Although the central role of Fidel Castro to the Cuban revolution cannot be overstated, socialism in Cuba has tracks deeper than the imprint of one man regardless of the magnitude of his stature. The legal reforms of the past decade may provide the basis to sustain Cuba's socialist system as well as its social achievments. If the economic transition is successful, so may be the renovation of leadership.

PREFACE TO THE FIRST EDITION

For more than ten years I have traveled to Cuba to learn something about the concept, function and content of law in the Cuban revolution and to understand the role of jurists, in all the many facets of that term, in the process. I found, of course, that my inquiry raised many more questions than could be answered, questions that have taken on more profound meaning since 1989 when Cuba was challenged by international events to either reinvent its socialist system or give it up. As I write, Cuba has accelerated the pace of reform and experimentation under the pressures of both a dire economic situation, which is deepened by the aggressive hostility of the United States, and a natural disaster, which flooded large portions of the island in March 1993.

Speculation abounds that the Cuban economy will soon collapse, sweeping away the revolution and its leader, Fidel Castro. The assumption underlying these predictions is that the revolution is a confinable, definable object, personified by Castro himself. The premise not only dismisses more than thirty years of history, it also masks the inevitable complexities of the present situation and ignores the profound differences between the Cuban revolution and the former socialist systems of Eastern Europe. Without doubt, the Cuban revolution has made a distinct imprint on Cuban society. Just as aspects of the pre-revolution social and political order continue to echo in Cuban society, the transformations and achievements of the past three decades will resonate into the future.

For those like myself who are sympathetic with the humanistic goals of the revolution, the intensity of this critical moment itself suggests that the most important question is not simply whether the system will endure under the crushing pressure of events, but rather, what has a generation of revolution accomplished. What internal contradictions and failures have impeded the effort, and what lessons and achievements become the basis for future developments in Cuba and elsewhere? This book tries to address these questions and others by looking at the development of the Cuban legal system; that is, the evolution of the framework of law and legal process that establishes and regulates the complex interrelationships between the structures of the state and the collective and its individual members.

From well before the triumphant march into Havana in January 1959, the Cuban revolution was premised on egalitarian and humanistic goals:

racial and gender equality; equitable distribution of wealth including land reform; fulfillment of basic social rights to education, health care and housing; and the democratization of Cuban society. The measures employed to implement these goals were indeed radical, abruptly dismantling the structures and tenets of bourgeois capitalism and replacing them with a socialist system based on Marxist philosophy. The socialist revolution would, in the words of Che Guevara, "create the new man." Yet, in the early years, there was no clear ideological construct defining these decisions. Although one of the first tasks was to bring to trial the collaborators of the previous regime who were responsible for torture, assassinations and other abuses, virtually no attention at all was paid to the legal system in general except to remove obstructive justices. Lawyers were considered at best unimportant and at worst parasites. The study of law itself was deliberately permitted to atrophy. By and large, law in the first decade of the revolution consisted of major enactments and hundreds of decrees authored by the revolutionary leadership that were intended to obliterate the old order and redraw the social, economic and political landscape. These dictates were legitimized by both the moral authority of the revolution itself and the popular fervor that ratified the process by enthusiastic participation.

It was not until the early 1970s that the leadership began to elaborate a juridical basis for the revolution that would both reflect its principles and direct the evolution of socialism in Cuba. This process, frequently called the "institutionalization" of the revolution, produced the 1976 Constitution as well as new codes to replace the old pre-revolutionary laws, which had been modified piecemeal to serve the revolution's objectives. Many institutional models were adapted from the Soviet Union and other socialist countries, but the Cuban versions reflected their own national character and frequently contained important innovations. Legislation, which was often presented for discussion directly with the population through its various organized sectors, was expressly seen as the primary instrument of social change required for the achievement of socialism. Laws were adopted that governed most facets of Cuban society including family relations, labor, criminal justice, housing and property, the judicial system, legal procedure and the legal profession, as well as economic and political organization. In the early 1980s, after the institutional structure had begun to mature and the impact of previous legislation could be assessed, a series of reforms began to take place to strengthen and improve the measures undertaken in the 1970s. By this time the legal profession had been rehabilitated and was emerging as an increasingly important participant in the process.

Since 1989, the sweeping transformations in the former socialist bloc countries and their adoption of free market economies have compelled Cuba to change its commercial relations with these former trading partners and to compete in the international market. It is inevitable, as its leaders acknowledge, that Cuba continue to adapt to this new economic context. At the same time, Cuba has responded to internal needs to broaden popular participation in its political system. Moreover, pragmatism obliges the leadership to concern itself with future political transition. Reforms as well as economic pressures engender new dynamics in Cuba, but whether these forces make Cuba's reversion to a capitalist system inescapable is still open to question. At the moment Cuba resists abandoning socialist principles.

At the heart of the revolutionary effort has been the attempt to create a system that would provide economic well-being based on the equitable distribution of resources as well as conditions for social and personal development. The revolution's impressive accomplishments in universal, free education and health care, gender and racial equality and in developing popular participation were unmatched in the eastern European socialist countries and remain unmatched in most of this hemisphere. These social and economic advances have taken root in the public consciousness as fundamental rights, some more deeply than others. Ideally, expansion of democratic participation would have also progressed, but space for political exercise remains limited by the present crisis as the government strives to survive without sacrificing its social achievements.

Resolution of the tension between the collective good and individual interests is a challenge in every society. In Cuba, the revolution's accomplishments have required collective commitment and the subordination of some measure of individual autonomy and freedoms. The equation is decidedly weighted toward the collective. Though certainly limited, however, individual autonomy and freedom have not been completely subsumed by collective prerogatives. The law establishes the right to due process, which is generally respected. Moreover, the benefits of the system, particularly in education and culture, have expanded opportunities for individual growth. An assessment of the experience of the past thirty-four years, however, requires consideration of how and where the balance has been struck.

This book is not specifically about human rights in Cuba, although any treatment of law inevitably is connected to the subject of human rights. It is not my purpose to either defend or condemn. It is undeniable that there are limitations on freedom of expression and political association of those who oppose the socialist system in Cuba today. But this does not make Cuban law a sham, and it certainly does not place Cuba among the most egregious violators of human rights in the hemisphere worthy of harsh sanctions. By attempting to present a broad view of law in Cuba, I hope that this book will provide a more useful perspective on human rights in Cuba, one that is proportionate to the seriousness of the rights limitations and one that illuminates the possibilities for full enjoyment of political, civil, social, economic and cultural rights.

From January 1, 1959, until today, Cuba has lived with both direct and indirect interference from the United States. Within a very short time after the triumph of the revolutionary forces, the United States armed counter-revolutionary movements, provided a base for air attacks, and sponsored the invasion at the Bay of Pigs in April 1961. Since then, the United States has continuously striven to destabilize Cuba's socialist government. These efforts have included infiltration by U.S. agents, assassination attempts against Fidel Castro, sabotage, a near total embargo on commerce and travel between Cuba and the United States and direct interference with Cuba's economic and diplomatic relations with the rest of the world. Although U.S. hostility does not explain everything that has occurred in Cuba, it has been an ever-present factor that cannot be ignored.

The U.S. embargo is not simply unilateral. Its extra-territorial reach has and continues to deprive Cuba both of opportunities to market goods to third countries and of the ability to make purchases from capitalist countries at prevailing market prices. The continuing embargo is largely responsible for today's severe shortages of food, medicine and other necessities, endangering the very lives of Cuban citizens, and it threatens to undo the achievements of the revolution. Moreover, the relentless hostility of the United States also succeeded in maintaining varied levels of tension internally. The Institute for Economic Research of JUCEPLAN (the central planning board of Cuba) estimates that the total economic cost of the embargo for the period 1960-1990 was approximately $38 billion. However, it is impossible to calculate the cost of U.S. hostility in political terms. It is plausible to project that the Cuban revolution might have developed very differently, both economically and politically, had the United States simply been neutral toward its existence.

The inspiration for this book came as a result of my first visit to Cuba in April 1982 – one month before the Reagan administration imposed restrictions on travel by U.S. citizens to Cuba. During that visit I met a number of provincial court judges as the result of a letter of introduction to Enrique Marimón, then a judge of the Cuban Supreme Court. During several hours of conversation, these judges explained the structure of the court system and patiently answered my many questions with impressive candor. One of the major concerns these judges voiced was the need to improve both the quality of Cuba's courts and the quality of its bar. In fact, they underscored the insufficient number of trained lawyers. I was intrigued by the challenge of developing an entirely new legal system to support a revolutionary agenda, and I decided to continue the inquiry.

My research has focused not only on the role of Fidel Castro but also on the many others whose work and ideas have influenced the development of law, the legal profession and legal institutions in Cuba. Fidel Castro is undoubtedly the single most important figure in the Cuban revolution, and he has exercised, and continues to exercise, considerable power and authority. Because of his stature he is often portrayed, both outside and inside Cuba, as the omnipotent leader who oversees all policy and legislative decisions. Although no major policy decision is made without Castro's approval, and he is known to sometimes intervene in even small matters, there are many individuals and institutions that have played significant roles in the development of the legal system and legislation in Cuba, and they will continue to do so in the future.

As a professional engaged in research on Cuba, I am among the few U.S. citizens exempted from the U.S. government ban on travel to Cuba, and I have taken advantage of that small opening to return to Cuba numerous times to study the transformation of the legal system. During these visits I interviewed scores of Cuban lawyers, scholars and officials and spent time studying the structure and function of Cuba's legal institutions. In addition, I attended innumerable conferences, symposia and seminars sponsored by Cuban institutions. The Cuban jurists and officials were extremely generous with their time and willingness to assist my project, and the librarians at the Library of the Supreme Court, the National Library and the National Union of Cuban Jurists offered invaluable assistance locating materials and documents.

Coincidentally, I embarked on my study at the same time that the Cuban legal system was undergoing profound reform, which enabled me to study both the changes in the law as well as the process of reform itself. Many important reforms have taken place just in the last year, including significant modifications to the 1976 Constitution. Some changes have been motivated by the pressing need to reorganize economic planning, to open up investment opportunities and to expand international trade. Others, such as the enactment of a new criminal code in 1987, are the product of several years of thoughtful analysis. Even in the midst of the current crisis, Cuba is moving toward very progressive reforms of its criminal procedure and continues to modernize its judicial system.

Because of the transformative mission of socialist law, each specific substantive area must be placed in its historic as well as its revolutionary context. Therefore, some information and concepts may be repeated to various degrees in several chapters of this book. After presenting a brief review of the legal history of Cuba prior to the revolution, the first chapter describes the transformation to socialist legality. Chapter two discusses the Cuban Constitution and the concepts of socialist democracy and individual and collective rights. Chapters three and four describe the development of the institutions and professions concerned with the implementation of law: the judicial system, the Office of the Attorney General, the Ministry of Justice and the legal profession. The remaining chapters analyze specific substantive issues and areas of law: equality, family law, criminal justice, private property and economic law.

Portions of the material in this book have been published previously, but because of the pace of change the material has been substantially updated. Moreover, since developing an understanding of the Cuban system is a process in itself, I have had to revise some of the analyses as well as the conclusions drawn in these earlier writings. To be sure, changes will continue to take place, and I expect that some details in this book will also soon be outdated. It is my hope, however, that this analysis of the development of legal norms and institutions in Cuba may give some insight into the direction of the Cuban revolution, past and present.

ACKNOWLEDGEMENTS

Many friends and colleagues gave their encouragement and support to this project. I owe special thanks to Dr. Ramón de la Cruz for his valuable assistance and commentary in the areas of criminal law and judicial reform; to Oscar Montoto Diaz for carefully tracking down and sifting through volumes of legislation; to Mercedes Estany for her patient and thorough research; to Gail Reed for providing her thoughtful insights; to the many Cuban lawyers, professors, judges and researches who gave so generously of their time and resources; and to the Office of the General Counsel, Sherritt International Corporation for the generous financial assistance which made the research for this revised and updated edition possible.

Debra Evenson

Chapter 1

TRANSFORMATION TO SOCIALISM

> [A] revolution consists in the first phase in the destruction of the unjust laws of the old society; there is no doubt that our revolution has been a destroyer of laws. More just laws, the new juridical order of the new society, that is what we are trying to create now.
>
> Fidel Castro, speech at Limonosev University, Moscow, May 21, 1963.

It was clear well before 1959 that the objectives of the Cuban revolutionary leadership went far beyond the defeat of Batista. The manifesto issued by the July 26th Movement outlined a radical social and economic program that would redistribute both wealth and power in Cuba.[1] Some have interpreted these pronouncements as reformist rather than Marxist and argue that implementation would not have required fundamental restructuring of property ownership and political institutions in Cuba. However, the inherent contradiction between fulfillment of this program and the constraints posed by private property rights should have been apparent to any observer who took the manifesto seriously. Such far-reaching reforms would inevitably collide with vested interests in the status quo. Perhaps foreseeing these obstacles, Castro predicted in 1953 that, in order to carry out a revolutionary program, the legislative, administrative and judicial powers would have to be put in the hands of the revolutionary forces: "A government acclaimed by the mass of rebel people would be vested with every power, everything necessary to proceed with the effective implementation of popular will and real justice."[2]

Indeed, once in power, the revolutionaries proceeded with breathtaking speed and determination. They promulgated hundreds of laws and decrees

---

[11] "Manifesto No. 1 del 26 de Julio al pueblo de Cuba," issued on August 8, 1955, from Mexico, called for the same radical reforms that Fidel Castro iterated in his famous defense speech at the 1953 Moncada trial, known as "History Will Absolve Me." These reforms included, among other things, the outlawing of *latifundio* (large landholdings) and redistribution of land to small farmers and laborers, worker participation in the profits of large, commercial and mining enterprises, drastic reduction in al rents, nationalization of public services (telephone, electricity and gas), extension of education and increases in pay to public employees. The manifesto is printed in English translation in *Revolutionary Struggle* (Cambridge, Mass: The MIT Press, 1972), Rolando E. Bonachea and Nelson P. Valdés, eds., pp. 259-271.

[2] Fidel Castro, *History Will Absolve Me* (New York: Center for Cuban Studies, undated), p. 25.

in the name of the masses of people who felt empowered by the victory and who cheered decisions that lowered rents, redistributed land and punished those who served the dictatorship. By the end of 1960, the socialist character of the revolution began to take shape, within a few years, the leadership had almost completely dismantled the old economic and political order.

The revolution dramatically affected the legal order as well. Swift, radical transformation could not be accomplished utilizing the existing law, which had served to legitimize and maintain the previous system. Similarly, since the legal profession, as well as the judiciary, was most likely to be aligned with the propertied interests, they were not to be trusted to support the transition. Lawyers in general were thought to be of little use, and those who had served the capitalist system were considered parasites. Moreover, the judicial system, virtually unaltered since independence from Spain, had never been either strong or autonomous, and it was notoriously corrupt.[3] Dishonest judges, as well as those who set themselves against the policies of the revolution, were purged. Many fled to Miami; a good number of lawyers, whose client base had evaporated with the nationalization of private enterprises, joined them.

Those jurists who stayed to support the revolution, however, were not prepared to fill the juridical void and to develop a coherent legal construct for the revolution. Only a handful were schooled in Marxism/Leninism or socialist philosophy. Although courses on Marxist theory were introduced into the law school curriculum in the 1960s, very few Cubans attended law school during this period.[4] Further, most trained lawyers left legal practice for administrative positions in the government.

It is not surprising, therefore, that during most of the 1960s little attention was paid to the development of a revolutionary theory of law. Although the means of production had been converted to social property, the process of developing a juridical framework to guide the transformation of society to socialism was not initiated until the late 1960s. It has taken decades to establish a credible judicial system, to produce a generation of competent lawyers, judges and legal scholars, and to develop a coherent legal order. The evolution of law has been marked by significant gains and success, but also by reversals and failures. In sum, the construction of the "new juridical order" has proved far more difficult than the "destruction of unjust laws."

---

[3] See Chapter 4.

[4] See Chapter 3.

I. A BRIEF LEGAL HISTORY

Cuba was the first important territory colonized by Spain in the western hemisphere, and it was the last to gain its independence. After years of armed struggle, the Cubans finally won their independence in 1898, only to find themselves under the rule of the United States which imposed a military government from 1899-1902. Rather than permit the Cubans to govern themselves, the United States assigned General Leonard Wood to oversee the establishment up of a new government. As a result, Cuba's legal system has dual origins. Its primary parentage is Spanish law and the European civil law tradition, but it reflects some aspects of U.S. law as well.

Even as Cuban patriots were fighting the war of independence, Spain continued to introduce new laws and codes, some of which remained in effect until well after independence and even after the revolution of 1959. For example, the Spanish Penal Code—the substantive criminal law—remained in effect and served as the basis for the 1936 Social Defense Code, which was not repealed until 1979; the Spanish Civil Code of 1889 remained in force until 1987, although with numerous modifications. The Cuban judicial system was also modeled after the Spanish system, with one important innovation—the creation of a court of constitutional review—which reflected U.S. influence. Further, the presidential system of government and the principle of the separation of powers, patterned after that of the United States, were incorporated in the first Constitution of the Republic adopted in 1901. United States jurisprudence also influenced the introduction of certain elements of criminal procedure, specifically protections for the accused, such as the right not to testify.

From the time it gained its independence to the time of the revolution in 1959, Cuba adopted four constitutions: 1901, 1934, 1935 and 1940. Each of these constitutions provided for representative government and liberal protection of individual rights, but none served to establish a stable, democratic system, and they were frequently amended and/or suspended in response to political pressures. For example, the Constitution of 1901 was suspended during the second U.S. military intervention from 1906 to 1909, and it was substantially amended in 1928. After the fall of the Machado dictatorship in 1933, the 1928 amendments were repealed and the 1901 Constitution reinstated. The second constitution, adopted in 1934, was amended twelve times before it was suspended in 1935 and ultimately replaced by another constitution later that same year.[5]

---

[5] For a history and the full texts of Cuba's constitutions before 1959, see Andrés M. Lazcano y Mazón, *Las Constituciones de Cuba* (Madrid: Ediciones Cultura Hispánica, 1952).

In 1940, as a result of public pressure, Cuba adopted yet another constitution. Hailed as one of the most progressive and modern in the hemisphere, the 1940 Constitution was drafted by a popularly elected constituent assembly that included a substantial number of delegates representing liberal and progressive constituencies, including the Communist Party. Indeed, it contained provisions giving rights to Cuban workers and women that have never obtained constitutional footing in the United States.[6]

The 1940 Constitution, however, failed to fulfill the aspirations of the liberal/progressive political forces that brought it about. First, many of its provisions remained empty promises because implementation required complementary legislation, which was never enacted by the legislature. Second, the governments elected in 1944 and 1948 were notoriously corrupt, and there was little or no public accountability. Corruption did not abate after Batista usurped power in 1952 either, and, in fact, the island became a haven for organized crime controlled by U.S. mafia figures. In sum, Cuba's political, judicial and legal institutions and processes, never acquired sufficient stability and legitimacy to have inspired popular respect and confidence.

José Martí, the intellectual and political leader of the nineteenth century independence movement that fought for liberation from Spain, espoused democratic ideals, which included principles of political freedom as well as social and economic justice. The ideas of Martí have had, and continue to have, strong influence in Cuban philosophy. Thus, within the framework of representative government formally established by Cuba's several constitutions, the democratic impulse enjoyed its moments of expression, but it was always overpowered by either corruption or authoritative regimes. Moreover, large sectors of Cuban society never truly participated in governance or politics. They were the working poor and the unemployed who survived at the margins of the political system.

The legitimacy of Cuban governments was also undermined by frequent U.S. intrusions on Cuban national sovereignty. In the early years of the republic, the United States intervened directly in Cuban affairs as a matter of legal prerogative derived from the infamous Platt Amendment.[7] Military

---

[6] For example, the 1940 Constitution prohibited gender discrimination (Art. 20) and contained a provision guaranteeing equal pay for equal work (Art. 62). It also guaranteed to each worker a one month vacation a year for each eleven months worked (Art. 67). Although extremely progressive, many of these provisions required implementing legislation that was never forthcoming.

[7] The Platt Amendment was attached to the Cuban Constitution as a result of a treaty between the United States and Cuba, signed in May 1903. The withdrawal of U.S. occupational forces from the island was conditioned on the Cuban acceptance of this amendment by which Cuba consented that "the United States may exercise the right to intervene for the preservation of

interventions occurred in 1906, 1912 and 1917. Direct interference was less important after the repeal of the amendment in 1934 because by then both the Cuban economy and the Cuban capitalist class were dependent on the United States. In 1958, Cuban trade was completely dominated by the United States which supported the Batista regime until the eve of his defeat. Needless to say, resentment toward U.S. domination runs deep in Cuban consciousness both before and after the Cuban revolution and has been a persistent theme in Cuban politics.

One of the banners under which the revolution was fought was the fulfillment of the principles of the 1940 Constitution. In many ways, the revolution made good on this promise although it never restored the prior structure of government. For example, the 1940 Constitution prohibited both racial and gender discrimination, but former governments neither enforced these provisions nor promoted equality. Although racial discrimination was a punishable offense, whether practiced by government or private individuals,[8] employers continued to discriminate freely without reproach, and many facilities remained off-limits to non-whites. Even Batista was denied admission to certain clubs because he was mulatto. In 1960, the revolution declared as two of its primary goals the achievement of racial and gender equality. Described in Chapter 5, the effort and results have been impressive, even if the project remains incomplete and imperfect in design. Further, the 1940 Constitution required abolition of *latifundio* (large landholding)[9] and restriction of foreign ownership of Cuban property.[10] It also recognized a public duty to improve public education[11] and to address the need for low-income housing,[12] but no action in these areas was forthcoming until after 1959.

Cuban independence, the maintenance of a government adequate for the protection of life, property, and individual liberty, and for discharging the obligations with respect to Cuba imposed by the Treaty of Paris on the United States." The amendment also imposed limitations on the Cuban government's ability to contract debt and prohibited Cuba from permitting any foreign power from having control of any portion of Cuba or use any portion for military purposes.

[8] Constitución de la República de Cuba (1940), Art. 20, *Gaceta Oficial,* No. 464, July 8, 1940.

[9] Ibid., Art. 90.

[10] Ibid.

[11] Ibid., Art. 51.

[12] Ibid., Art. 79.

II. THE FIRST YEARS

On January 1, 1959, neither Washington nor Cuba's propertied elite were capable of taking the lead after Batista's sudden departure, and they stood by virtually immobile as the revolutionary forces stepped into power buoyed by popular euphoria over the defeat of the dictatorship. Immediately, the revolutionary leaders began to assume control of political and legal institutions. A number of liberals, including some prominent lawyers, who had supported the overthrow of Batista in hopes of establishing a bourgeois democracy, joined the new government.

As previously agreed, Castro installed Manuel Urrutia Lleo, a former judge, as president on January 2, 1959. Urrutia had been chosen because of his prestige and acceptability to both the moderate middle-class backers of the revolution and to the guerrilla forces who took part in the alliance formed in Caracas in 1958.[13] In his brief tenure as president of Cuba, Urrutia presided over a cabinet comprising both prominent members of the middle-class who were moderates and members of Castro's July 26th Movement.[14] The moderates, including Urrutia, resisted the revolutionary program for reconstructing Cuba, but they were unable to pose an alternative or to solidify a base of support of their own. Fidel Castro and the revolutionary leadership had captured the hearts of the masses. Military and police power were in the hands of the revolutionaries. Thus, those expecting that defeat of Batista's tyranny would bring bourgeois democracy to Cuba were easily brushed aside by the tide of radical change. It is not surprising, therefore, that by mid-summer of 1959, many in the original cabinet, including President Urrutia, were gone.[15]

Yet, in the first six months of 1959, many fundamental legal changes took place with the approval of Urrutia and his supporters. Within weeks of Batista's abdication, the revolutionary government introduced

---

[13] Hugh Thomas, *Cuba: The Pursuit of Freedom* (New York: Harper & Row, 1971), p. 970. In 1957, as the presiding judge in the Santiago trial, Urrutia had dissented from the majority court decision to convict one hundred Castro supporters accused of sabotage. Urrutia argued that such actions against an unconstitutional government were justified. In December 1957, Urrutia went to Miami and joined a five-man government of Cuba in exile. Ibid., pp. 942, 970-91. Urrutia apparently was in little danger in Cuba even after voting against conviction of the rebels. Opponents of Batista had asked him to join the Miami group in November, but he stayed on until December in order to accrue his retirement benefits.

[14] Ibid., p. 1066.

[15] Ibid., pp. 1232-33, 1291-92. Although many members of the legal profession left Cuba in the 1960s, many also stayed and joined the revolutionary project. They went to work for economic institutions like the National Institute of Agrarian Reform and the National Bank. Others found positions in the Ministry of the Interior, the Ministry of Justice and the courts. See Chapter three.

comprehensive changes in Cuban law that radically altered Cuban society and politics and paved the way for consolidation of power in the hands of Fidel Castro and his supporters.[16] Although it reinstated much of the 1940 Constitution, the Fundamental Law of February 7, 1959 suspended the Congress and vested all legislative authority in the new Council of Ministers, which functioned under a prime minister appointed by the Council.[17] The first Prime Minister, José Miró Cardona, was also a political moderate and president of the Havana Bar Association. In addition, the Fundamental Law provided for the suspension of the non-removability of ministers and the judiciary.[18] These measures were signed by Urrutia and his associates, who also went along with postponement of elections that were to have taken place within six months.[19]

Controlled by the revolutionary leadership, the Council immediately set about transforming the social and economic order, enacting over one hundred new laws between 1959 and 1963. These laws included the first Agrarian Reform Law (May 1959), the Urban Reform Law (October 1960), the Nationalization Law (October 1960) which nationalized nearly every important private enterprise, the Nationalization of Education Law (June 1961) and the second Agrarian Reform Law (October 1963). In addition to this major legislation, the government issued hundreds of detailed decrees. In a formal sense, the government was very legalistic. No action was taken without first declaring a law, even if the law was modified numerous times as circumstances required. These decrees were in essence the dictates of a small elite, but their legitimacy emanated from the unfolding revolution that enjoyed massive popular support.

New institutional structures were established parallel to the existing ministries and the courts, giving Fidel Castro more flexibility to maneuver around the old bureaucratic structures. The most important of these was the National Institute of Agrarian Reform (INRA) which implemented land reform and agricultural policy. INRA enjoyed autonomy from the Council

---

[16] Failure to produce major institutional reform, as well as inability to wrest power from the military, led to reversal of the gains made by the provisional government which took power after Machado's fall. As a result of the liberal coalition which formed the new government, the more radical elements were isolated, and eventually the military under Fulgencio Batista re-established its control. Although some democratic reforms were instituted between 1934 and 1952, including the liberal Constitution of 1940, these were swept away by the military coup of 1952 which reinstalled Batista. Some of the radical student leaders in the 1933 revolt played important roles in the revolution that brought down Batista in 1959. For a discussion of the 1933 revolution, see Luís Aguilar, *Cuba 1933* (Ithaca, N.Y.: Cornell University Press, 1972).

[17] Ley Fundamental, Art. 119, *Gaceta Oficial*, Febraury 7, 1959.

[18] Ibid., Disposiciones Transitorias Adicionales, Quinta.

[19] Thomas, pp. 1084-1086.

of Ministers and had wide latitude for creative and flexible interpretation and application of the law. Osvaldo Dórticos Torrado, who succeeded Urrutia as president of the republic in July 1959, wrote in the first issue of *Cuba Socialista*, published in September 1961, that the INRA was created because the revolution needed a mechanism free of the obsolete, bureaucratic bottlenecks of the old system.[20]

In addition, the newly created Revolutionary Courts operated independently of and parallel to the ordinary courts. These special tribunals tried the hundreds of Batista collaborators who had committed acts of assassination, torture and other abuses. After July 1959, they were given jurisdiction to try those accused of counter-revolutionary activity. People's Courts were also established independent of the ordinary courts to hear local complaints and try misdemeanors. Although breaking with the pattern of existing, more traditional institutions, and infusing the system with a measure of popular justice, these innovations and others did not provide the basis for the development of an integrated, unified system of legal and government structures.

By the end of the decade the counter-revolution had been quelled. Armed attacks, terrorist bombings and acts of sabotage no longer posed a serious threat to security. Other factors, however, threatened the stability of the revolution: a faltering economy and a chaotic web of bureaucratic regulations and institutions. It became clear that the revolution could not simply rely on revolutionary zeal and sacrifice for its survival. The government had to define a coherent legal, economic and political framework that could provide direction and continuity for the aspiring socialist state. Further, growing dependence on the Soviet Union and Cuba's integration into the socialist market of eastern Europe governed by the Council on Mutual Economic Assistance (CMEA) necessitated the development of a centralized planning apparatus parallel to that of its new trading partners. Among other things, this meant the construction of a new juridical base, the creation of legal institutions and the production of lawyers and jurists trained to serve the socialist state. The era of radical experimentation came to an end, and the revolution looked to eastern Europe for stable models.

---

20 Osvaldo Dórticos Torrado, "Los Cambios Institucionales y Políticos de la Revolución Socialista Cubana," *Cuba Socialista*, No. 1, Sept. 1961, p. 29. The Institute's initial task was to carry out land expropriations that took place between 1959 and 1963. At the end of this phase INRA was converted into a state organ in charge of organizing, promoting and overseeing agricultural production. It also promoted socialist forms of farming such as the cooperatives and peoples' farms (granjas del pueblo), and it created the National Association of Small Farmers (ANAP). At first INRA functioned independently, but in 1962 when Cuba adopted its first national economic plan, INRA was integrated into the economic development of the country.

III. ELABORATING A SOCIALIST LEGAL ORDER

In the late 1960s the Central Committee of the Communist Party established the Commission on Juridical Studies to formulate the new legal framework. Chaired by Blas Roca Calderío, former general secretary of the pre-1959 Cuban Communist Party, this commission was composed of lawyers and academics who were trained under capitalism but who were committed to socialist doctrine. These jurists set out to rationalize the system and to create both the institutions and the legal tools for the transformation of society. Although the Cubans studied the legislation and experiences of the Soviet Union and the eastern European countries very closely, they did not simply copy them. In its legislation, institutions and legal procedures, the Cuban legal system exhibits a distinct national imprint as well as important innovations.

Over a six-year period, the commission studied every aspect of the juridical order. As a result of its work, several fundamental bodies of legislation were adopted, including the Cuban socialist Constitution of 1976, the Law on the Organization of the Judicial System, the Code of Criminal Procedure and the Family Code. This legislation was drafted by special commissions working both in coordination with the Cuban Communist Party and in consultation with mass organizations which had been created in the early 1960s, such as the Federation of Cuban Women (FMC), the Central Organization of Cuban Workers (CTC), the National Association of Small Farmers (ANAP), and the Committees for the Defense of the Revolution (CDRs).

Laxness about compliance with law had become epidemic, and recuperation of judicial process was considered essential to instill respect for and confidence in the law. Thus, the law on the judicial system itself was the first major piece of legislation to be drafted by these commissions, and it was adopted even before the constitution. The construction of a unified court system coincided with the adoption of a new Code of Criminal Procedure in 1973. Both developments contributed to greater fairness and consistency in criminal procedure, but development of a respectable, modern judicial system would take many years.

The process of institutionalization also included the restructuring of the legislative and administrative organs of government. The proposed structure of the Cuban socialist state approved at the First Congress of the Party in 1975, was set forth in the 1976 Constitution and subsequent legislation. The 1976 Constitution created Popular Assemblies (*Poder Popular*) at the municipal, provincial and national levels. Their creation marked the first time since the revolution that an elected body was formally given a role in governing the country. During the 1970s the government also laid the groundwork for the development of structures for the planning and management of the economy. Cuban jurists assert that the juridical foundation for these and subsequent measures rests on the concept of socialist legality, which defines the theoretical basis for the creation of the new society in Cuba.

IV. SOCIALIST LEGALITY

Far from being nihilistic or arbitrary in their attitude toward law, Cuban scholars were very concerned, on the one hand with interpreting and enriching the ideological framework and, on the other hand, with developing legal norms and procedures that not only were consistent with that framework but would contribute to the improvement of the socialist system. Legal theory, even if applied formalistically, has been central both to shaping the content of specific laws as well as to the evolution of a coherent doctrinal basis for the Cuban socialist state. This regard for socialist legal principle is expressly stated both in the constitution and other legislation.

Pursuant to the concept of socialist legality, law and government perform a positive, dynamic function in the creation of socialism. The objective of law is not only to regulate but rather to transform society. In the words of Lenin, "A law is a political instrument, it is political."[21] Thus, law is a tool to shape social behavior; it serves not to preserve the status quo but to provide the basis for the continuous evolution toward socialism.

In fulfilling its function, law must satisfy two potentially conflicting objectives essential to the transformation to socialism. Law must establish the basis for social stability, but it also must create the conditions for social development as well as for the continuous perfection of legislation itself. This dynamic quality of socialist legality represents a radical departure from the conservatism of the civil law system Cuba inherited from Spain. Civil law systems, based on detailed, lengthy codes, resist change as a matter of principle. As asserted by John H. Merryman, the civil law tradition elevated the value of certainty in the law "to the level of dogma."[22]

Even under U.S. common law tradition, in which law evolves through judicial interpretation, changes generally reflect custom or a consensus that

[21] "La Legalidad y la Cultura Jurídica en Cuba en la Etapa Actual," *Revista Jurídica*, No. 2, 1979, p. 4 (quoting Lenin).
[22] John Henry Merryman, *The Civil Law Tradition* (Stanford, Calif: Stanford University Press, 1985), p. 48.

has already emerged in society. Thus, in the United States and other industrialized countries, whose legal systems have evolved with the emergence of modern capitalism, law has been a stabilizing, regulating force that adjusts slowly to accommodate new circumstances. It functions both to enforce established norms and to resolve conflicts arising from these norms, but it rarely has the purpose of affirmatively changing society.

Like the evolution of common law, legislative reforms are not intended to significantly alter societal values. For example, the U.S. civil rights acts of the 1960s attempted to regulate behavior that impinged on accepted definitions of individual rights. The goal of these statutes was primarily to grant racial minorities and women the same formal rights enjoyed by white males, not to achieve substantive equality. Thus, in general, courts interpreted their provisions narrowly and imposed significant barriers to litigants seeking redress for discrimination.[23] When public institutions attempted to apply affirmative measures to remedy the historic impact of racial inequality—to bring about equality of results—conservative jurists and politicians acted to prevent an interpretation that would give law such a transformative role.[24] In contrast, the objective of law in socialist Cuba has been both to regulate and to transform.

In the process of developing a methodology for the development and implementation of socialist law, Cuban jurists struggled with the definition of socialist legality, an abstract expression that appears not only in the Constitution but also in other legislation. For example, the Constitution states that one of the primary roles of the courts is to "strengthen socialist legality,"[25] and the Office of the Attorney General (*Fiscalía*) is assigned to "enforce socialist legality."[26] The term connotes a distinction between "socialist legality" and what might be called "capitalist legality" beyond the difference in the substantive content of the laws of the respective systems. One such difference, of course, is the transformative function of socialist law.

One might conclude, as some Cuban jurists have, that socialist legality is coterminous with the content of socialist legislation.[27] Pursuant to such a narrow, formalistic concept, socialist legality would by definition

---

[23] Ibid.

[24] See, for example, *Regents of the Univ. of California* v. *Bakke*, 438 U.S. 265 (1978)(striking down the medical school's minority admissions program); *City of Richmond* v. *Crosan*, 488 U.S. 468 (1989)(striking down a minority set-aside program to promote minority-owned business).

[25] Constitución de la Republica de Cuba (1976), Art. 123(a), *Gaceta Oficial Ext.*, No.7, February 24, 1976.

[26] Ibid., Art. 130.

[27] "La Legalidad y la Cultura Jurídica en Cuba en la Etapa Actual," *Revista Jurídica*, No. 2, 1979, p. 4.

encompass any law or regulation promulgated by the socialist government. Some theorists, however, have considered this definition too limited and static. They argue for a broader principle that embraces not only the transformative content of law but the structures of enforcement and governance as well.[28] In the mid-1980s, the meaning of socialist legality was re-examined and given an even more inclusive definition that encompassed the very process by which the socialist system continues to transform itself, thus infusing the term with a juridical-political dynamic.[29] Understood in this way, socialist legality is more than just normative law that serves as an instrument to regulate society. It also includes the values and ethics according to which laws are evaluated and amended as well as the very method by which the state governs the society.

Accordingly, Cuban scholars have considered the constitution much more than a legal document. Dórticos, who became Minister of Justice in the late 1970s, asserted that socialist constitutions serve as dynamic agents in the evolution toward communism, an essential quality differentiating them from capitalist constitutions that preserve the status quo: "The Constitution in a socialist society is not just history which has taken place, but it is history which is still taking place."[30] By establishing the juridical organization of the state and society, the constitution also creates the conditions for the development of the social relations and objectives that are expressed in it.[31] In essence, it "creates the bases to propel the socialist society into the future."[32] Thus, while the constitution is foremost a legal document that establishes the norms for law and legislation, it also assumes a transformative mission that makes it a "transcendental" political document.[33]

Although a revolution is a process, not an event, Cuba attempted to design and implement a new legal order in less than two decades. The complex task of managing a socialist economy and mediating the social contradictions that emerged in the process of building socialism produced a permanent state of reassessment and reform. In the process, Cuba had to face more than one paradox. Consistent with Marxist theory and their own civil law tradition, Cuban jurists accepted the belief that law has a scientific basis. Yet the challenge of creating and applying new rules in untested

---

[28] Julio Fernández Bulté, "El Concepto Cientifico Ampliado de la Nueva Sociedad," *1er. Simposio Científico Acerca de la Política y la Ideología en sus Relaciones con el Derecho* (Havana: Ediciones Minjus, 1984), p. 4.
[29] Ibid.
[30] Osvaldo Dórticos Torrado, "Discurso Pronunciado en el Acto Central por el V Aniversario de la Constitución de la República," *Revista Cubana de Derecho*, No. 16, 1980, p. 6.
[31] Ibid., p. 7.
[32] Ibid.
[33] Ibid.

waters was daunting and required attention to the subjective aspects of law and its social impact. Further, there is an inherent tension between the need for stability and the drive to continuously perfect, but it is one that the state had to try to manage in order to generate a new society.

The response to changing circumstances since the late 1980s has resulted in minor adjustments, substantial alterations and at times complete reversal of established policy. For example, in 1987 the Cuban government substantially revised the Criminal Code it had adopted in 1979 and revised it again in early 1999. Cuba enacted a general housing law in 1984 that it repealed and replaced with a new statute in 1988. Farmers' markets, which were permitted to open in 1980, were closed in 1986 and reopened again in 1994.

The economic and political impact of the collapse of the Soviet Union and the socialist bloc in 1990 precipitated even more dramatic reforms. Cuba has introduced new forms of property and expanded legislation permitting foreign investments. It has also revised laws concerning private farms and cooperatives, and reorganized the judicial system a third time. Significant amendments to the Constitution in 1992 set the stage for further reform. Among the other changes that have taken place is the substantial reorganization of the Cuban banking system. A tax system was instituted in 1994 for the first time since the revolution. Other important legislative modifications are currently under consideration.

Although necessary to both correct past errors as well as to face current realities, reforms have created great uncertainty with negative effects on compliance: If the law changes from one day to the next, how can one be sure what it is today or what it will be tomorrow? The problem was highlighted in 1985 at the Third Party Congress, which approved a program of *rectificación* (correction) of the errors and deficiencies in the Cuban socialist system. According to one jurist, the Cuban legislative process has suffered from lack of systemization and coherence resulting from years of too much improvisation and spontaneity and too little research, analysis and planning.[34] Aggravating the problem, the pace of change since 1989 has left little time to study and to reflect on the reverberations of the measures in society. With few appropriate models to learn from, the tension created by the need to maintain stability in the face of rapid reform complicates the possibility of sustained conformity with and movement toward socialist goals.

The fit between theory and practice is rarely perfect in any system. In Cuba the gap has been hard to narrow because the theory itself is new and

---

34 Amado Guntin Guerra, "La Legalidad Socialista en el Proceso de Rectificación de Errores," *Revista Cubana de Derecho*, No. 34, 1988, pp. 145, 150.

unproven. Moreover, the experiments in eastern Europe, which served as a model for the Cuban system, failed and have been abandoned. In many ways the endeavor was also impeded by the formalistic nature both of the civil law tradition Cuba inherited from Spain as well as the bureaucratic mechanisms adopted from the former Soviet Union and other eastern European countries. Despite the constraints of this legacy and the want of alternative, theoretical and practical models, Cuba has nevertheless achieved significant progress in many areas of its legal system, and Cuban jurists have made important and interesting contributions to the development of socialist law. However, in order to continue to adhere to the basic premises of socialist theory regarding social and economic welfare and the role of the state in guiding the economy, Cuba must find new methods and approaches.

As socialist values stand in stark contradiction to the blind rules of the market, the inclination to allow pragmatism guide the development of legal norms is roundly rejected by Cuban jurists.[35] In a round table discussion published in the Cuban journal *Temas* in 1996, nine Cuban jurists debated the subject "What to expect of Law?" At the center of the debate lay the difficult challenge of introducing reforms in Cuban socialism in a social, economic and political context far more complex than that which prevailed during the first three decades of the revolution. Given the contemporary scenario, the ability to find and implement legislative solutions that preserve and further socialist principles becomes extremely difficult.

The debate among these nine distinguished jurists revealed a great divergence of opinion on the role of law in socialist Cuba today. In an effort to find a common thread in the debate, Narciso Cobo Roura, President of the Cuban Society of Economic and Finance Law, stated:

> If there is something that all of us, in one way or another, expect from the Law it is that Law should, given the transformations that we have awakened in the society, be capable of not only serving as an instrument of change, but at the same time embody the values and principles and contribute effectively to...the alternative ethical content that provides the possibility of a new paradigm corresponding to the aspirations of our social project.[36]

The search for this new paradigm is central to the survival of socialist law and the ethical values it embodies. Cuba continues to be the laboratory for this search.

---

[35] See, round table discussion published as "¿Qué esperar del Derecho?" in *Temas*, No. 8, 1996, pp. 80-94.
[36] Ibid., p. 85.

Chapter 2

DEMOCRACY AND RIGHTS

For years, the rationale relied upon by Cuba's detractors in the United States to justify economic sanctions intended to bring down Cuba's socialist government[1] is the lack of democracy and respect for individual rights. Much hostile propaganda produced since the 1980s portrays Cuba's socialist system as static and tyrannical. The Cuban Constitution is dismissed as not worth the paper it is printed on. For their part, Cuban officials argue that democracy in Cuba is superior to other systems and provides greater opportunities for popular participation. Further, they contend that individual rights should be understood differently in Cuba than in capitalist countries because of the social and economic rights guaranteed by socialism. At the core of the polemic are deep ideological differences. This chapter attempts to explore some of the key issues of debate: constitutionalism, democracy and rights.

I. THE CUBAN SOCIALIST CONSTITUTION

The 1976 Constitution was drafted by a commission appointed by the Party in 1974. Like the Family Code and other major legislation of the 1970s, it was circulated in draft form among all the mass organizations for discussion and recommendations. Although changes made as a result of these discussions were minor, the process played a very important role in educating the public to the content and implications of the socialist order

[1] A comprehensive economic embargo established by the United States in 1963 prohibited all commercial relations between the countries and interfered with Cuba's trade relations with third countries as well. In the 1990s, these economic sanctions were tightened successively by the Torricelli Bill of 1992 and the Helms-Burton law of 1996. Congress carved out an exception in 1988 allowing free trade in informational products, and in 2000 voted to permit sales of food and agricultural products, but imposed impediments to such sales by prohibiting any US source financing and credits.

embodied in the Constitution. The Constitution was approved in a special national referendum on February 15, 1976.

Content

The content of the Cuban Constitution is overtly ideological, but it is also juridical. It embraces the essential core of socialist legality in contemporary Cuban jurisprudence. Then Minister of Justice Osvaldo Dórticos Torrado commented on the fundamental role of the socialist constitution on the occasion of the fifth anniversary of its adoption:

> As a juridical instrument, a legal instrument, it is the principal form and source of expression of State Law. In effect, the State creates all norms basing them in the Constitution, which is the juridical support of all legislation. The constitutional norms condition all drafting and realization of state legislation and condition the legitimacy of laws. The constitution also establishes the basis of the life of the state.[2]

Consistent with this view of the affirmative role of the constitution to define the objectives and character of the society, the 1976 Constitution declared Cuba to be a "socialist state" and provided that the economic system be based on the social ownership of the means of production.[3]

Central to the constitutional scheme is the state's obligation to assure the economic and social well-being of the collective. Thus, the Constitution entrusts the state with the responsibility to organize and direct the national economy.[4] By virtue of its control over production and distribution, the state guarantees a great many positive social and economic rights to the citizens. These guarantees include the right to work, to leisure time and to vacations,[5] the right to social security protection.[6] the right to free health care[7] and the right to free education.[8] Accordingly, the state must manage

---

[2] Osvaldo Dórticos Torrado, "Discurso Pronunciado en el Acto Central por el V Aniversario de la Constitución de la República," *Revista Cubana de Derecho*, No. 16, 1980, p. 6.

[3] Constitución de la República de Cuba (1976), Arts. 1, 14, *Gaceta Oficial Ext.*, No. 7, February 24, 1976. The Constitution was amended in 1992, changing the enumeration of some articles. Where they differ, the article numbers corresponding to the Constitution as amended are in parenthesis.

[4] Ibid., Art. 16

[5] Ibid., Arts. 44-45 (45-46).

[6] Ibid., Art. 46 (47).

[7] Ibid., Art. 49 (50).

[8] Ibid., Art. 50 (51).

economic resources to assure fulfillment of these rights and the well-being of the collective.

Since egalitarian values are at the core of Cuban socialism, the 1976 Constitution also establishes both equality of rights and duties for all citizens and prohibits discrimination based on race, color, sex or national origin.[9] The state's obligation with respect to equality goes far beyond simply guaranteeing equality before the law. It must affirmatively "create all the conditions which help to make real the principle of equality" and to assure equal treatment,[10] including equal pay for equal work.[11] Special attention is given to the equality of women. Constitutional provisions accord women not only social, economic and political equality but also establish equality in family relations.[12] The Constitution also makes provision for individual liberties such as the right to freedom of speech and of the press "in keeping with the objectives of socialist society;"[13] the rights to assembly,[14] demonstration and association;[15] the right to petition authorities;[16] the right to freedom of conscience and religious belief;[17] and the rights to privacy of home and mail,[18] freedom from arbitrary arrest,[19] personal property, [20] due process of law[21] and other rights.

As the fundamental law governing society, the constitution also establishes the framework for political processes and governmental structure. It declares the Communist Party of Cuba "the highest leading force of the society and state, which organizes and guides the common effort toward the goals of the construction of socialism and progress toward a communist society."[22] Power to legislate, however, is vested in the National Assembly of Peoples Power [23] and its executive committee, the Council of State.[24] Administrative authority is conferred on the Council of Ministers.[25]

---

[9] Ibid., Arts. 40-41 (41-42). The latter provision was expanded in 1992 to prohibit discrimination based on religious belief and "any other motive harmful to human dignity." Art. 42.
[10] Ibid., Art. 42 (43).
[11] Ibid.
[12] Ibid., Art. 43 (44)
[13] Ibid., Art. 52 (53).
[14] Ibid., Art. 53 (54).
[15] Ibid.
[16] Ibid., Art. 62 (63).
[17] Ibid., Art. 54 (55).
[18] Ibid., Arts. 55-56 (56-57).
[19] Ibid., Art. 57 (58).
[20] Ibid., Art. 22 (21).
[21] Ibid., Art. 58 (59).
[22] Ibid., Art. 5.
[23] Ibid., Arts. 68, 73(b) (69, 75(b)).
[24] Ibid., Art. 88(c) (90(c)).
[25] Ibid., Arts. 93, 96(i) (95. 98).

When Cuban lawyers embarked on the project of developing the juridical base for the revolution, particularly the constitutional framework, they naturally depended greatly on contemporary socialist jurisprudence, particularly the works of Soviet legal scholars. Although the content of the Cuban Constitution of 1976 closely resembled the Soviet Constitution of 1977, sharing broad concepts and the same general structure of political institutions and organization of the state, the Cubans did not simply imitate. Methods of governance, procedures of implementation and the articulation of some rights were distinctly Cuban. For example, unlike the Soviet Constitution, the Cuban Constitution gave express recognition to social organizations such as the Central Organization of Cuban Workers (CTC), the Committees for the Defense of the Revolution (CDRs), the Federation of Cuban Women (FMC), the National Association of Small Farmers (ANAP), the Federation of University Students (FEU) and the Federation of Students of Intermediate Education (FEEM) and granted them a role in carrying out state policy. The difference suggests that from the beginning the Cubans intended to incorporate a higher level of popular participation in the development and implementation of policy. The Cuban Constitution also contains stronger provisions regarding equality, particularly that of women, than did the Soviet Constitution.

1992 Modifications

Faced with the need to integrate fully into the world market and to adjust to a new political and economic context, the Cuban government adopted significant modifications to the Constitution in July 1992. The result of more than two years of discussion and debate,[26] these amendments redefine some basic constitutional norms. The process began with public debates held in the spring and summer of 1990 pursuant to a broad call by the Party for broad popular discussion of the problems confronting the country in preparation for the Fourth Party Congress held in October 1991. Although discussions were not directed toward specific constitutional changes, opin-

---

[26] Susana Lee, "Report on the imminent debate of the modification to the constitution," *Granma*, June 9, 1992, p. 3. At the same time, a commission created by the Central Committee of the Party, headed by Carlos Rafael Rodríguez, worked together with a commission of the National Assembly to finalize the proposed modifications. The work involved frequent meetings and discussions of drafts in the capital and in the provinces as well. Copies of the final proposal were circulated among all the assembly delegates in early June, five to six weeks before the assembly was to meet. A number of amendments to the language of the provisions were made during the National Assembly debate.

ions and concerns raised during these debates found expression in the modifications adopted in 1992.

In order to allow greater flexibility in economic reforms, amendments qualified the socialist ownership of property to encompass the "fundamental means of production"[27] as opposed to simply "the means of production," as stated in the 1976 Constitution. Further, unlike the 1976 Constitution, the 1992 revisions expressly recognize certain forms of non-socialist property.[28] In addition, the amendments forbid discrimination on the basis of religious belief and guaranty freedom of religious belief and the separation of the state and religious institutions.[29] They also expanded popular participation by permitting direct election of both the National and Provincial Assemblies.[30] Previously, representatives to the National and Provincial Assemblies were elected by members of the municipal assemblies who had been chosen by direct elections.

Although the charter remains fundamentally the same as the document adopted in 1976, the modifications are far more than mere minor adjustments and have enormous transformative potential. Observers who characterized the changes as merely cosmetic because they did not signal rejection of socialism have missed their significance. It was never the intention to abandon socialism even if these amendments mark Cuba's abandonment of the Soviet model. Rather, the alteration in the economic and political dynamic embodied in these amendments creates the conditions for important reforms in the Cuban socialist system.

Amendment to Make Socialism Irrevocable

In June 2002, in response to perceived threats articulated by President Bush in a speech demanding Cuba convert to a free-enterprise economy with a multi-party political system,[31] the National Assembly adopted further

---

[27] Constitución de la República de Cuba (as modified on July 7, 1992), Art. 14.

[28] Ibid., Art. 23 ("The State recognizes the property of joint ventures, corporations and economic associations which are constituted in conformity with the law.")

[29] A new Article was added to the Constitution which states: "The State recognizes, respects and guarantees religious freedom. In the Republic of Cuba, religious institutions are separated from the State. The different beliefs and religions enjoy equal consideration." Ibid., Art. 8. For further discussion of these rights, see Chapter 5.

[30] Ibid. Arts. 71, 135.

[31] In a speech given in Miami on May 20, 2002 marking the 100th anniversary of the Cuban republic (the date of US withdrawal of its military occupation), President Bush opposed the momentum gathering in the US Congress to lift certain aspects of the Cuban embargo and reaffirmed his administration's policy of pressuring Cuba to abandon its socialist system. Bush's vitriolic critique of Cuba was also preceded by ominous and unfounded accusations

amendments to the Constitution that make central aspects irrevocable: the socialist economic, political and social system[32] A paragraph added to Article 3 of the Constitution reads:

> Socialism and the revolutionary political and social system established in this Constitution, proven by years of heroic resistance against all types of aggressions and economic war of the governments of the most powerful imperial power that has existed, and having demonstrated its capacity to transform the country and create an entirely new and just society, is irrevocable, and Cuba shall never revert to capitalism.

These amendments are not simply a matter of political rhetoric. Although for years various proposals for a new Cuban Constitution have circulated in Miami and Washington, the imposition of any such a project would require full scale removal of the current Cuban government, a remote if not impossible scenario in present conditions. But assuming that a significant movement for total or partial dismantling of socialism should arise, the Constitution now poses a significant barrier to such change forcing opponents to have sufficient strength to overturn the system completely. There is no room after these amendments for a strategy of "chipping away," whether or not such a strategy is even feasible or would be successful.

Cuba is not alone among nations that have clauses in their Constitutions making certain aspects of the political system irrevocable. For example, the Brazilian constitution makes the federal system irrevocable as well as the system of direct election of the president. The constitutions of the Dominican Republic and El Salvador make the form of government irrevocable, and in the case of El Salvador, the system of alternating presidential terms may not be changed. The Italian system of republican government may not be the object of constitutional reform. Numerous other countries have provisions making aspects of their governmental or electoral systems beyond the reach of constitutional amendment.

Prior to this time, the Constitution empowered the National Assembly to approve, by a two thirds vote, total or partial amendments to the content of the Constitution.[33] Pursuant to the latest amendment, the National Assembly may not adopt any constitutional amendments that revoke the socialist economic, political and social system. Certainly, the debates and the language

---

by administration officials that Cuba was trafficking in biological weapons and providing technology to other countries on the US terrorist list so that they could produce them as well.

[32] Amendments were added to paragraphs 3, 11 and 137. They were reprinted in *Granma*, June 27, 2002.

[33] Constitución (1992), Art. 137.

employed make clear that pursuant to the Constitution no Cuban government may transform Cuba into a free-enterprise, capitalist system. However, whether and what reforms may be introduced into the economic, electoral and political system will be a matter of interpretation as to whether the reforms enhance rather than change their essential character. Under the Cuban system, authority to determine constitutional validity resides exclusively with the National Assembly.[34]

As Cuban socialism evolves, the Constitution may continue to be, in the words of Dórticos, "history in the making."[35] Specific provisions of the Constitution are discussed more fully in the following section and in subsequent chapters.

II. SOCIALIST DEMOCRACY

Cuban legal scholars have shown little regard for capitalist democracy which, in their view, is a hypocritical system.[36] The capitalist constitution is described as a classist document that expresses the interests of the dominant class and assures its supremacy: "In essence the bourgeois state is the dictatorship by the bourgeoisie, but it remains democratic for the capitalists."[37] Former dean of the University of Havana Law Faculty, Julio Fernández Bulté, criticizes representative democracy, which he asserts is "each day less representative, and it never was democratic."[38] Certainly, although even bourgeois democracy is acknowledged to have its own dialectic that may broaden representation within a range tolerable to the dominant class, the Cuban experience with it was not a happy one.

The Cuban disdain for bourgeois democracy may be partly attributed to its critique of its failures and deficiencies, but it also springs from a completely different concept of democracy. Socialists argue that there is dicta-

---

[34] For a discussion of constitutional review, see Chapter 4.

[35] Dórticos, p. 6.

[36] Emilio Marill Rivero, "Acerca de la Dialéctica de la Democracia y la Legalidad Socialista," *Revista Cubana de Derecho*, No. 16, 1980, p. 105. See also, Dórticos, pp. 5-35.

[37] Marill, p. 104. Similar sentiments are found in remarks of Cuban scholars participating in 1997 seminar on election and human rights in Havana sponsored by the Institute Interamericano de Derechos Humanos. Prof. Angel Mariño Castellanos observed: "The electoral systems in almost all capitalist countries are legal and political mechanisms by which the elite minorities, "democratically," reaffirm their power...while the popular masses are reduced to giving legitimacy to these minorities." *Seminario sobre elecciones y derechos humanos* (Costa Rica: IIDH, 1998), p. 168.

[38] Julio Fernández Bulté, "Reflexiones acerca del Estado de Derecho," *Revista Cubana de Derecho*, No. 6, 1992, p. 14.

torship and democracy in all systems. What characterizes "true democracy" is the measure of equality and popular participation in decision-making: Democracy requires at the outset "a society founded on equality...free of discrimination of all types (including economic and social)."[39] Thus, socialist democracy mandates the elimination of class divisions between the exploiter and the exploited, because there can never be political equality between the two. Liberty for one inevitably means oppression of the other.

Accordingly, to promote true equality before the law, socialist democracy requires not only the destruction of the capitalist class by eliminating the tools of domination but also the suppression of all the manifestations of the bourgeois past such as individualism, personal greed and irresponsibility toward the collective and social property. The struggle against the deformations of the past is a long-term project, not one to be accomplished overnight with the defeat of the capitalist state.[40] Thus, the transformation to socialist democracy requires repression of past values and cannot succeed without the dictatorship of the proletariat.

In addition to uprooting the corrupting vestiges of the past, the achievement of socialist democracy requires both the construction of collective productive forces and the elevation of the political and cultural education of the masses. As a result, socialist democracy will not put the masses in charge of the organs of government from the beginning. Rather, the leaders who are the vanguard of the proletariat will govern on behalf of and in the name of the workers on the basis of democratic centralism. To achieve full democracy, however, political and juridical mechanisms must be developed and employed by the vanguard to promote the continuous incorporation of workers' participation in governance. By this definition, the process is not static; socialist democracy creates the conditions for the progressive expansion of popular democracy.

Egalitarianism is fundamental to socialism requiring the appropriation of the means of production, which allows for both the equitable distribution of resources and the employment of resources to benefit the collective, as opposed to private interests. The elimination of private interests competing for resources and, hence, influence, is essential to socialist democracy. In addition, education and physical and material well-being are requisites to the development of the socialist citizen creating the material base essential to the realization of popular democracy.

In pursuit of these goals, the Cuban government has progressively raised educational levels. The massive literacy campaign of 1961 sent thousands

---

[39] Comments of Miguel Alfonso Martínez, *Seminario sobre elecciones y derechos humanos*, p. 153.

[40] Marill, p. 109 (quoting Lenin).

of Cuban youth into the countryside to teach reading and writing and to learn about rural life. Since then the Ministry of Education has striven to increase the national educational level to a minimum of ninth-grade achievement. Universal health care has increased life expectancy of Cubans to almost 75 years. The government also promotes and develops the arts, culture, and recreational and sports activities.

The first decades of the revolution were a time of social effervescence and popular participation. Beginning in the early 1960s, the mass organizations took on special tasks in the development of the new society and became vehicles for massive grassroots involvement in public affairs. Millions of Cubans engaged in social change efforts for the first time in Cuban history, participating in health and sanitation projects, neighborhood associations, citizen militia, workplace assemblies, etc.

However, until recently, the system of democratic centralism implanted in the 1970s progressively limited the parameters for public debate and channels for popular influence over decisions and policy. As the system of government, patterned on the Soviet model, became increasingly centralized and bureaucratized, so too did the structures that had been developed to promote popular participation, including the mass organizations and the legislative assemblies. Rather than encouraging creativity and innovation in these organizations, the Party monopolized policy making and utilized the mass organizations primarily as instruments of implementation. The resulting rigid hierarchy and formalism of these institutions led to widespread criticism in the late 1980s that they were losing touch with and were not responsive to their base membership.

The failure or reluctance to broaden participation might be attributed to several different factors. The infancy of the socialist state compelled dependence on strong leadership to transform the country and free it of bourgeois ideas and values. Moreover, the historic antagonism of the United States toward Cuba's independence, unrelenting since 1959, presented a constant threat of political and economic destabilization exacting unity behind the government. Limited channels of popular influence may also reflect a lack of confidence on the part of the political elite in the people to steer the socialist state, as well as a simple refusal to relinquish control by those in power. Whatever the true explanation, the result over time was a tendency to entrench paternalism and reinforce the hold of the bureaucracy rather than to extend popular democracy.

Constraints on participation and the limited boundaries of permissible debate created a fundamental contradiction: Instead of fulfilling its role of elevating the masses to a position where they could govern, the vanguard created and maintained a dichotomy between the ruling elite and the non-reliable masses. The fact that the governors may be wise, humanitarian and sensitive to the interests of the masses does not diminish the danger posed to prospects for "true democracy." Even on its own terms, the progressive strengthening of socialist democracy requires a steady broadening of participation.

Advances in Popular Participation

Ironically, the disappearance of the Soviet Union opened the way for important reforms as the ensuing economic and ideological crisis forced reappraisal of the Cuban system. The search for solutions to the economic crisis and the survival of socialism required broad popular consultation in order to build a consensus around necessary reforms. The Party and the CTC organized public meetings called "workers' parliaments" for Cubans to identify problems, voice criticisms and make recommendations. All over the island, Cubans gathered at what were open, free wheeling gatherings, resembling "town hall" meetings. The meetings were televised nationally thereby expanding the audience. Many of those participating severely criticized the progressive bureaucratization and formalism that afflicted the system and impeded initiative. A clear consensus emerged that the top-down approach to decision making of the past had to be reversed in favor of stimulating initiative at the grassroots.

Direct Elections

One outcome of these public discussions was the decision to reform the electoral process to provide for direct elections to the Provincial and National Assemblies. Direct elections was one of the constitutional reforms adopted in July 1992. After considerable debate and discussion over how candidates would be nominated and how both regional and national representation would be accommodated, the National Assembly approved an electoral law in October 1992[41] that was implemented in the elections for delegates to the Provincial and National Assemblies that took place in February 1993.

It was decided at the outset that the Party would not formally participate in the nomination of candidates for election. As the nominating mechanism,

---

[41] Ley No. 72 (Ley Electoral), *Gaceta Oficial Ext.*, No.9, November 2, 1992.

the law established national and provincial candidacy commissions organized to select candidates.[42] Over a three-month period prior to the 1993 elections, the national commission, composed of representatives from the mass organizations, received more than 60,000 nominations from their membership and the population at large, from which 589 were to be selected as candidates for the National Assembly.[43] Diversity of age, gender and social sector figured prominently among the criteria for nomination. The final selection of candidates for the February 1993 elections was made in consultation with the municipal assemblies that had been elected on December 20, 1992.

The new electoral process gave the population the first opportunity to vote directly for its national and provincial representatives. It did not, however, provide for contested elections; nor could candidates other than those nominated by the commission be placed on the ballot. Voters could either vote for all or some of the candidates selected, not vote at all, or cast a blank or defaced ballot as a way of expressing opposition to the candidates, and by extension the government. However, half the candidates for the National Assembly were to be chosen from among the delegates elected to the municipal assemblies. Since municipal delegates are nominated in open neighborhood assemblies and elected in contested elections, the population did have a direct say in who those potential candidates might be.

Despite the limitations of choice, the election was widely viewed internally as well as from outside as a "referendum" on the Castro government and the socialist system. Prior to the elections, Miami based radio stations beamed into Cuba regularly exhorted Cubans to emulate the 1990 "no" vote that deposed Chilean dictator Agustus Pinochet by casting spoiled ballots or by writing "no" on the ballot as a way of expressing their opposition to the Cuban government. The Cuban government too perceived the election as a kind of referendum and launched a campaign to encourage a vote for "unity."

According to official statistics, over 98 percent of the population voted. Nationally, a little over 3 percent of ballots were reported blank and 4 percent spoiled. Foreign journalists who witnessed ballot counting reported that the percentage of those voting "no" by either spoiling their ballot, leaving the ballot blank or writing an anti-government slogan varied, reaching to

---

[42] Ibid., Arts. 16-41.

[43] The British Broadcasting Corporation, Summary of World Broadcasts, February 10, 1993 (broadcast of speech by Fidel Castro, February 6, 1993).

20 percent in some voting districts.[44] In Havana, where the greatest discontent appeared to be concentrated, the percentage reportedly reached 30 percent in one district. Thus, although Cubans may have felt compelled to cast ballots to avoid the approbation of their neighbors, many apparently did not fear reprisal for expressing their disapproval by voting against the official slate.

Some outside observers characterized the new electoral process as fraudulent appeasement of internal and external pressures for democratization. The vote, however, demonstrated that, for whatever reasons, the government maintained substantial support. The 1998 elections demonstrated even firmer support for the government. The same nomination and voting procedures were used; the government once again called for a "unity" vote while Miami broadcasts again urged protest votes. As in 1993, over 98% of the population voted, but what was surprising was that the percentage of spoiled ballots was about half that of the previous elections (1.66%) and blank ballots remained about 3%.[45] The percentage of spoiled ballots in Havana declined even more sharply from 10.43% in 1993 to 3.42% in 1998.[46] A little more than 4% of the voters in Havana cast blank ballots in 1998.[47] The most plausible explanation for the results is that, despite the prolonged crisis, the Cuban population confirmed its support of the process of transition taking place in Cuba and/or rejected interference from the north that threatened Cuban sovereignty.

The new electoral process produced a substantial number of new faces in the National Assembly as well as in the Council of State. In 1993, only ninety-eight former delegates to the National Assembly were re-nominated; more than half of the thirty-one member Council of State was new.[48] The 1998 elections resulted in the replacement of almost two thirds of the delegates elected in 1993. In addition, the Assembly is increasingly younger and includes a greater percentage of women (27.62%) than before.

Even if the nomination and electoral procedures employed were imperfect, the change may very well provide the basis for further expansion of participation of the electorate in the future. Consistent with the theory of "socialist legality," these measures are viewed as steps in a continuing proc-

---

[44] For reports on the elections see "The Scene Behind the Elections," *Latin America Weekly Report*, March 4, 1993, p. 4; Agence France Press, "Younger Faces Grace Cuba's Assembly-Elect," February 26, 1993.

[45] Arnold August, *Democracy in Cuba and the 1997-98 Elections* (Havana: Editorial José Martí, 1999), pp. 360-364. Similar reductions in spoiled ballots were reported personally by persons who witnessed the opening of the ballot boxes.

[46] Ibid.

[47] Ibid.

[48] Ibid. pp. 365-67.

ess, which, if allowed to continue, will create its own dynamic for further reform. Indeed, debate continues on how to improve the system. Equally important, there is genuine concern in Cuba, not just among members of the top leadership, but at other levels as well, that survival of the socialist system requires greater flexibility and inclusiveness in the political system. Arguing for a renewed dedication to the strengthening of popular democracy in 1992, Julio Fernández Bulté, forcefully expressed the immediacy of the task:

> We are in a moment, in which the falsities and errors of one model of socialist society have limited the credibility of the Marxist-Leninist project of socialism. For that reason today more than ever we Marxist-Leninists are pressed to clarify not only the theoretical bases of the socialist model but also to enrich it with real practice, so that we Cubans will enjoy the almost absolute privilege of being able to shape our own society and our own state model.[49]

Consultation With the Population

Direct elections have not been the only means by which the Cuban population has participated in decision making. Since the early 1990s, as the government has been compelled to undertake difficult economic measures, some of which reversed past policies, it has done so through a process of consultation with national organizations, particularly the labor unions. In the absence of models or easy solutions to the problems facing the country, the "workers' parliaments" of the early 1990s per force were shed of the dogma and routine characteristic of similar gatherings of the past. As in the early years of the revolution, no significant measure was undertaken without first presenting it to the workers and other civic and professional organizations both as a way of consulting them on the changes as well as measuring public reactions.

Since 1990, the influence of the national organizations on legislation and policy has grown. They are consulted by the government and the legislative assemblies on issues relevant to their concerns. For example, officials of the Ministry of Labor and Social Security report that they do not develop any regulations without input from the unions.[50] The national organizations

[49] Fernández Bulté, p. 17.

[50] There are many examples demonstrating the decisiveness of union participation. For example, a draft proposal on modifying the social security law was shelved in the face of union opposition. See, Evenson, pp. 11-12.

also take legislative initiative. For example, the FMC has frequently initiated and promoted changes in regulations affecting women in addition to participating in the drafting of the Family Code. ANAP drafted and submitted a new law on agricultural cooperatives to the National Assembly in December 2001.

As a matter of course, the legislative process in Cuba entails numerous and broad consultations outside of the National Assembly before a proposed law is submitted to a vote. The objective is to air concerns and critiques in search of a consensus. For example, work on the proposal on agricultural cooperatives presented by ANAP began in 2000.[51] Yet, when submitted to the National Assembly at the end of 2001, the draft was rejected by the commissions primarily because a significant number of delegates in the provinces and the cooperatives that reviewed it had substantial critiques or reservations concerning some aspects of the legislation. ANAP reconvened meetings with the cooperatives to discuss the proposal and work out revisions. The proposal as revised was resubmitted to the National Assembly in 2002. As another example, the drafting of a new Labor Code began in the year 2000, entailing discussions in the Ministry of Labor and Social Security, the trade unions, the labor bar and the courts. Within two years it had gone through numerous drafts and continues to be debated and amended. Before being submitted to the National Assembly, the Labor Code will have been presented for discussion by all Cuban workers at local union meetings.

Once proposed legislation has been approved by the commissions of the National Assembly for submission to the legislative body, it is then debated by the elected delegates in meetings held in the provinces in which they reside. Thus, by the time proposals go through this lengthy process of consultation and public discussion there is generally a consensus for approval when the proposal is finally submitted to a vote at the National Assembly although, even there, minor amendments are often made from the floor and adopted.

This process of direct consultation may explain in large measure why there has not been significant growth of internal opposition which one might expect during such difficult times. Although the government continues to exercise substantial control over political activities and those who oppose the socialist system and its leadership will find themselves marginalized, or even prosecuted in some instances, it is not fear which forges the basis of support. Opposition groups in other countries far more repressive, such as El Salvador or Guatemala did not shrink from active resistance despite the brutal consequences of death squads and military reprisals. The basis of support for the Cuban government today rests largely on continued identity

---

[51] "Parlamento campesino," *Trabajadores*, August 5, 2002, p. 7.

with the collective project that has brought many benefits to the Cuban people and continuing confidence in the government to further that project,[52] coupled with an intense nationalist spirit.

Cubans are not at all reticent to voice their discontents with the current economic situation, with the bureaucracy or even with specific decisions of government. Complaints are as plentiful as mangos in June. However, for a substantial number, the gains achieved as well as fear of the turmoil and potential violence that might accompany any destabilization of the current government far outweigh such discontents. Even more important, there is broad consensus that Cuba must resist attempts of the United States and the hostile elements of the exile community to dictate Cuba´s future. Any concessions to the pressures from either source are perceived as surrender of Cuban sovereignty.

Reforming the Legislature

At the same time that the new electoral process was instituted in 1993, leadership in the National Assembly began to consider measures that would enhance the deliberative functions of the legislature. With the exception of the officers of the National Assembly, the delegates maintain their current employment and have neither legislative offices nor staff to assist them. had been primarily non-professionals with neither offices nor staff to assist them. However, the National Assembly has permanent commissions composed of delegates elected to the Assembly. Regulations adopted by the National Assembly in 1996 define the role of these commissions and detail their authority.[53] Since 1998, there have been nine permanent commissions, each having jurisdiction over a different subject area.[54]

The commissions hold meetings throughout the year to debate issues, draft legislation and review proposed legislation submitted to the National Assembly. It is generally up to the relevant commission to decide when a particular bill is ready to be presented to the legislature. In addition, they may convene meetings with officials at all levels of the political and eco-

52 This confidence appears to have been strengthened since 1994 when the free fall of the economy was brought to a halt and a modest recovery began. Since then, Cuba has progressively been able to improve conditions even if it has not yet been able to recover all the losses suffered since 1990.

53 Reglamento de la Asamblea Nacional del Poder Popular, *Gaceta Oficial*, December 27, 1996.

54 The nine commissions are: Constitutional and Legal Affairs, Economy, Local Organs, Productive Activity, Services, Defense, Health, Education, and International Relations.

nomic system, hold public hearings, undertake studies and program site visits to institutions.[55] To carry out these tasks, the commissions have offices in the capital, administrative staff and access to professional consultants.

Thus, although the assembly itself convenes only twice a year for sessions lasting only two or three days, the short duration of the sessions does not indicate the extent of deliberation. The permanent commissions work throughout the year. Further, by the time legislation reaches a vote at the National Assembly it has been reviewed and discussed not only by the commissions but also by the delegates in meetings convened in the provinces and by the relevant ministries, agencies and non-governmental organizations, depending on the subject matter, as well as by the executive branch, the Council of State.[56]

Another aspect of the Cuban political system that enhances public participation is the obligation of all members of the National Assembly to report to their respective Municipal Assemblies.[57] The content of the report is determined by the municipal assembly. In addition, the term of an elected deputy to the National Assembly may be revoked by those who elected him or her.[58]

III. POLITICAL ASSOCIATION AND PLURALISM

Fundamental to the Cuban socialist system is the concept of collective social goals. Notions of conflicting interests or "balance of powers" are alien ideas. Accordingly, the Constitution states that the Communist Party "is the supreme guiding force of the society and the State, that organizes and guides common efforts toward the goal of constructing socialism."[59] The Party does not have legislative initiative or authority;[60] rather it provides

---

[55] Ibid., Arts. 26-42.

[56] The Council of State, elected by the National Assembly, exercises executive power and is empowered to enact legislation when the National Assembly is not in session. Such legislation, known as decree-laws, take effect immediately but must be submitted to the National Assembly for ratification at its next scheduled session. Unfortunately, there is virtually no information available regarding how the Council of State functions, how often it meets, or what procedures govern its deliberations.

[57] Reglamento de la Asamblea Nacional, Art. 102.

[58] Constitución (1992), Art. 85.

[59] Ibid., Art. 5.

[60] The Party is not among the persons or entities granted legislative initiative by article 88 of the Constitution.

political leadership, determining the broad policies that guide the society. Although the Party does not govern, administer or legislate, there is a close and interdependent relationship between the government, the Party and the social and professional organizations. It is this unity of purpose that provokes some observers to conclude that Cuba is a dictatorship that excludes effective participation.

In response to criticism that a one party system does not allow for pluralism, Cuban officials suggest that democratization of the Cuban Communist Party and other social organizations creates greater opportunity for expression of diverse views than a multi-party system in which minority interests dominate the political process.[61] Cubans critique modern multi-party systems for the minimal participation of the public in the nomination and choice of candidates and for the distortions created by the exorbitant costs of campaign financing that limits rather than broadens pluralism.[62] But the fundamental argument is ideological: socialism requires consensus around collective goals which emerges from recognition of common interests as opposed to negotiating conflicting interests. Pluralism, it is argued, requires respect for diversity of opinion and creating channels for communicating the perspectives of the various sectors of society, not necessarily competing parties.

While the Party establishes the broad policy framework, the government, in consultation with the national organizations and other institutions in the civil sector, determines the strategies and tools of implementation. The process of decentralization begun in the 1990s breathed new life into the internal dynamic of the national organizations, making them more independent and better able to develop and represent the distinct perspectives of their constituents and members. Thus, it is not unusual for an organization like the trade unions to oppose certain measures or call for modifications in proposed legislation or regulations. Many have increased their capacity for research and policy development which contributes to the national debate on issues of public concern.

The Party itself has undergone a reassessment both of its internal make-up and its role. To begin with, participants in the 1991 pre-Congress debates almost uniformly criticized the dogma and formalism that afflicted the Party and stifled creativity and initiative. In addition, its membership and leadership were not representative of major segments of the population, particularly youth and religious believers. At the Congress, the Party amended its statutes to permit religious believers to become members. At

---

[61] See, e.g., *Seminario sobre elecciones y derechos humanos* (Costa Rica: IIDH, 1998), pp. 162-63, 289-95.

[62] Ibid. (commentaries of various Cuban participants).

the same time, many younger members were elected to the Central Committee and the Political Bureau.[63] The resolution on the Party statutes also called on the Party to promote respect for diversity of opinion.[64] Further, internal election of leadership, at least at the lower levels has also been democratized incorporating contested elections for leaders by secret ballot.

Although the Party and the government are not synonymous, the Party came under fire for the confusion that had developed over the years between the Party and the organs of government and administration, particularly at the municipal levels.[65] Clarifying the role of the Party and disengaging it from administration is not only important as a political/legislative matter, but key to the success of the decentralization of the state enterprise system where management decisions must be based on profitability and efficiency. These changes are consistent with the decision to confer the task of nominating candidates for the National and Provincial Assemblies on the national organizations, not the Party. Although the leadership of the mass organizations is almost entirely composed of Party members, the establishment of this role outside of formal Party control is an important step in furthering popular democracy and pluralism.

Further, there has been substantial growth in the activity of non-governmental organizations. In the 1990s more than 2,500 new associations emerged creating a new sector of non-governmental organizations.[66] Religious organizations, particularly the protestant organizations, became increasingly active not only in their religious activities but also in social programs. These are positive developments that encourage greater participation as well as diverse points of view to bear on policy decisions. What is excluded from the Cuban concept of democracy is the emergence of a sector representing private property interests that conflict with socialist values and goals. Survival of socialism depends, however, not only on preventing fragmentation, but on developing and sustaining a broad consensus. To achieve the latter requires the continual expansion of popular participation.

---

[63] *Este Es el Congreso Más Democrático*, report of the Party Congress, October 10-14, 1991 (Havana: Editora Polítca, 1991), pp. 6-32.
[64] Ibid., p. 7.
[65] See, e.g., *Seminario sobre elecciones y derechos humanos* (Costa Rica: IIDH, 1998), p. 181.
[66] Juan Valdéz Paz, "The Cuban Political System in the 1990s: Continuity and Change," in *Socialism and Democracy*, Vol. 15, No. 1 (2001), p. 110.

IV. RIGHTS AND DUTIES OF CITIZENS

The Cuban Constitution contains the full panoply of rights recognized in the Universal Declaration of Human Rights: those defined as economic, social and cultural rights as well as political and civil rights. Under international human rights law, these two branches of human rights are considered co-equal and interdependent. For example, the preamble to the International Covenant on Civil and Political Rights states that "the ideal of free human beings enjoying civil and political freedom and freedom from fear and want can only be achieved if conditions are created whereby everyone may enjoy his civil and political rights as well as his economic, social, and cultural rights." Similar language appears in the preambles to the International Covenant on Economic, Social, and Cultural Rights and to the American Convention on Human Rights. Articles 22-27 of the Universal Declaration of Human Rights set out the economic, social and cultural rights that are characterized as indispensable for human dignity and the free development of personality. These rights, which include the right to "a standard of living adequate for the health and well-being...including food, clothing, housing and medical care," are to be realized not by individual autonomous action but through national effort and international cooperation.[67]

Consistent with these principles, Article 1 of the Cuban Constitution, as revised in 1992, declares that the purpose of the Cuban socialist state is to provide "political liberty, social justice, individual and collective well-being and human solidarity." To fulfill these objectives, the Constitution contains certain material guarantees, such as the right to work, to social security, to medical care, to education and access to sports and culture. In return for these guarantees, able adult citizens have a moral duty to work although there is no penalty for not doing so.[68] The Constitution also sets forth a wide range of individual rights as noted at the beginning of this chapter.

In concept, the Cuban constitutional text is closer to the ideal expressed in international human rights instruments than is the U.S. Constitution. Stated in its most simple terms, the fundamental tension between socialism and free enterprise systems lies in the protection given private property rights. The socialist state guarantees rights to private personal property, but the state controls the use of resources on behalf of the public good thus striving to guarantee equitable distribution of wealth and social benefits. In contrast, capitalist systems protect private economic property and the exploitation of resources to the benefit of individual interests. International

---

[67] International Covenant on Economic, Social and Cultural Rights, Article 2.

[68] Ibid., Art. 45.

human rights doctrine recognizes the right to private property, but does not raise private enterprise to the level of fundamental human rights. Further, Cubans argue that private control of resources distorts democratic institutions by weighting them in favor of the minority with the greatest resources.

While arguably imperfect in many respects, the protection of individual liberties is more extensive in the United States than in almost any other country. In many instances, however, individual liberties, particularly property rights, are guaranteed at substantial expense to the collective. The very broad protection given private property and the thrust of U.S. jurisprudence generally place individual autonomy and private property above group rights and the public welfare. Nevertheless, the collective good is not entirely suppressed in favor of the individual liberty. Law must occasionally balance individual rights against the public interest, as when certain speech is prohibited because it is obscene or may endanger the public safety. Property uses may be regulated, albeit in very limited ways, to serve the public good.

The U.S. Constitution, however, does not recognize economic and social rights as positive rights. Consequently, the state has no obligation to create employment, to provide health care, to assure minimal nutrition, or even to provide public education. Ideologically, the system is based on the notion that greater social well-being will be derived from private competition and individual initiative than from public efforts. Yet, the U.S. record with respect to tangible social and economic well-being is remarkably deficient given its wealth of resources: Access to health care is very unevenly distributed; infant mortality is higher than in most industrialized countries;[69] hundreds of thousands are homeless;[70] public education is in crisis;[71] and poverty levels are rising.[72]

Socialist legality, on the other hand, strives first and foremost to provide for the collective well-being based on egalitarian values. Cuba's achievements in the areas of free quality health care, education and social benefits have been exceptional, particularly given its economic underdevelopment.[73]

---

[69] James S. Rawlings and Michael R. Weir, "Race and Rank Specific Infant Morality in a U.S. Military Population," *American Journal of Disabled Children*, March, 1992, pp. 313-316.

[70] Steve Kerch, "Ground Broken to Help Homeless," *Chicago Tribune*, January 29, 1989. Estimates of U.S. homeless range up to more than three million.

[71] Katherine Boo, "Reform School Confidential," *Public Education*, October, 1992. In many cities only half of high school students pass state examinations; in Chicago in 1988, half of the students dropped out before graduation.

[72] "U.S. Poverty Rate Highest since 1980s," *Chicago Tribune*, September 4, 1992.

[73] Sarah M. Santana, "Whither Cuban Medicine? Challenges for the Next Generation," in *Transformation and Struggle: Cuba Faces the 1990s* (New York: Preager, 1990), Sandor Halebsky and John M. Kirk, eds., p. 267. Cuba's infant mortality rate rivals that of the United States and Canada. Life expectancy in Cuba rose from 65.10 in 1965 to 73.97 in the

Although essential to the process of democratization and full exercise of political and civil rights, these achievements have been accompanied by limitations on individual autonomy. The balancing of these interests, usually weighted in favor of the collective, creates inherent tensions between the two. While some commentators might minimize these contradictions because the "new citizen" would willingly sacrifice self-interest for the common good, they cannot be easily denied.

Each society must decide where the appropriate balance is to be struck based on its social and ethical values. Any resolution of the competing considerations requires concessions on one side or the other. At the extreme ends of the scale, the sacrifices of one to the benefit of the other may create conditions that will eventually destabilize the social consensus. In Cuba, the balance is decidedly on the side of the collective, although certain individual rights are given very broad protection, particularly in the area of equality, family law, personal property rights and criminal justice. In addition, positive rights such as health care, education and employment benefit the individual as well as society. The tension between individual and societal interests can perhaps been seen in highest relief in two different areas: in the treatment of persons who tested positive for HIV prior to 1994 and in the constitutional limitation on freedom of expression.

AIDS: Reconciling Individual and Collective Rights

The Cuban government has committed enormous resources to the development and delivery of national health care services. All Cubans have access to the full range of quality health care services, including dental care. Moreover, medical care employs first world technology and procedures. As a result, Cuba has eradicated many infectious diseases and parasites common in other developing countries. Not only is Cuba's system admired as a model for the developing world, but its achievements rival many industrialized countries, including the United States.[74]

The right to such quality health care, however, carries with it certain impositions on individual autonomy generally valued in U.S. society. For

---

period 1985-1990. Mortality rates from infectious and parasitic diseases, a common killer in underdeveloped nations, plummeted from 94.4 (per 100,000 population) in 1962 to 9.4 by 1987 as a result of the revolution's efforts. Ibid. These achievements have even withstood the devastating economic crisis which began in 1990. See, e.g., Jim Lobe, "Learn from Cuba, Says World Bank," Inter Press Service, April 30, 2001.

[74] Ibid.

example, during the winter 2002 campaign to stamp out dengue fever, Cubans were obligated to permit multiple fumigations and health inspections of each home. Mothers of infants will be called and even visited at home if they fail to bring their children in for regular examination and inoculation. Although such insistence is beneficial to both individuals and society, it might be viewed elsewhere as an invasion of privacy and individual autonomy.

In the case of AIDS, the Cuban government made the decision when the first AIDS case was diagnosed in Cuba in 1986 to quarantine all persons who tested positive for HIV. Total quarantine was considered necessary to prevent the spread of the virus in the population. At first, the "patients," as they were called, were sent to hospital-like facilities resembling a prison more than a sanatorium. They were virtually isolated from normal life and enjoyed few amenities. Within a short time, the harshness of quarantine was tempered by the construction of attractive, comfortable sanatoriums that provided community-like surroundings equipped with recreational facilities and other services. Patients lived in private apartments and could continue doing useful work at the sanatorium. In addition, they received intensive medical attention and access to the latest drug therapies, thus prolonging of their lives. They also received an enriched diet, superior to that of their friends and families on the outside. All of this required an enormous allotment of public resources.[75]

At first, the residents were not permitted to leave the sanatorium at all, although they did receive regular visits from family and friends. Then a system of escorted furloughs was introduced, and subsequently, passes for one to seven days free of supervision for those who demonstrated responsible attitudes. Finally, in 1994, Cuba eliminated the coercive character of its quarantine program. After an initial medical and psychological evaluation and counseling period of six months, most patients are permitted to leave the sanatoriums. A substantial number, however, voluntarily decide to stay because they prefer the living conditions at the sanatoriums. The six month obligatory stay at the sanatorium for purposes of evaluation and counseling is designed to assist HIV positive persons to reintegrate into society.

Health officials estimate that Cuba spends approximately $15,000 a year to maintain a patient at the sanatorium. However, the change in policy had to do with the questions other than resources since those who are HIV positive continue to receive intensive medical attention and a special diet to boost their immunity. Reevaluation of policy brought into question the

---

[75] For a general description of Cuba's response to AIDS see Sarah Santana and Karen Wald, "Human Immunodeficiency Virus in Cuba: The Public Health Response of a Third World Country," *International Journal of Health Services*, Vol. 21, No. 3, 1991, p. 511.

benefit of quarantine and concern for the lives of those who are infected who have survived with the infection for increasingly long periods of time as well as concern for their families.

Some accused Cuba of "criminalizing AIDS" by its program of forced quarantine. They also criticized the premise of the policy that quarantine will control the spread of the disease. In fact, they argue, it may have had the negative effect of undermining educational efforts since people on the outside may have considered themselves safe from becoming infected.

Certainly the policy imposed a profound limitation on individual autonomy, but the Cubans contended that their responsibility was both to care for those who were infected and to do everything possible to protect society and the individuals who were not infected, even if that meant limiting the freedom of those who tested HIV positive. Moreover, Cuba also undertook measures other than quarantine, including extensive, compulsory testing of individuals, screening the blood supply and expanding educational efforts. Until 1994, Cubans were tested routinely whenever they came into contact with the health care system. Further, those who traveled abroad for extended periods of time were tested upon their return. Between 1986 and 1992 more than thirteen million tests were performed.[76]

As of 1992, only 892 cases had been detected, an extremely low number given the size of the population (eleven million) and the fact that most adults are sexually active.[77] In contrast, in the state of Illinois, with a population size and urban/rural dispersion comparable to Cuba, there were well over 6,000 reported cases as of 1992.[78] Some of the difference is explained by the absence of intravenous drug abuse in Cuba, a major source of HIV infection in the United States. Also, the first case in Illinois was detected in 1981,[79] five years before the first case appeared in Cuba giving the disease many more years to spread. In addition, until the mid-1980s foreign tourism was quite limited in Cuba. Still, 892 cases is very low, particularly given the potential to exposure in Southern Africa where over 50,000 Cuban troops spent tours of active duty from 1976 to 1989. Thus, widespread testing and quarantine may have kept the spread of the infection in Cuba to levels significantly below those in other countries.

Since 1992, with the growth of international tourism, the number of Cubans infected with the HIV virus has almost tripled from 892 to 2,482 in

---

[76] Ciro Bianchi Ross, "SIDA se condiciona el placer," *Cuba International*, No. 274, October, 1992, pp. 13-16.

[77] "Cuba Says It Slows AIDS by Quarantining Patients," *Chicago Tribune*, December 3, 1992, p. 7.

[78] Gail Schmoller, "Belief About AIDS: Conflict with Reality," *Chicago Tribune*, August 16, 1992, Womanews, p 1.

[79] "County Hospital Plans AIDS Ward," *Chicago Tribune*, July 22, 1987, p. 1.

1999, more than half of which are found in the City of Havana.[80] The figure is still relatively low, but officials are concerned and have stepped up preventive measures, concentrating on educational programs in the media and among youth and giving special attention to prostitutes.

Without doubt permanent quarantine was an extreme measure. Even if those considered psychologically stable and responsible are permitted to return to their homes, some argue that forced quarantine even for six months is indefensible, both legally and morally, under any conditions. The Cubans, however, are not at all apologetic about a decision they perceive as having prevented an epidemic of disastrous proportions that would not only take the lives of thousands of citizens but would potentially bankrupt the medical system, creating other equally serious health dangers. Moreover, the economic crisis created dire shortages of condoms in the early 1990s, making it difficult for individuals to protect themselves. Given this context, there is no easy solution to the equation. At the same time, however, Cuba's continuing efforts to provide care and treatment for all those infected and its ongoing evaluation of its own policy are indeed laudable.

Freedom of Expression

The Cuban Constitution protects freedom of speech and the press but limits that freedom by the phrase "in keeping with the objectives of the socialist society."[81] Well before the 1976 Constitution was adopted, political expression had been restricted when it conflicted with state policy. In 1961 Castro issued his famous dictate: "Within the revolution everything; outside the revolution nothing."[82] The statement has generally been interpreted in Cuba to mean that everything that supports the development of socialism is permitted; efforts to oppose socialism will not be tolerated.

The definition of the boundaries of the permissible has expanded and contracted with events. In the 1960s, thousands of counter-revolutionaries were jailed for attempting to bring down the socialist government. Most were actively engaged in anti-socialist/anti-Castro conspiracies, but some got into trouble not for advocating capitalism but for criticizing the policies

[80] José de la Osa, "Lo nuevo en SIDA", *Granma*, August 27, 1999, p. 2. Since the first case was detected in 1986, 893 of the 2,482 persons who have tested positive to the HIV virus have become ill with AIDS and 632 have died. Ibid.

[81] Constitución (1992), Art. 53. See also, Art. 62.

[82] Fidel Castro, "Palabras a los Intelectuales," (Havana: Ediciones del Consejo Nacional de Cultura, 1961).

and methods employed to achieve socialism. Even speech meant to be supportive could arouse disapproval at times if it strayed too far from the party line. In the 1970s, scores of intellectuals and activists were either prosecuted or, more often, marginalized for opposing Party policy and/or the leadership of Fidel Castro. During the mid-1980s the government relaxed its attitude toward certain forms of opposition, and a small number of independent groups emerged whose activities were tolerated.

Political space narrowed again after 1989 in response to both external and internal events. Revelations of serious corruption among high level officials, including drug dealing by some military officials, rocked public confidence. These revelations were followed by the collapse of the socialist bloc that deepened an already growing economic crisis and shook ideological faith. At the same time, the United States intensified its aggressive policies against Cuba. Following the invasion of Panama, the United States initiated military maneuvers in the Caribbean that were interpreted in Cuba as rehearsals for air attacks against the island. In the early 1990, it strengthened and extended the extra-territorial reach of the economic sanctions, began a program of overt aid to dissident groups on the island and stepped up its international campaign to isolate Cuba.[83] With some justification, Cuban officials linked all efforts to organize internal dissent either directly or by implication to the U.S. effort to overturn the government.

With the very survival of socialism at stake, the government has not been friendly to suggestions that it should provide room for those they believe to be the agents of its destruction. Official actions are generally not targeted at ordinary individuals who express criticisms but at groups and budding organizations, particularly those that cooperate with Radio Martí[84] or with opposition groups in Miami or that receive assistance and aid from the United States Interests Section in Havana.[85] Some members of the "dissident" groups have been arrested and sentenced for periods ranging from

---

[83] In 1992, the United States adopted what is known as the Toricelli Law which, among other things, prohibits US subsidiaries from trading with Cuba. The passage of this law dealt a severe blow to Cuba´s faltering economy making it very difficult for Cuba to obtain the medications and food products it needed since most such trade had been with US subsidiaries. The passage of the Helms-Burton bill in 1996 was meant to deprive Cuba of critically needed investment capital by punishing foreign investors who entered into deals with Cuba. At the same time, the United States embarked on an overt program of support to dissident groups inside Cuba and continued funding Radio Martí and TV Martí.

[84] Radio Martí is a federally funded radio station that transmits directly from Miami to Cuba. It is not blocked by the Cuban government, but its audience in Cuba has dwindled to about 5% in 2001.

[85] Although normal relations between the two countries have been disrupted since the 1960s, both countries opened what are called "Interests Sections" in the corresponding capital city. The Interest Sections primarily handle consular affairs but also engage in other activities.

one to four years in prison. Unlike the repression practiced by other regimes in Latin America, however, no political opponents have been "disappeared" or executed in Cuba, and jail sentences rarely extend beyond two years.[86]

In general, the measures against organized opposition have not deterred individuals from expressing candid criticisms of the government both publicly and privately. For the time being, the government is trying to navigate a path between, on the one side, preventing actions intended to destabilize the social order and, on the other side, broadening discussion and, hence support for, the economic, institutional and democratic reforms that the socialist state must undertake if it is to survive. The persistent threat of subversion from the outside makes this path quite narrow. The conclusion drawn by the Special Rapporteur appointed by the United Nations Human Rights Commission in 1991 to study the situation of human rights in Cuba reflects this dilemma:

> While not overlooking the urgent need for specific measures . . . any analysis concerning the situation and implementation of human rights in Cuba must, as a point of departure, accept the fact that the Government is, and has for a long time been, surrounded by an international climate extremely hostile to many of its policies and, in some cases, even to its very existence. . . . [T]he abrupt breakdown in the flow of aid previously received from abroad, as well as the almost total exclusion of Cuba as a beneficiary of the multilateral financing and technical assistance agencies, have not given the Government much scope for maneuver in this field.[87]

It is clear thus far that certain political activities will not be tolerated: those that support the United States policy of subverting the socialist system of Cuba or facilitate the application of United States economic sanctions against Cuba; or those that discourage or interfere with investment or other economic cooperation with Cuba. In February 1999, the National Assembly

---

[86] The March 1999 trial of four dissidents created an international furor as the United States Interests Section personnel and other foreigners were barred from the courtroom. Among other charges, the four were accused of cooperating with Radio Martí, receiving support from opposition groups in the United States, supporting the US embargo against Cuba and attempting to discourage foreign investment in Cuba. The four were tried under provisions of the Cuban Criminal Code in force at the time of their arrest in 1998. No one, however, has given an explanation for the delay in bringing them to trial, which far overextended the period allowed by Cuban law in the absence of justifying circumstances.

[87] "Situation of Human Rights in Cuba," *Human Rights Questions: Human Rights Situations and Reports of Special Rapporteurs and Representatives*, United Nations, General Assembly, Doc. A/47/625, November 19, 1992 (Interim Report of the Special Rapporteur for Cuba), p. 21.

adopted the Law on the Protection of the National Economy and Independence.[88] The provisions make it a crime to intentionally engage in actions that facilitate implementation of those aspects of U.S. policy hostile towards Cuba. To date it has not been applied to anyone.

On the other hand, outside of political organizing and activities perceived as cooperating with interests in the United States adverse to the survival of the socialist system, the scope of public debate has expanded in Cuba. Discussion of subjects that had been previously discouraged, such as religious belief, racial disparities or homosexuality, have found increasing acceptance both officially and socially. Academic centers, freed from dogma, are exploring new ideas and theories in a wide range of disciplines, including economics, political science, women's studies, ethics and philosophy. New journals of critical thought are emerging and growing.[89]

Information, like education, is essential to a flourishing democracy. Despite efforts by the United States to isolate Castro, Cuba has never closed its borders to the outside world. To the contrary, Cuba has maintained academic and cultural exchanges with most countries of the world, including the United States. Since as early as the mid-1980s, there has been an explosion of such international exchange programs, all of which broaden the knowledge and perspectives of Cuban artists, professionals and academics. Moreover, Cuba annually hosts scores of international festivals and conferences that attract foreign artists, professionals and intellectuals, even those from capitalist countries (including the United States if travelers qualify under U.S. regulations regarding travel to Cuba).[90]

In some areas access to information in Cuba is quite open, as in scientific and technical investigation, at least where disclosure would not com-

---

[88] This law was enacted to implement the Las Reaffirming Cuban Dignity and Sovereignty. Ley No. 80 (Ley de Reafirmación de la Dignidad y Soberanía Cubana), *Gaceta Oficial Ex.t*, No.2, December 24, 1996.

[89] See, for example, *Temas*, *Contracorriente*, *Nuestra America*, all of which are available to the Cuban population in Cuban pesos.

[90] After a brief opening during the Carter presidency, the Reagan/Bush administrations reimposed travel restrictions on U.S. citizens wishing to travel to Cuba; they also prevented most academic and cultural exchanges by severely restricting visas to Cubans. These measures were made even more restrictive in September 1994. Only in May 1999 did the Clinton Administration reinstate the general travel permission previously granted to United States academics prior to 1994. Although liberalizing procedures for accredited academic and religious institutions to obtain specific licenses (US government permits) to take groups to Cuba, the measures maintain restrictions on individual travel as well as limitations on freelance journalists and limit Cuban Americans to one visit a year for humanitarian purposes. The travel regulations are codified at 31 CFR 515 which contains the US Treasury Department´s embargo regulations against Cuba.

promise potential patents. Moreover, access to the internet is expanding rapidly in all research centers and public entities, including access on a pay for time basis at post offices and other centers. However, access to internal government information is still problematic in Cuba. High-level deliberations are generally hidden from public view, and until very recently, the government ministries have kept tight control over information concerning their policies and operations.

The media in Cuba are a mixed bag. The major national newspapers are *Granma*, the official organ of the Party, *Juventud Rebelde*, the paper of the UJC, and *Trabajadores*, the paper of the CTC. *Granma* rarely presents debate on complex issues. Rather, it is paternalistic in tone and generally reports on official decisions only after they have been taken. The subject matter of debates in the National Assembly are reported, but viewpoints are not aired in advance in the mass media to inform the public of the issues being discussed or even afterwards to reflect points of disagreement during debates. Moreover, for many years, *Granma* ignored negative local news, preferring to focus on the positive. However, since the last Congress of the Journalists Union in early 1999, the newspapers have expanded coverage of social and economic problems and incorporated more analysis of important issues. They also carry criticisms in opinion pieces and letters to the editor.

In contrast, radio and television have improved substantially. Television broadcasts present documentaries and specials on important and complex social issues. Television also offers a broad range of entertainment programs including regular screening of U.S., European and Latin American films, without commercial interruption. Since 1989, Cuba has broadcast the weekly CNN Latin American report. In 2001, Cuba launched a new channel dedicated entirely to educational programming. Programs include courses in languages, history, art, culture and science as well as documentary films.

Radio is the most dynamic forum for public debate and features popular news and information programs as well as lively, uncensored call-in shows. In addition, Cuban media are "supplemented" by U.S. radio transmissions beamed at Cuba—both the U.S. government-sponsored "Radio Martí" and private broadcasts.[91] The purpose of these broadcasts is to provide the Cuban people with information and analysis not provided by the Cuban government. These radio broadcasts are not jammed, but listenership is quite

[91] Although Radio Martí is not jammed by the Cuban government, its companion, TV Martí, a U.S. government sponsored station transmitting from Florida directly to Cuba, is almost entirely blocked by Cuban interference. Both the radio and TV transmissions have been criticized internationally as violating international norms governing the electronic media.

small: A recent study showed that only 5% of Cubans listen to Radio Martí.[92]

Fidel Castro, famous for lengthy discourses on both the domestic and international economy, as well as politics, has been perhaps the richest source of information and education for the population. While the length of his speeches has been the brunt of innumerable jokes, Castro's vocation for thorough, coherent and comprehensible explanations of complex economic and political issues has had enormous effect. Less lengthy in their presentations, ministers and other officials such as Carlos Lage, First Secretary of the Council of Ministers, and Ricardo Alarcón, President of the National Assembly, provide comprehensive analysis of conditions and government policies. Media interviews with these officials and others provide the population with detailed information on the economy, public affairs and culture. Yet, despite receiving increasingly comprehensive and detailed explanations of policy, at least from some quarters, the general population has not been given entree to the official discussions and debates that precede adoption of key economic and political decisions. Further, no independent investigation apparatus or mechanism exists.

Finding the proper balance in all of these areas touching on expression and information is critical to the development of socialist democracy. The current tensions, intentionally exacerbated by the aggressively hostile policies of the United States, limit rather than create the propitious conditions for liberalization. Still, with the exception of checks on (and in some cases repression of) "dissidents" who launch frontal attacks on the legitimacy of the Party or the socialist state, there are signs that Cuba is giving more room to new ideas and debate on a broad range of economic and social issues. Continued progress in this direction is essential if Cuba is to further democratize its socialist system and sustain the conditions for its survival.

---

[92] "Too much TV/Radio Martí static in Miami," *The Atlanta Journal-Constitution*, July 8, 2002.

Chapter 3

THE JUDICIAL SYSTEM

The three institutions primarily responsible for promoting and guarding socialist legality in Cuba are the court system, the Attorney General's Office (Fiscalía) and the Ministry of Justice. Although each was fairly weak and riddled with corruption under the prior regime, they did not fare very well in the early years of the revolution either. The change in personnel effected by the new government eliminated officials known to be corrupt, but it did not bring vitality to the role of these institutions in the legal system. Unfortunately, the deliberate neglect of the judicial system and the legal profession in general in the 1960s impeded the development of legal culture leaving Cuba with an inefficient court system and a poorly trained judiciary.

Moreover, the role of the established courts as centers of private dispute resolution diminished. Centralization of authority in the state, the nationalization of the economy and the prohibition of most private economic relationships including the rental of property, eliminated many areas of private controversy over which the courts previously exercised jurisdiction. Simultaneously, new political and social institutions emerged that would play an increasingly important role in dispute resolution. Rather than seek redress for grievances in the courts, Cubans began to turn to institutions like the Communist Party, the Office of the Attorney General, the Committees for the Defense of the Revolution (CDRs) and the Central Organization of Cuban Workers (CTC) to resolve problems. Thus, in the first two decades, other institutions, particularly local party organs and work place councils, became the primary forums for dispute resolution, thereby reducing the role of the courts in civilian affairs, outside of criminal trials.

It was not until in the 1970s, that the courts and the judiciary began a process of transformation and modernization that is still unfolding. Since then, the courts have steadily gained greater prominence in the legal system as their jurisdiction has expanded in response to the evolution of substantive law. At the same time, Cuba continues to experiment with and develop non-judicial forums for the resolution of claims in the areas of labor rights and domestic relations.

I. THE PRE-REVOLUTIONARY JUDICIARY

One of the early acts of the revolutionary government was to bring the judiciary under its control and influence. The Constitution was amended in early January to permit removal of judges tainted by association with the Batista regime.[1] In addition, Revolutionary Courts were established outside the jurisdiction of the ordinary courts, initially to try war criminals and later to try persons accused of counter-revolutionary acts. These and other actions converted the judicial system into an instrument of the revolution. It cannot be said, however, that by doing so the revolution destroyed a judicial system that had legitimacy or a tradition of independence. To the contrary, Cuba's judiciary was historically allied with the ruling political interests, and in the decade before the revolution it was notoriously corrupt.

At the very beginning of the Republic in 1902, influenced by the U.S. occupation at the turn of the century, Cuba granted the Supreme Court the power to determine the constitutionality of laws, decrees and regulations. The court, however, rarely challenged government action except when legislation affected its own authority or jurisdiction. Moreover, despite its power of judicial review, the court was not only powerless to stop Batista from suspending the Constitution and violating the rights of Cuban citizens, but it expressly declined to hear a challenge to Batista's coup of March 10, 1952, and made no pronouncements in opposition to the dictatorship.[2] One of the few judges who questioned the legality of Batista's actions was forced into exile.[3]

The alliance of the judiciary with the dominant political forces, however, was not the court's only defect. The system's structure was antiquated and woefully inefficient. The nineteenth-century judicial system bequeathed by colonialism had progressed little since the beginning of the Republic. Although the population grew appreciably, the number of courts was exactly the same in 1959 as it was in 1911, leaving large portions of the population outside the major cities without effective access to the courts.[4] Even the provisions of the liberal Constitution of 1940 that were intended to strengthen judicial power did not breathe life into the court system; the Supreme Court, which supervised the functioning of lower courts, made no proposals for improvement during the entire period from 1940 to 1959.[5]

---

[1] *Gaceta Oficial, Edición Especial*, January 13, 1959.

[2] Jorge Domínguez, *Cuba: Order and Revolution,* (Cambridge, Mass.: The Belknap Press, 1978), p. 111.

[3] Hugh Thomas, *Cuba: The Pursuit of Freedom* (New York: Harper & Row, 1971), p. 1347.

[4] Francisco Alabau Trelles, La Revolución y el Poder Judicial, Proyecto de Ley Orgánico del Poder Judicial (Havana: Editorial Luz-Hilo Luz, 1959).

[5] Ibid.

Perhaps one explanation for the judiciary's reluctance to exert its independence is that the 1940 Constitution, while declaring the independence of the judiciary, also provided for a system of political appointment to the Supreme Court. Prior to 1959, judges of the Supreme Court were chosen by the President from a list of three names proposed by a nine-member electoral college. Members of the electoral college were appointed by the full bench of the Supreme Court (four members), the President (three members) and the University of Havana (two members).[6] Judicial appointments were then submitted to the Senate for approval.[7] The general lack of legitimacy of Cuba's political institutions historically, however, precluded the development of a strong, independent judiciary. As would be expected, the result was a Supreme Court representative of and subservient to the dominant class interests as reflected in the government.

Typical of continental civil law systems, the lower-level judges were civil servants who rose through the ranks on the basis of seniority. Although judges were criticized for being passive and politically dependent, the greatest concern with respect to the lower courts was widespread corruption.[8] Decisions were routinely purchased through bribery. In a few instances, judges who went against the prevailing political power were forced from the bench.[9] Prosecutors were also notorious for corruption and extortion, demanding payment or favors in exchange for relief from prosecution or fines.[10]

II. CONFICT AND CHANGE

Not surprisingly, in early 1959, there was broad consensus among Cuban jurists that the halls of justice were rotten to the core and substantial reform was needed. Even moderates, who eventually condemned the more radical policies of the revolution, believed it was necessary to carry out an extensive purge of judges and court officials loyal to Batista as well as those "who because of their aristocratic mentality" obstructed reform.[11] In the

---

[6] Constitución de la República de Cuba (1940), Art. 173, *Gaceta Oficial*, No. 464, July 8, 1940.
[7] Ibid., Art. 180.
[8] Stories of corruption are recounted by many lawyers who practiced before the revolution. See also, Domínguez, p. 116; Thomas, p. 1348.
[9] Interview with Emilio Marill, October 13, 1992, Havana, Cuba.
[10] Interview with Manuel Herryman, former police official under the Batista government, June 10, 1988, Jaimanitas, Cuba.
[11] Alabau Trelles, p. 5.

view of Francisco Alabau Trelles, a magistrate of the Supreme Court who was himself removed in the judicial purge of December 1960,[12] the pre-1959 judicial system required "complete reorganization" if it were to become independent, honest and effective in the administration of justice.[13] Thus, there was little opposition to the January 13, 1959, decree that suspended the non-removability of the judiciary. The authority to remove judges was granted for limited periods of thirty to forty-five days at a time[14] and this authority was renewed when necessary.[15] New judges were named by the Council of Ministers.

Thus, the rationale behind the principle of the non-removability of the judiciary notwithstanding, its suspension was acceptable under the prevailing political context. Opposition to the removal of judges emerged only when the socialist goals of the revolution surfaced at the end of 1960. Thus, the liberals, who supported the revolution at the beginning and condoned the removal of judges sympathetic to the Batista regime, later insisted on the guarantee of non-removability and protested removal of newly appointed judges who resisted the revolutionary agenda of the new government.

Emilio Menéndez y Menéndez, a close associate of Urrutia, was appointed president of the Supreme Court in January 1959. By all accounts he was a decent man, untainted by collaboration with the Batista regime, although undistinguished as a jurist. He was a moderate who, in his address to the opening of the 1959 court session in September, exalted the liberal philosophy of Descartes.[16] Menéndez argued that justice lay in the inherent value of individual freedom and exercise of free will, principles he believed did not vary with changing social context.

In contrast to Menéndez y Menéndez and other liberal reformers, José Santiago Cuba Fernández, who had fought in the revolution and had been appointed public prosecutor of the Supreme Court, projected a much more radical vision of the role of the judiciary. At the same 1959 inauguration of the court session, Santiago Cuba espoused that the laws of the revolution should be applied and interpreted "according to revolutionary criteria."[17] Judges could not be blind instruments:

---

[12] Decreto No. 2896 (Ministry of Justice), *Gaceta Oficial*, December 21, 1960.
[13] Alabau Trelles, p. 5.
[14] Ley Fundamental (February 7, 1959), Provisiones Adicionales Transitorias, Quinta.
[15] The non-removability provision was suspended again in November 1960 in order to purge opposing justices from the courts. International Commission of Jurists, *Cuba and the Rule of Law* (Geneva: ICJ, 1962), p. 110.
[16] Dr. Emilio Menéndez y Menéndez, *Discurso en la Apertura Solemne de los Tribunales Celebrada el 1 de Septiembre de 1959*, (pamphlet, undated).
[17] Memoria leído por el Fiscal del Tribunal Supremo, José Santiago Cuba Fernández en el acto de la Apertura Solemne de los Tribunales Celebrada el 1 de septiembre de 1959 (pamphlet, undated).

> Society demands less blindness and more vision of the people, a vision which makes possible that the Revolutionary Law is applied not as a cold norm but as living law dictated by the Revolutionary Power to serve the people.[18]

The conflicting legal philosophies of Santiago Cuba and Menéndez manifest the fundamental incompatibility of the bourgeois concept of the judiciary and the radical nature of revolutionary justice. The moderates who came from middle- and upper-class backgrounds saw themselves in the lofty role of "impartial" interpreters of the revolutionary laws applying "neutral" principles rooted in the precepts of individual and property rights of bourgeois democracy. The revolutionaries, on the other hand, argued that the judiciary must be an instrument of the revolution obligated to apply the law in a manner consistent with revolutionary goals and principles to which other interests were subordinated.

Demand for establishment of a judiciary independent of the legislative power began to emerge in late 1959. The National Association of Judicial Officials convened a forum on judicial reform in November. At the forum, representatives of the National College of Lawyers argued that judges should be named by the Supreme Court, the Law Faculty and officials of the bar association.

Conflict mounted when the judiciary began to impede the social and economic policies of the revolution. In early 1960, the Supreme Court opposed some of the government's laws and frequently ruled in favor of landowners in disputes arising under the agrarian reform law.[19] Antagonisms within the legal profession increased as the Havana Bar Association tacitly aligned itself with the propertied interests as well. In reaction to these developments, lawyers loyal to the revolution took over the association in July 1960, unseating its former leadership and issuing harsh verbal attacks against the judiciary for undermining government policy. Increasing polarization led to a final purge of the judiciary in late 1960. By late fall most of the judges who had not joined cause with the revolutionary government had left the country. They wrote a stinging condemnation of the revolution from exile in Miami.[20]

New judges loyal to the revolution were appointed, including Enrique Hart Ramírez, a practicing Roman Catholic, who remained president of the

---

[18] Ibid.

[19] Luís Salas, "The Judicial System of Postrevolutionary Cuba," *Nova Law Journal*, Vol. 8 (1983), pp. 43-70.

[20] The International Commission of Jurists report, *Cuba and the Rule of Law*, contains numerous statements of former members of the Cuban judiciary exiled in Miami that condemn the revolutionary government for violations of human rights and the rule of law.

Supreme Court for almost twenty years from 1961 to 1980.[21] Hart opened the 1961 court session with a statement embracing the task of constructing the socialist state. In his address, he declared his loyalty to the revolutionary government and warned that the judicial system was in a transitional period that necessitated cautious attention to the strict application of the law.[22] Further, he expressed his support for the removal of the justices who were opposed to the social and economic reforms of the government.

Not surprisingly, the newly appointed judiciary was uncritical in its support of the socialist regime. This loyalty did not necessarily mean, however, that all prosecutions resulted in conviction. The Supreme Court insisted that lower courts apply the law and follow procedure faithfully, reversing their decisions when they did not. A substantial number of trials ended in acquittal, and many convictions were overturned.[23]

However, like their predecessors, the new judiciary passively retained the structure of the colonial system. In fact, the modifications to the Organic Law of Judicial Power that were enacted in December 1960 retained the pre-revolution structure of the ordinary courts, although the power of judicial review had been eliminated.[24] Aside from the creation of the Revolutionary Courts and the People's Popular Courts, the ordinary courts remained virtually unchanged in structure and jurisdiction until 1973.

The People's Popular Courts

The People's Popular Courts, on the other hand, reflected the idealistic desire to democratize justice, at least at its most popular level. These courts were neither developed in consultation with the existing judiciary nor were they supervised by them. Rather, they were established by a commission organized by the law faculty in October 1962 at the urging of Fidel Castro.[25]

---

[21] Enrique Hart Ramírez was the father of Armando Hart, one of the early student leaders jailed with Fidel Castro after the Moncada attack. Armando Hart first served as Minister of Education and was later named Minister of Culture, a position he continues to hold.

[22] "Discurso leído por el Dr. Enrique Hart Ramírez, Presidente del Tribunal Supremo," 1 de septiembre de 1961, La Habana, Cuba (pamphlet, undated).

[23] Salas, p. 46.

[24] In the Supreme Court, the civil law chamber was joined with the chamber on administrative law, but the chambers on criminal law and on constitutional and social guarantees remained. Law No. 898, *Gaceta Oficial,* December 3, 1960, Art. 2. The latter chamber, however, no longer was empowered to review acts of the Council of Ministers.

[25] *Tribunales Populares,* pamphlet published by the School of Juridical Sciences, Faculty of Humanities, University of Havana (1963). This pamphlet contains documentation pertaining to the formation and functions of the organizing commission.

These courts represented an innovative experiment designed both to develop mass participation in the justice system and to educate the population to the new socialist ethic. As stated by Castro, the goal of the popular courts was to correct antisocial behavior "not with sanctions, as in the traditional style, but rather with measures that would have a profound educational spirit."[26]

The first such courts were established in 1962 in rural areas not previously served by the judicial system. Staffed by part-time judges who were elected from the neighborhood or workplace, these courts handled private disputes and charges of petty crimes.[27] The use of judges selected from the community introduced a lay participation in the judicial system in Cuba for the first time. Candidates for positions as judges were screened for moral fitness and revolutionary commitment, and those selected received training of up to forty-five days. The establishment of these courts was frequently supervised by young lawyers and law students. By the end of the decade, there were more than 2,200 such courts functioning in all parts of the country, including the cities.

There are numerous accounts of the positive impact of these courts in the communities they served and on the development of concepts of popular justice.[28] The tools to resolve disputes were not found in codes of law, but emerged from common experience and community values. Trials were public and attendance was encouraged to maximize their educational function.

The duality of judicial systems, however, caused much confusion, overlapping jurisdiction and inconsistency in the application of law. As criticisms of the system emerged in the late 1960s,[29] a number of jurists perceived the need to rationalize the system in order to create greater predictability and fairness in the resolution of disputes. Analysis of the problems and development of a proposal for a unified court system were entrusted to the Commission on Juridical Studies appointed by the Party in 1965.

Revolutionary Courts

Another system of courts outside the jurisdiction of the ordinary courts

---

[26] José Santiago Cuba, "Los Tribunales Populares," *Verde Olivo*, October 16, 1966, p. 24.
[27] For a discussion of the development of the Popular Tribunals, see Adele Van Der Plas, *Revolution and Justice: The Cuban Experiment* (Amsterdam: Forris Publications, 1987); Luís Salas, "Emergence and Decline of Cuban Popular Tribunals," *Law and Society Review*, Vol 17, No. 4 (1983), pp. 588-612.
[28] See, generally, Van Der Plas; Salas, "Emergence and Decline;" and Harold J. Berman, "The Cuban Popular Tribunals," *Columbia Law Review*, Vol. 69 (1969), p. 1317.
[29] Salas, "The Judicial System," p. 51.

was that of the Revolutionary Courts, established in January 1959 to try Batista's henchmen and collaborators, who were accused of atrocities and criminal acts during the struggle against the dictatorship. A continuation of similar courts created by the rebel forces in the Sierra Maestra to prosecute war crimes during the armed rebellion, the Revolutionary Courts were placed under the control of the military rather than the ordinary criminal courts. The jurisdiction of the Revolutionary Courts was suspended in early July 1959 when most of Batista's supporters had either been convicted or had fled. In November, however, with the emergence of sabotage and armed resistance to the revolution, these courts were re-opened and given jurisdiction over crimes designated as counter-revolutionary.[30]

The Revolutionary Courts used a summary procedure that substantially limited the opportunity for trial preparation. Defendants frequently did not communicate with defense attorneys until shortly before trial. Yet there was by some accounts a genuine effort to establish the guilt or innocence of the accused, and not all of those arrested were convicted.[31] Because of public outrage over the atrocities of the Batista regime, even moderates deemed the Revolutionary Court proceedings justified under the circumstances.[32] More than one observer has noted that the Revolutionary Courts, despite having meted out death sentences to hundreds, spared Cuba a repeat of the bloodbath that followed the fall of the Machado dictatorship in 1933[33] or that erupted in Venezuela following the fall of Pérez Jiminez in 1958. Nor has Cuba experienced institutionalized mass killings as took place in Chile in 1973, or extra-judicial executions and disappearances reported in Argentina, Colombia, El Salvador, Guatemala and other Latin American countries.

Although the Revolutionary Tribunals and the ensuing executions grabbed headlines in the United States, fueling anti-Castro sentiments in Congress, it was the loss of power and property, not the Revolutionary Tribunals, that inspired the counter-revolution.

---

[30] Ley No. 634 (Normas para el pase de los juicios y causas por delitos contrarevolucionarios de la jurisdicción ordinaria a los Tribunales Revolucionarios), *Gaceta Oficial*, November 23, 1959.
[31] Thomas, p. 1074.
[32] In his biography of Fidel Castro, Tad Szulc quotes several people connected with these Tribunals who had since left Cuba and who felt the tribunals were justified since they prevented mobs from taking justice into their own hands. Tad Szulc, *Fidel: A Critical Biography* (New York: William Morrow, 1986), pp. 482-485.
[33] Ibid.

III. REFORM OF THE JUDICIAL SYSTEM

By 1967, the turmoil ensuing from revolutionary transformation had subsided and most counter-revolutionary violence had ended. The revolution entered a new phase, and as institutionalization of the revolutionary regime continued, the Party began to pay attention to the long-neglected legal system. The Commission on Legal Issues developed a program for reform and modernization of the judicial system, resulting in a new law on the organization of the judicial system adopted by the Council of Ministers in 1973.[34]

The 1973 law was the first renovation of the Cuban judicial system since the revolution. This law re-established a unified court system that provided for four levels of jurisdiction: base, district, provincial and national (the Supreme Court).[35] The People's Courts were abolished, as were the Revolutionary Courts. Although the 1973 statute maintained the principle of judicial independence by which judges owe obedience only to the law, judges were no longer appointed by the Council of Ministers for life but rather for a renewable term of years.[36] Further, the statute separated the Office of the Attorney General administratively from the Court System and set out a new structure for its functions.[37] The Attorney General, however, maintained a seat on the governing body of the Supreme Court.

The Chamber for Constitutional and Social Guarantees was eliminated, and violations of such rights were reviewed by other chambers when cases arose relevant to their jurisdiction. The Supreme Court was given appellate review over all judicial proceedings, even those of the military courts. Although the Revolutionary Courts were eliminated, crimes against state security continued to be treated apart from the criminal justice system, and special chambers in the provincial courts and in the Supreme Court were created to hear and review such cases. Thus, there were four chambers of the Supreme Court: civil and administrative, criminal, state security and military.[38]

In addition, the statute outlawed the private practice of law.[39] Henceforth, all lawyers wishing to provide legal services to individuals and to represent individuals before the courts were required to join the *bufetes colectivos*, which functioned as law collectives supervised by the Ministry of Justice. Most of the lawyers remaining in Cuba joined the *bufetes*. The Ministry of Justice also maintained the registry of lawyers.

---

[34] Ley No. 1250 (Ley de Organización del Sistema Judicial), *Gaceta Oficial*, June 23, 1973.
[35] Ibid., Art. 2.
[36] The term for the presidents of the courts was seven years, for professional judges five years, and for lay judges it was three years. Ibid., Art. 85.
[37] Ibid., Art. 3.
[38] Ibid., Art. 19.
[39] Ibid., Art. 171

The 1973 law on the judicial system introduced an important innovation to the Cuban court system—the lay judge. The inclusion of lay judges, who served on the bench along with professional judges preserved the popular participation in the judicial process initiated by the People's Courts. This unique feature is considered by Cuban officials to be one of the democratic attributes of the system. The selection and role of the lay judge is discussed below.

Although the 1973 law represented an attempt to strengthen the judicial system, insufficient attention had been given to the internal administration of the courts and the training of judges. Incompetence, particularly at the trial level, was widespread and impeded improvement of the judicial system for many years.

A second, more thorough, overhaul took place in 1977, when a new statute on judicial organization adjusted jurisdictional lines to the new political administrative districts established in the 1976 Constitution. Moreover, the 1977 statute more clearly defined administrative accountability. Whereas the Supreme Court had previously been appointed by the Council of Ministers, under the 1976 Constitution judges of the Supreme Court were to be elected by the National Assembly,[40] and judges of the provincial and municipal courts were to be elected by the corresponding legislative body.[41] The new law also contained sections strengthening the structure of the Office of the Attorney General[42] (even though it was no longer affiliated institutionally with the courts), provisions governing the *bufetes colectivos*[43] and a provision establishing the National Union of Cuban Jurists.[44] Thus, all three institutions were considered to be functionally part of the judicial system even if administratively independent. In the case of the *bufetes*, they were evolving into an increasingly autonomous institution.

Although the Ministry of Justice is not mentioned in either statute, it continued to exercise supervisory responsibility over the organization and general administration of the courts as well as over the *bufetes*. In addition to these supervisory and administrative tasks, the Ministry of Justice was responsible for the training and screening of judicial candidates to be proposed to the respective legislatures.

The 1980s brought more comprehensive reforms that began an era of modernization of the court system. The retirement of Enrique Hart in 1980,

---

[40] Constitución de la República de Cuba (1976), Art 75(m). *Gaceta Oficial,* No. 7, February 24, 1976.

[41] Ibid., Art. 105(h).

[42] Ley No. 4 (Ley de Organización del Sistema Judicial), Arts. 119-142, *Gaceta Oficial,* August 25, 1977.

[43] Ibid., Arts. 145-153

[44] Ibid., Art. 154.

after nineteen years as president of the Supreme Court, opened the way for younger judges to assume leadership in judicial administration. The governing council of the Supreme Court began to work closely with the Ministry of Justice to analyze deficiencies in the judicial system, which were numerous: poorly trained judges, inefficient organization and procedures and lack of mechanisms for analysis and evaluation of the court system. Reform of the judicial system in the 1980s paralleled important developments in Cuba's legal system in general, not only in substantive and procedure law, but in legal education as well.

Advancement in reform and modernization continued in the 1990s. In 1990, the National Assembly adopted yet another comprehensive law on the structure and administration of the judicial system, entitled simply "Law on the Popular Courts," to replace the 1977 law.[45] Its express goal was to improve further the court system. In particular, it recognized the necessity to "institute a judicial organization that enables, by its structural flexibility, solutions to new situations," to develop mechanisms for the continuous evaluation of the effectiveness of the system and to "strengthen . . . the quality of judicial work, with a view towards its constant perfection."[46] Law No. 70 of 1990 and subsequent modifications to the municipal and provincial courts have revised jurisdictional lines, clarified and strengthened administrative functions, and increased access to judicial process.

Seven years later this law was replaced by yet another statute governing the court system. This statute, enacted as part of a general process of decentralization taking place in Cuba, made the court system an autonomous institution, separated from the Ministry of Justice.[47] In addition, a provision governing the Office of the Attorney General, which had been an independent institution since 1977, was eliminated from the legislation governing the court system and enacted as a separate law.[48]

The Courts Today

The evolution of the courts in Cuba parallels other developments in the legal system. Starting in the mid-1980s, Cuba undertook a number of steps to improve the quality of the legal system. In particular, attention was given to increase access to and respect for the courts and the legal process. These

---

[45] Ley No. 70 (Ley Sobre Los Tribunales Populares), *Gaceta Oficial Ext. Esp.*, No. 25, July 24, 1990.
[46] Ibid., third *Por Cuanto*.
[47] Ley No. 82 (De los Tribunales Populares), *Gaceta Oficial Ext.*, July 14, 1997.
[48] Ley No. 83 (De la Fiscalía General de la República), *Gaceta Oficial Ext.*, July 14, 1997.

measures coincided with efforts to improve legal education and to increase the number and quality of lawyers as well as the efficiency of legal services.[49]

Cuba has not been immune to the problems of overcrowded court calendars and backlogs that negatively affect the quality of justice both because of delays and because of insufficient time for analysis of individual cases. Some of the backlog has resulted from the increasing numbers of cases of increasing criminal activity paralleling the economic crisis; some of it is attributable to the expanding role of the courts in resolving civil matters. On the practical side, an additional, and equally serious, problem was created by the lack of fuel and spare parts that paralyzed both public and private transportation in the early 1990s, making it extremely difficult for litigants, witnesses and attorneys physically to get to the courtroom.

In response to the situation, the procedure for handling misdemeanors was streamlined in the municipal courts,[50] and the jurisdiction of the municipal courts as courts of first instance was expanded to relieve crowded court dockets in the provincial courts. Moreover, some cases were removed from court jurisdiction altogether. For example, labor disciplinary matters as well as protection of workers' rights are now resolved by workplace hearing boards with right of appeal to the courts when the dispute involves a disciplinary measure which affects continued employment or a right of the worker.[51] Further, non-adversarial cases, such as uncontested divorces, may now be handled administratively.[52] On the other hand, the system of state arbitration boards, which ruled on contract and economic disputes between state enterprises, was eliminated in August of 1991.[53] Jurisdiction over such disputes has been entrusted to new Economic Law Chambers of the provincial courts and the Supreme Court.

To alleviate the problems created by the deterioration of the public transportation system as a result of the economic crisis, Law No. 70 permitted provincial and municipal courts to hold trial in locations outside the official court building when it is necessary to serve justice.[54] Whereas

---

[49] See Chapter three

[50] Decreto-Ley No. 132, *Gaceta Oficial*, April 9, 1992.

[51] Decreto-Ley No.176 (Sistema de Justicia Laboral), *Gaceta Oficial*, No.28, August 15, 1997. For a description of the labor grievance procedures in Cuba, see Debra Evenson, *Workers in Cuba: Unions and Labor Relations* (Detroit, MI: Guild Law Center, 2001), pp 62-73.

[52] Interview with Dr. Carlos Amat Fores, Minister of Justice, Havana, Cuba, October 12, 1992; interview with Drs. Emiliano Manresa and Juan Mendoza, National Directorate of the *Bufetes Colectivos*, Havana, Cuba, October 12, 1992.

[53] Decreto-Ley No. 129 (De extinción del Sistema de Arbitraje Estatal), *Gaceta Oficial Ext.*, No. 9, August 19, 1991.

[54] Ley No. 70 (1990), Art. 12.

changes in jurisdiction require legislative action, the Governing Council of the Supreme Court was empowered to propose to the Ministry of Justice the creation of new chambers of the provincial courts and new municipal courts or sections of these courts.[55] In mid-1992, trial courts were opened in each of the Popular Councils, special councils established in districts of larger municipalities to address local administrative issues.[56] These courts are considered sections of the respective municipal courts and hold sessions three days a week. The other two days are devoted to continued training and preparation of the judges.

Thus, trials were held closer to the domicile of the litigants to reduce the burden of travel and to better assure the presence of the parties and necessary witnesses. To some extent, these new neighborhood courts, opened to enhance access and efficiency, recall the popular courts of the 1960s. But there are some important differences. The contemporary courts lack the informality of the popular courts. First, trials are presided over by professional judges as well as lay judges. Second, procedure and applicable substantive law are strictly governed by legislation.

Although the Ministry of Justice did not monitor or evaluate the judgments of the courts in particular cases, it did have an important role in overseeing the selection of the judiciary and in the financing and general administration of the courts. The Ministry of Justice (as well as the Governing Council of the Supreme Court) increased its supervision of the administrative aspects of the courts and developed and regularized procedures for evaluating their performance. To this end, staff at the Ministry of Justice designed computer systems for data processing and record keeping with respect to the courts. The Ministry of Justice also devoted considerable attention to the evaluation and training of judicial candidates.

The efforts of the Ministry of Justice were supported by parallel developments in the courts themselves. Regulations adopted in 1991 as a result of the joint work of the Governing Council of the Supreme Court and the Ministry of Justice set out the framework for the internal administration of the courts.[57] The regulations outlined and strengthened administrative responsibilities of court officials and established a system of reporting, analysis and evaluation at all levels.

All of these measures were designed and undertaken with a view to improve the efficiency and the quality of the judicial system. The efforts of the Supreme Court and the Ministry of Justice in this regard were impres-

---

[55] Ibid., Art. 20.1(m).

[56] Interview with Carlos Amat Fores, Minister of Justice, Havana, Cuba, October 13, 1992.

[57] Acuerdo No. 5 (Reglamento de los Tribunales Populares), *Gaceta Oficial Ext.*, No. 2, February 22, 1991.

sive, and officials devoted substantial time and resources to the project of modernizing the court system. The reform process involved frequent exchange and dialogue with judges and court officials at all levels. Moreover, many judges and officials traveled abroad to study the judicial systems of other countries, and Cuba invited foreign judges to visit its institutions and engage in discussions on judicial administration. There is considerable enthusiasm among officials that Cuba will be in the forefront of developing countries in achieving a professional, modern judicial system.

In 1997, as a further step in strengthening the courts, a new law was enacted which separated the judicial system from the Ministry of Justice. As a result, the Governing Council of the Supreme Court became the authority responsible for the administration, organization and finances of the courts. While increasing the autonomy of the courts, the measure has imposed an enormous administrative burden which judges and judicial staff did not have to deal with before. Now, in addition to the judicial work carried out by court administrators, they must concern themselves with construction, physical plant and similar issues concerning court facilities. It has taken several years for the courts to develop efficient systems for drafting budgets and controlling costs.

IV. THE JUDICIARY

Development of a professional judiciary has taken decades and efforts are just beginning to show results in the improvement of the quality of court procedures and the drafting of sentences. In addition, the task of training is ongoing as legal reform since the 1990s has advanced at a steady pace in all spheres of the legal system. A number of provisions of the 1997 law augment the professionalism and independence of the judiciary.

Professional Judges

As in most systems based on the civil law tradition, the vast majority of professional judges in Cuba enter the judicial ranks after receiving special training during or immediately following law school. In 1991, entry to the judiciary was opened to the legal profession to help ease the shortage of judges. Somewhat more than 150 lawyers sought positions on the bench in

1992.[58] At the same time, the Ministry of Justice initiated a competitive examination for all those applying to enter the judiciary. Those who pass and meet the other requisites for judicial positions are further screened by the Ministry of Justice, which presents slates of candidates to the respective legislatures for election.

Until 1997, professional judges were elected for five year terms by the corresponding legislative body. Under current law, they are elected for unlimited terms and serve as long as they are physically able unless they voluntarily retire or are removed for cause by the legislative body which elected them. Along with making the courts an autonomous institution, this reform is aimed at reinforcing the independence of the judiciary.

The requirements for the judiciary are set out in the governing regulations.[59] In addition to age and citizenship requirements, candidates must demonstrate good moral character and have the requisite years of legal experience either as a judge or lawyer: The requirement is ten years for the Supreme Court, five for the provincial courts and two years for the municipal courts. Those who are elected from the list of proposed candidates undergo further training at an institute established by the Ministry of Justice. Special continuing courses are also offered to judges at the University of Havana and at the National Union of Cuban Jurists to assure that judges stay current on legal developments. In addition to increasing time for study of case files, the reductions of the workload for judges is also intended to provide time for continuing education.

Party membership has never been a requirement for the judiciary, but prior to 1976 the Party did review the nominees. Today, the members of the judiciary are increasingly less likely to be members of the Party. One study found that 43 percent of lay judges were not members of the Party in 1988.[60] In contrast, all judges in the former Soviet Union were Party members,[61] and in other former Marxist systems the percentage was substantially higher as well.[62] Moreover, in 1990, previous provisions requiring that all judges, either lay or professional, demonstrate "active revolutionary involvement were eliminated." Removal of this requirement may reflect either the difficulty in assessing "revolutionary involvement" or the general move away from dogmatism since the late 1980s. Party membership is not a requisite for the judiciary, and, according to one study, a substantial proportion of the

---

[58] Interview with Dr. Carlos Amat Fores.

[59] Ley No. 82 (1997), Art. 42.

[60] Marjorie Zatz, *Producing Legality, Law and Socialism in Cuba,* (New York: Rutledge Press, 1994), p. 275.

[61] George Ginsburgs, "The Soviet Judicial Elite: Is It?" *Review of Socialist Law*, Vol. 11, 1985, p. 300.

[62] Inga Markovits, "Law and *Glasnost*: Some Thoughts About the Future of Judicial Review Under Socialism," *Law & Society Review*, Vol. 23, No. 3, 1989, p. 424, n. 32.

professional judges are not members of the Party.[63]

Lay Judges

One of the innovations of the Cuban revolution was the introduction of lay judges, who serve along side professional judges in all cases.[64] The Cuban practice is comparable to the mixed courts of Germany and France but with important differences. In Cuba, lay judges serve at all levels of the judicial system and participate in almost all cases brought to the courts. They are an integral part of the system, participating both in trial and appellate proceedings. In contrast, German lay judges primarily serve the function of juries and participate only in trials of serious crimes;[65] in France lay judges serve only in trials involving misdemeanors and in special tribunals such as those dealing with labor and commercial disputes.[66]

With some exceptions, sessions of the courts are presided over by three judges: In the Supreme Court there are two professional judges and one lay judge;[67] in the provincial and municipal courts one professional and two lay judges preside.[68] In the provincial courts an additional professional judge sits in all criminal cases where the maximum penalty is eight years or more, when the amount in dispute in civil matters is considerable and in other special instances. On the other hand, in the case of a misdemeanor in a municipal court, the accused will be tried by a single professional judge.

Like professional judges, lay judges are elected by the corresponding legislature, but in the case of the lay judge the term is five years. Since lay judges continue their regular employment, each lay judge serves a maximum of thirty days a year.[69] At the municipal and provincial levels, lay judges are selected from within their local communities. Nominations of candidates for lay judges are made by the mass organizations, the most important of which is the Central of Cuban Workers. Candidates are nominated made at workplace assemblies. Nominations are screened by the Ministry of Justice to assure that the candidates meet the formal requirements.

---

[63] Marjorie Zatz, p. 171.

[64] The use of lay judges was generally practiced in all former European socialist countries, but, as in other spheres, the Cuban model developed its own distinct character.

[65] John Langbein, "Mixed Court and Jury Court: Could the Continental Alternative Fill the American Need?" *American Bar Foundation Research Journal*, No. 1, 1981, p. 198.

[66] John Henry Merryman, *The Civil Law Tradition* (Stanford, Calif.: Stanford University Press, 1985), pp. 40-41.

[67] Ley No. 82 (1997), Art. 23.3.

[68] Ibid., Arts. 35.1, 38.

[69] Ibid., Art. 53.4.

Those who are elected as lay judges receive special training before participating on the bench.

By law, lay judges have the same rights and duties as professional judges to participate in the trial and to ask questions as professional judges. Only a professional judge, however, may be designated as president of the session.[70] There is a natural tendency for lay judges to be persuaded by the superior knowledge of the professional judge on issues of law, but according to several accounts, it is not extraordinary for the lay judges to prevail over the professional judge.[71] As representatives of the community, lay input seems to be most significant in the area of sentencing. In contrast to Soviet lay judges, who seemed to simply rubber-stamp the decisions of professional judges, the Cuban lay judges appear to play a more dynamic role and are respected by their professional colleagues.[72] Attitudes of other members of the legal profession, as well as the general population, towards the lay judiciary is an area ripe for analysis.

Thus, although lay judges, as well as professional judges, are likely to share the values of the system, there is no overtly political measure of their qualifications. In addition, they fairly reflect the population at large and are diverse both with respect to race and gender.[73] Almost all have attained a ninth-grade education or higher, and most occupation categories are well represented.[74]

Judicial Autonomy

Cuban law expressly states that judges are independent in their judicial function. The 1990 law on the courts incorporated language that had been part of the law governing judicial power from well before the revolution: Judges exercising their function of imparting justice are independent and owe obedience only to the law."[75] Not only are judges free of required membership in the Party, but they have also shown themselves to be independent from other organs of government in their deliberations.

The new law sets forth defined reasons for the revocation of a judge's

---

[70] Ibid., Arts. 8.2, 23.3; Constitución (1992), Art. 124.

[71] Zatz, p. 270; interview with Dr. Jorge Bodes, President of the Criminal Law Chamber of the Supreme Court, May 10, 2002.

[72] Ibid.

[73] Zatz, p. 275.

[74] Ibid.

[75] Ley No. 70 (1990), Art. 2. The same language appears in the 1997 statute as well. Ley No. 82 (1997), Art. 2.

mandate.[76] None of the circumstances justifying removal involves lack of political orthodoxy. The statutory reasons include physical or mental incapacity to continue his or her judicial function; demonstrated negligence or incompetence; and becoming the subject of criminal prosecution. Only the legislative body that elected the judge may revoke the mandate, and revocation is a legislative, not an administrative process. There is, therefore, no appeal. On the other hand, disciplinary measures taken against sitting judges are appealable. One of the contributions of the 1990 law was to establish guidelines and procedures for disciplinary proceedings, setting forth an administrative process in which the judge is to be informed of the charges and given an opportunity to both rebut them and appeal the final decision if it should be adverse.[77]

Observers of the former socialist countries in Europe have noted the lack of judicial independence illustrated by what was termed "telephone justice,"[78] that is, the direct interference with the judicial process by officials who order a specific outcome by making a timely telephone call to the presiding judge. Studies of judicial behavior in Cuba demonstrate substantial autonomy in ordinary criminal cases. According to Salas, in 1977, the courts dismissed 43 percent of all criminal cases filed by the Office of the Attorney General for lack of sufficient evidence.[79] Further, defendants were acquitted in 39 percent of the cases tried in the base courts, 37 percent in the regional courts and 28 percent in the provincial courts.[80] Similar statistics for dismissals (31.5 percent) and acquittals have been reported in a more recent study of sample cases handled by a large *bufete* in Havana in 1991.[81] In the more than 7,000 cases appealed to the municipal courts from the labor grievance boards in 2000, the courts overturned or modified decisions in 25.8% of disciplinary cases and in 41.7% of those involving benefits and rights.[82]

Clearly judges in all societies, socialist or otherwise, are influenced by the social and political environment in which they live and work. Thus, even though they do not receive direct interference, sentences can and do reflect the prevailing social ambiance. For example, in Cuba, when political leaders make a point of denouncing theft of state property, especially organized black market activity, courts are likely to respond by meting out stiffer

---

[76] Ley No. 82 (1997), Art. 67.
[77] Ibid., Arts. 71-76.
[78] See, for example, Markovits, p. 424.
[79] Salas, "The Judicial System," pp. 59-60
[80] Ibid.
[81] Raymond Michalowski, "Socialist Legality and the Practice of Law in Cuba" (unpublished manuscript, 1992), p. 45.
[82] Mimeographed evaluation of the labor grievance boards for the year 2000 undertaken by the CTC.

penalties for those found guilty of such crimes. On the other hand, there are cases in recent years, where those tried for the crime of "enemy propaganda" or other crimes against state security have been acquitted or, if found guilty, received sentences lighter than those requested by the prosecutor.[83]

Judicial Interpretation

Cuba's legal system follows in the tradition of the Spanish civil law system. Unlike common law systems, such as the United States, in which judges have broad powers to interpret the law and those very interpretations become legal precedent for future cases, judges in civil law systems are generally obligated to apply the written law as strictly as possible to the case at hand without reference to prior decisions. Although many civil law systems have begun to introduce greater judicial discretion in interpreting laws, the foundation of civil law systems remains the written law.

In Cuba, the Supreme Court is empowered to supervise the lower courts in pursuit of consistency and coherence in judicial decisions. When the Supreme Court becomes aware of particular errors or conflicts among lower courts arising on appeal, the Governing Council of the Supreme Court may issue an instruction regarding the correct interpretation of a particular statute. The Council may also issue a policy guideline regarding the application of certain provisions. For example, in response to public concern over increasing crime, the 1999 amendments to the Criminal Code raised sentences for many crimes. The Council, in recognition of the negative social consequences of imposing undifferentiated harsh sentences, issued a statement that judges should look for elements that allow application of the lowest sentence permissible.[84] The statement of the Council reflected a policy of the court to seek rationality in decision making in service of the social interest.

This concern for rationality and logic with respect to judicial outcomes became the object of discussion and debate in 2000. A pamphlet issued to judges by the Supreme Court in May, 2002, entitled "The Importance of the

---

[83] For example, Elizardo Sánchez and two others, who were tried in November 1990 for spreading false information, received sentences of two years and eighteen months. The maximum sentence provided in the Criminal Code, Art. 115, is four years. Maria Elena Cruz Varela, was sentenced in November 1991 to two years in prison on similar charges. In both cases, the accused were released before the termination of their prison sentences. Defense attorneys have reported to me that they have been successful in some cases of obtaining acquittals of their clients.

[84] Interview with Dr. Jorge Bodes, President of the Criminal Law Chamber of the Supreme Court of Cuba, May 10, 2002.

Social Interest and Rationality in Judicial Decisions," admonishes judges that correct interpretation and application of the law, must never lead to "absurd, irrational decisions or those that harm the general interests of the population." In explaining the directive, the President of the Supreme Court, Rubén Remigio Ferro, described instances where slavish application of the black letter had lead to absurd results because the judges did not analyze the facts and circumstances sufficiently to achieve a rational result within the law.[85] The pamphlet concludes with a quotation from José Martí:

> It is true that judges must adhere to the law, but they should not be servile in adherence because then they would not be judges but slaves. They are not placed in this position in order to shackle their intelligence, but to do justice, but freely. They must follow legal precept, but they also have the power to interpret it.

The Court increasingly plays a role in advocating for just results even outside the courts. For example, as described in Chapter 7, judges may impose alternative sentences for first time offenders including mandatory work for the same period of years as the minimum statutory prison sentence. The Supreme Court encouraged lower court judges to avail themselves of this provision in appropriate cases. However, the unions were not in favor of giving convicted criminals jobs with the same rights, salaries and privileges of regular workers. Judges of the Supreme Court met with union leaders to discuss the problem and persuaded them to accept the placement of first time offenders in regular jobs. However, the unions have not yet come to consensus on whether these workers may become union members.

This advocacy on the part of the courts is a far cry from the passivity that afflicted the judiciary since before the Cuban revolution. In addition, the Supreme Court has set annual goals for achieving greater efficiency in the courts such as decreasing the average time for resolving appeals from more than120 days to less than 90 days in the Supreme Court. Such initiatives are reflective of positive changes taking place in the Cuban court system.

IV. JUDICIAL REVIEW

As part of the legislative process, all draft legislation must be sent to the Commission on Constitutional and Legal Issues, a permanent commission of the National Assembly to determine the constitutionality of the proposal.

---

[85] Interview with Dr. Ruben Remigio Ferro, President of the Supreme Court of Cuba, April, 2002.

The commission then submits a written opinion to the National Assembly detailing any perceived violations of or conflicts with the Constitution. Reforms of the National Assembly could strengthen the work of this commission. The president of this commission for the legislative period 1998-2003 is also the dean of the Faculty of Law at the University of Havana. In addition, it has been the practice for prominent academics and lawyers to serve as technical advisors to the commission.

Cuba's rejection of judicial authority to review constitutionality goes against the general trend in Latin America and other parts of the world where the empowerment of the judiciary is seen as an important guarantee of constitutional and human rights. In fact, judicial review was introduced in Cuba in the first Constitution of the Republic, drafted during the U.S. military occupation and effective May 20, 1902. However, as noted previously, the judicial power was rarely, if ever, an important countervailing force to the executive or legislature. Similar experience with judicial review is reported in other Latin American countries.[86]

Although the courts have become increasingly viewed as an important pillar in the Cuban legal system, there has been little evidence to suggest consideration of granting the courts independent powers of constitutional review. Current thinking respecting judicial review is reflected in a recent article entitled "Reflections on the 'Rule of Law,' " by Julio Fernández Bulté, former dean of the University of Havana Law School. Bulté derides what he considers "false formal measures of democracy," which are defined by regimes that themselves have not achieved democratic results.[87]. Although he does not specifically refer to judicial review as one of these formal measures, Bulté does suggest that Cuba must improve its democratic system and rescue from history the true basis of democracy derived from "the direct and non-delegable power of the people."[88] At the same time, however, he acknowledges that the "Rule of Law" requires mechanisms to assure absolute guarantees against arbitrariness and the "abuse of the power or ignorance of the will of the governed."[89] This is to be achieved not simply by establishing the appropriate balance of authority within the machinery of government, but by the constitution of state power which presupposes the active and direct participation of the people, the Rousseauian "permanent plebiscite."[90]

Consistent with this view, the 1992 modifications of the Cuban Consti-

---

[86] Merryman, p. 156.

[87] Julio Fernández Bulté, "Reflexiones acerca del Estado de Derecho," *Revista Cubana de Derecho*, No. 6, 1992, pp. 9, 14.

[88] Ibid., p. 17.

[89] Ibid.

[90] Ibid.

tution did not expand judicial power but rather took steps to broaden popular participation in the election of national and provincial representatives by instituting direct elections.[91] In addition, there is continuous consultation with the civil sectors on legislation and regulatory matters in an effort to arrive at consensus on measures to be taken.

Judicial review is a fundamentally conservative force, preventing government from stepping outside accepted principles. In addition to the ideological rationale given by Bulté for rejecting judicial review, there are other factors that disfavor its adoption in Cuba now or in the near future. Socialist law in Cuba has been anything but stable. It continues to evolve and change. Fairly radical changes have taken place since 1990 in response to the economic crisis. Even the fundamental principle of exclusive state ownership of the means of production was modified in the 1992 constitutional revisions. In a context of continuous evolution and experimentation, there are few cornerstones on which to base judicial review of legislative action. Nor is there any persuasive argument for imposing conservatism of a particular institution in a situation that demands simultaneously bold experimentation and pragmatism.

What is important to the future of the Cuban judicial system is its continued professional and administrative development. The seriousness with which officials now approach the role of the judicial system augurs well for its self-governance and independence.

VI. THE OFFICE OF THE ATTORNEY GENERAL

Over the past twenty years, the Office of the Attorney General, known as the Fiscalía, has developed into an independent institution with an increasingly important function in the Cuban legal system. Prior to 1973, the government maintained the pre-revolution structure in which the Office of the Attorney General was administered by the courts and was dependent on them for its budget. Although the law said that the Office of the Attorney General was independent, its fundamental role as prosecutor in criminal cases and the fact that its offices were located in the court buildings necessitated its close ties to the court system.[92] In 1975, the Office of the Attorney General came under the administration of the Ministry of Justice and, in 1977, was made completely independent, both legally and administratively

[91] Constitución (1992), Art. 135.

[92] Interview with Miguel Angel Garcia Alzugaray, Director, Department of International Relations of the Office of the Attorney General, December 16, 1992, Havana, Cuba.

of the judicial system.[93] It was not until 1997, however, that the National Assembly enacted separate legislation to govern the Office of the Attorney General.[94] Although not part of the judicial system, the Attorney General participates as a member of the Governing Council of the Supreme Court[95] to facilitate interchange on questions pertaining to procedure and criminal justice, but, its participation does not indicate institutional influence in either direction.

Pursuant to Article 127 of the Constitution, the Office of the Attorney General is the body of the State responsible to assure that the laws are enforced and carried out in strict compliance with the Constitution and to represent the State in criminal prosecutions. Thus, its primary function is not only to prosecute criminal activity in the name of the society but to guarantee socialist legality by insuring strict compliance with the law by government and economic institutions and agencies, officials and individuals. To fulfill this responsibility, the Office of the Attorney General has authority to carry out investigations and to request information from officials and institutions. When it finds infractions it reports them to the body that is administratively superior to the one found in non-compliance. It also has authority to bring legal action against those who are in violation of the law and to enforce compliance with regulations.

In 1978, as part of its function of promoting and protecting socialist legality, the Office of the Attorney General established Departments of Public Attention throughout the country. These departments receive and investigate complaints by citizens who feel their rights have been violated. The complaints may be resolved in a number of ways. First, the official may explain to the citizen that given the facts and circumstances there has been no violation. Second, if there is some question, the official will communicate with the agency against whom the complaint has been lodged to get clarification. If there has been a violation, the official will seek compliance. In other cases, the official will suggest to the citizen that he or she take legal action or pursue administrative remedies. Over the years, this department has become quite active, primarily assisting citizens in understanding their rights and procedures for vindicating them within the law. Between 1988 and June 2001, these departments attended to complaints by approximately 209,000 citizens, 30% of which were found to be valid and resolved by the Office of the Attorney General.[96]

In addition, the Office of the Attorney General oversees the carrying out

---

[93] Ley No. 4 (1977), Art. 108.
[94] Ley No. 83 (1997).
[95] Ley No. 82 (1997), Art. 19.
[96] "Informe Rendición de Cuenta, Fiscalía General de la Republica," presented to the National Assembly, August 4, 2001, p. 9.

of criminal sanctions and is responsible to assure that the rights of those detained or imprisoned are protected. It is authorized to carry out inspections of correctional institutions, review documents pertaining to the accused or those detained and to interview prisoners and detainees. If it finds infractions, it is empowered to issue orders requiring corrective action.[97]

Similar to other national institutions, the Office of the Attorney General has a vertical structure with national, provincial and municipal offices. The Attorney General and the vice-attorneys general are elected by the National Assembly, and as a measure to strengthen their independence, the 1997 law makes appointment for an indefinite period which may only be revoked pursuant to prescribed procedures for reasons set forth in the governing statute.[98] The Office of the Attorney General receives a separate budget from the national government. Like other public institutions it has labored under difficult physical and material conditions as a result of the economic crisis. Shortages of supplies and deteriorating buildings and offices have impeded improvement of the services its provides the public. Since 1991, the government has taken steps to assist in remedying some of these problems.

Further, like the legal profession and the judiciary, the Office of the Attorney General suffered for many years from the neglect of rigorous training of its personnel, particularly prosecutors functioning in the municipal and provincial offices and courts. Parallel to improvements in the law curriculum, the Office of the Attorney General has developed special advanced training programs to increase the level of expertise and professionalism.

---

[97] Ibid., Art. 28.
[98] Ibid., Arts. 34-48.

Chapter 4

DEVELOPMENT OF THE LEGAL PROFESSION AND THE PRACTICE OF LAW

The upheaval of 1959 had a dramatic impact on the legal profession. The nationalization of private businesses decimated the client base of most Havana law firms, and by 1962, a great number of lawyers had left Cuba.[1] At the same time, the legal profession, which had previously enjoyed both prestige and influence among those with political power, fell from grace. The practice of law itself came to be considered a parasitic bourgeois profession that would be unnecessary in the "new society" in which corruption, crime and exploitation would disappear. Castro, himself a lawyer, exhorted young people to study more useful things like medicine, engineering or science, instead of law. To the observer, it could have appeared that the revolution was following, in a figurative way, the Shakespearean phrase "[t]he first thing we do, let's kill all the lawyers."[2]

As the role of the courts and legal institutions in Cuban society shrank, legal education as well as the legal profession began to atrophy. In 1962, as part of the process of reorganizing the newly nationalized educational institutions, the Faculty of Law lost its status as an independent faculty of the University of Havana (the only law faculty in the country at the time) and became merely a school within the Faculty of the Humanities. The number of university students matriculating in the study of law dwindled, and in 1964-1965 no new students enrolled in the law school.[3] Between 1965 and

---

[1] For a description of the disintegration of one of Havana's leading law firms in 1959, see, Augustín Cruz, "It Took Only Three Years: The Destruction of a Law Firm," *American Bar Association Journal*, Vol. 50, January, 1964, p. 63.

[2] *Henry VI*, Part 2, Act IV, scene ii.

[3] Interview with Julio Fernández Bulté, former Dean of the Faculty of Law at the University of Havana, December 21, 1988. Enrollment in the Faculty of Law, the nation's only law school, dropped precipitously from 2,853 in 1958-59 to 159 in 1971-72. Luís Salas, "Emergence and Decline of Cuban Popular Tribunals," *Law & Society Review*, Vol. 17, 1983, p. 598.

1980 the median number of graduates from full-time study was fewer than fifty annually; none graduated in 1978 and 1979.[4]

Moreover, the law curriculum became very limited, partly as a result of the lack of concern for the replenishment of the profession and partly because traditional courses were no longer considered useful or relevant. For example, private enterprise law completely disappeared from the curriculum. Other courses that were regarded as having continuing but lesser value to a socialist society, such as contracts and commercial law, were reduced in scope. New courses on Marxist theory and economics were introduced. As in the past, the teaching methodology remained rigid and formalistic.[5]

Despite these adverse circumstances, the practice of law did not disappear altogether. Those who remained in private practice became occupied with a myriad of property issues, domestic relations problems and criminal defense cases. In 1965, consistent with the socialist policy of the new government, the Ministry of Justice approved, on an experimental basis, the establishment of collective law offices (*bufetes colectivos*) in Havana that would provide legal services at modest rates or free to those who could not pay. These were small law offices that functioned as profit-making collectives, the lawyers sharing their fees and expenses. In addition, lawyers took positions outside the practice of law. Many lawyers who were sympathetic to the revolution began working as advisors to and administrators of the institutions of the new government. Law students and young lawyers were called on to assist in the organization of the Popular Courts of the 1960s, which were presided over by lay judges and did not envisage a role for lawyers in the proceedings.[6]

Although it was already acknowledged by the mid-1960s that lawyers not only had a role in the development of the socialist system and were important to the process of institutionalization, recovery of the legal profession, in terms of both prestige and quality, would take several decades. In 1965, the Party appointed a Commission on Juridical Studies to analyze the laws and institutional framework of the new Cuban socialist system and to propose legislation that would provide the system with a firm juridical base. Blas Roca Calderío, a leader of the former Cuban Communist Party, presided over the commission. A shoemaker by trade, not a lawyer, Blas Roca is credited with promoting the legal institutionalization of the revolution.

As a result of the commission's work, the importance of the judicial system and the legal profession gained recognition. The First Congress of

---

[4] *Tesis Sobre la Vida Jurídica del País*, (Havana: Unión Nacional de Juristas Cubanos, 1987), pp. 19-21.

[5] Interview with Manuel Hevia, January 6, 1992, Havana, Cuba.

[6] For a description of the Popular Tribunals, see Chapter 4.

the Party in 1975 specifically noted the role of lawyers in the future development of the socialist system:

> The role of jurists must grow with the progress in perfecting our State and the new mechanisms of the System of Directing the Economy. We need more jurists better prepared and specialized in all the distinct branches of Law.[7]

In 1976, the law school was returned to its former status as an independent faculty in the University of Havana.

Today, the legal profession has emerged as a vital sector in contemporary Cuba. Legal services offices have expanded providing counsel to individuals and enterprises. Most substantial companies have enlarged their in-house legal staff. Moreover, efforts to prepare lawyers to assist in Cuba´s insertion into the international economy have included revamping the law school curriculum, a national program of post graduate courses and extensive professional and academic exchange programs with foreign lawyers and universities from Europe, Latin America and Canada.

I. THE BUFETES COLECTIVOS

The first significant legislation drafted by the Commission on Juridical Studies was the Law on the Organization of the Judicial System. Adopted in 1973, this law established a unified court system eliminating both the Revolutionary Tribunals and the lay Popular Tribunals.[8] The statute also abolished the private practice of law. Henceforth, all legal services to the population were to be provided through collective law offices, known as *bufetes colectivos*, organized and supervised by the Ministry of Justice since the mid 1960s.[9] Thus, in order to practice law, a lawyer was obligated to join one of the *bufetes colectivos.*[10]

By May 1973, a month before the new law on the judicial system was enacted, the number of *bufetes colectivos* had grown to thirty-eight, distributed among the six provinces.[11] These offices were staffed by 227 law-

---

[7] "Informe Central," *Primer Congreso del Partido Comunista de Cuba* (Havana, 1975), pp. 151-52.

[8] Ley No. 1250 (Ley de la Organización del Sistema Judicial), *Gaceta Oficial*, June 23, 1973.

[9] Ibid., Arts. 171, 173.

10Ibid., Art. 171

[11] The distribution was as follows: Pinar del Rio, 1; Havana, 16; Matanzas, 3; Las Villas, 8; Camagüey, 2; and Oriente, 8. Report of Dra. María Luisa Arteaga Abréu, president of the

yers.[12] Building on the experience of the *bufetes* in the 1960s, the Ministry of Justice designated a national organizing commission to develop both a plan for a national structure to administer the *bufetes colectivos* and a code of conduct for the lawyers. The National Organization of Bufetes Colectivos (ONBC) was created in 1974 to organize and oversee the network of collective law offices. At the same time, the Ministry of Justice invited eligible lawyers in private practice to join a *bufete* and issued regulations that broadened the types of judicial and administrative procedures in which lawyers were authorized to participate.[13]

The founding of the ONBC as a national institution was remarkable in several respects. It became the only vehicle through which lawyers could continue to provide legal services to individuals, thus bringing all lawyers under the code of ethics adopted by the ONBC governing bodies. It also created one of the first autonomous institutions in Cuba. Although the Ministry of Justice maintained oversight, the ONBC began to direct its own policy and administration. Blas Roca explained the importance of this independence in a speech at the founding of the ONBC: The lawyer could not be considered a public employee, subject to outside administrative authorities, if he were to fulfill his mission of representing the interests of his client before the courts.[14] It was not until 1984, however, that the legal basis for the independent status of the ONBC was created by statute. Adopted at a time when substantial reforms were taking place in virtually all areas of the legal system,[15] the law is reflective of continuing concern for improvement of the legal system in general.

The substantial deficit in lawyers, both in quantity and quality, posed a significant problem to the development of the *bufetes*. Great attention had been given to drafting new laws in the 1970s and to reorganizing the courts, but the replenishment of the legal profession had been completely ignored. At the same time, the demand for legal services was increasing as new laws,

---

provisional National Board of Directors of the Bufetes Colectivos, published in *Discursos en el Congreso de Constitución de los Bufetes Colectivos* (Havana, 1974), p. 20. In 1973, Cuba was still divided into six provinces; the 1976 Constitution increased the number to fourteen.

[12] Ibid.

[13] Acuerdo No. 34 (Reglamento de los Bufetes Colectivos y Código de Ética Profesional (Abogados)), *Gaceta Oficial*, March 7, 1974.

[14] Speech of Blas Roca at the closing of the National Constitutive Congress of the Bufetes Colectivos, January 13, 1974, in *Discursos en el Congreso de Constitución de los Bufetes Colectivos* (Havana, 1974), p. 34.

[15] In 1984, the Criminal Code, including the sentencing structure, underwent review for modification leading to a new Code in 1987. Other important legislative developments included the adoption of a Labor Code (1985), a national housing law (1984), a new Civil Code (1987) and the development of the arbitration system.

such as the Housing Law of 1984,[16] gave individuals new rights and responsibilities. The meager number of law graduates was clearly insufficient. In order to address the shortage of qualified lawyers, the Political Bureau of the Communist Party proposed that new law faculties be created to train more lawyers. In addition, the curriculum of the law faculties was overhauled.

Increasing the numbers and quality of law graduates, however, was not sufficient to assure competent and efficient legal services. The newly appointed Minister of Justice, Juan Escalona Reguera,[17] along with the leadership of ONBC, worked to expand and strengthen the ONBC as an institution. Developed jointly by the Ministry and the ONBC, Decree-Law 81, "On the Exercise of the Practice of Law and the Organization of Bufetes Colectivos," which became effective on Jurist's Day, June 8, 1984,[18] sets forth the structure and role of the ONBC as well as the regulation of the practice of law.[19] Article 5 affirms the autonomy of the ONBC:

> The ONBC is an autonomous national entity serving social interests and of a professional character, with its own juridical personality and property, consisting of jurists who join voluntarily, and governed by the present Decree-Law.

The law authorized the Ministry of Justice to issue more specific regulations governing the practice of law and the organization of the *bufetes colectivos*.[20] These regulations, issued in December of 1984, further defined the autonomous status of the ONBC:[21]

> Art. 6. The National Organization of Bufetes Colectivos develops its activities autonomously in conformity with its goals, is subordinate only to the law and is directed solely by the organs of direction recognized in its by-laws and in the present Regulation.
>
> Art. 7. The National Organization of Bufetes Colectivos has juridical personality and its own patrimony, the capacity to acquire and dispose of its property and to enter into contracts on its own behalf; it is entitled to rights and obligations and to exercise legal actions that correspond to it. The representation of the National Organiza-

---

[16] Ley No. 48 (Ley General de la Vivienda), *Gaceta Oficial Ext.*, No. 22, December 31, 1984.
[17] Juan Escalona Reguera is currently the Fiscal General of the Republic of Cuba.
[18] June 8 commemorates the date that the 19th century patriot and lawyer Ignacio Agramonte presented his thesis for his license in law.
[19] Decreto-Ley No. 81 (Ley Sobre el Ejercicio de la Abogacía y la Organización Nacional de Bufetes Colectivos), *Gaceta Oficial Ext.*, No. 12, June 8, 1984.
[20] Ibid., Disposiciones Especiales, Primera.
[21] Resolución No. 142 (Reglamento sobre el Ejercicio de la Abogacía y la Organización de Bufetes Colectivos) (Ministry of Justice), *Gaceta Oficial*, December 18, 1984.

tion of Bufetes Colectivos is exercised by its organs of direction in conformity with their respective legal authority and by the present regulation.

Thus, although the Ministry of Justice was to maintain some oversight functions,[22] the ONBC was given authority to direct its own affairs. As an institution, the ONBC is governed by a General Assembly of delegates elected by members of the local *bufetes*. The assembly, which meets annually, elects a seven-member National Board of Directors that develops policy and administers the organization for five-year periods. The ONBC provides the Ministry of Justice with periodic reports on its activities and any disciplinary actions taken against lawyers.

The Cuban system of *bufetes colectivos* bore some resemblance to the Soviet colleges of advokatura, but it was not patterned after the Soviet colleges and differed substantially. Both the Soviet colleges and the Cuban *bufetes colectivos* were supervised by the respective ministries of justice and were the exclusive providers of legal services based on state-established fees. The Soviet colleges, however, never functioned with the degree of self-governance that the Cuban *bufetes* have and were subordinated to local party institutions.[23] Nor did they take an active role in developing policy and legislative proposals as have the *bufetes colectivos*. Until the late 1980's, the Soviet colleges remained passive, bureaucratic institutions of aging practitioners, a good portion of whom did not even have law degrees, and who enjoyed little prestige.[24]

As an indication of the difference in their status, salaries of Cuban lawyers were consistently higher than their Soviet counterparts relative to average salaries among workers. Even in 1974, however, Cuban lawyers received a very substantial monthly salary of 231 pesos, which was almost double that of the average worker, an indication of their newly acknowledged importance and rehabilitation as a profession.[25] Whereas the average monthly income of a Cuban lawyer in 1989 (460 pesos) was more than

---

[22] Ibid., Art. 42. The primary areas of oversight concern programs of continuing legal education, evaluating performance of lawyers before the courts and other tribunals. The Ministry of Justice also has the right to review and approve changes in the fees charged, the number of *bufetes* and lawyers assigned to each. By law, and in practice, these functions are carried out in coordination with the ONBC and the Ministry rarely, if ever, sets aside an ONBC decision. It also conducts an audit of the financial activities of the ONBC.

[23] Eugene Huskey, "The Limits to Institutional Autonomy in the Soviet Union: The Case of the *Advokatura*," *Soviet Studies*, Vol. 34, No. 2, April 1982, pp. 200-227.

[24] Ibid., pp. 202, 217. See also, Peter Solomon, "The Role of Defence Counsel in the USSR: The Politics of Judicial Reform Under Gorbachev," *Criminal Law Quarterly*, Vol. 31, December, 1988, p. 84.

[25] Arteaga Abréu, p. 24.

twice the salary of the average worker,[26] Soviet lawyers' salaries in the late 1980s were only slightly higher than the average income.[27] Legal services in Cuba also were about twice as expensive for clients relative to their monthly salaries than they were in the Soviet Union in the late 1980s.[28]

Over the years the ONBC has not only become self-governing in terms of establishing internal policies, but it has become completely self-financing from fees charged to clients. The ONBC receives no government funding and has even occasionally contributed funds to public projects.[29] In addition, although salaries were initially set by the Ministry of Justice, today the ONBC controls these salaries which are paid out of income from client fees. According to Dr. Emiliano Manresa, former president of the National. Board of the ONBC: "The lawyer represents the interests of a citizen, at times against decisions of an administrative nature, against a public official or another citizen. If paid by the state he would be a public official, and the independence of his function would be compromised."[30] Thus, unlike education and health care services, the costs of which are assumed by the state, legal services in Cuba are contracted for on an individual basis. Clients sign a contract with a lawyer for specific services and pay a set fee ranging from 10 pesos for drawing up a simple document to as much as 100 pesos for more complicated matters involving litigation.[31] There is no charge for the initial interview or consultation. Those unable to pay for services may be provided counsel for free

Although Cuba has experimented with various kinds of bonus programs as material incentives to factory workers, the situation of lawyers is indeed unique. Today, as a result of ONBC policy changes since 1988, their income is entirely dependent on the number and complexity of the cases handled. The greater the number of cases handled, the more money a lawyer will earn. Fees are higher for more complicated legal problems, and even in simpler cases lawyers earn a higher percentage of the fee if the case turns out to be unusually time consuming. In the latter case, the fee proportion is worked out with the director of the local *bufete*. Moreover, there is no ceiling on how much a lawyer can earn; some may earn as much as 600 pesos

---

[26] Interview with Emiliano Manresa Porto, December 29, 1989, Havana, Cuba.

[27] Robert Rand, *Comrade Lawyer* (Boulder, Col.: Westview Press, 1991), p. 12. Solomon suggests that the low salaries and prestige of lawyers in the Soviet Union posed a barrier to reform even in the late 1980s. According to Solomon Soviet lawyers themselves opposed reforms which would give defense counsel greater participation in the criminal process because it meant more work for no extra pay. Solomon, p. 88.

[28] Raymond Michalowski, "Socialist Legality and the Practice of Law in Cuba," (unpublished manuscript, 1992), pp. 29-30.

[29] Interview with Emiliano Manresa.

[30] Esther Mosak, "En la Balanza," *Cuba Internacional*, No. 267, March, 1992, pp. 37-42.

[31] Michalowski, pp. 29-30.

or more—as much or higher than the highest salary range for any professional in Cuba.[32]

Decree-Law 81 sets forth the rights of lawyers and requirements for admission to practice in the *bufetes*. First, the term *abogado*, or lawyer, refers only to those who represent and defend the rights of individuals or juridical persons before the courts, organs of arbitration or administrative agencies, both nationally and internationally.[33] The practice, however, encompasses giving consultation as well as representation.[34] Members of the judiciary, prosecutors, administrators or arbitrators may not practice law.[35] To join a *bufete*, one must graduate from a law faculty in Cuba or in a foreign country with recognition or validation in Cuba, and be admitted to practice by the ONBC.[36] However, the Ministry of Justice may under extraordinary circumstances authorize someone to practice law during a determined period.[37] In addition, to be admitted to practice, an applicant must demonstrate good moral character and must not have been convicted of an intentional crime that would call him or her into public disrespect or be subject to criminal process for such a crime.[38] Lawyers are required to keep current with legislative developments and to continue perfecting their knowledge and skills, but there is no specific requirement of certification for continuing legal education.[39]

To join a *bufete*, a lawyer applies to the respective provincial director who evaluates the application and sends a recommendation to the ONBC. Once admitted, a lawyer can practice anywhere in the country regardless of the *bufete* to which he belongs. Similarly, clients have the right to choose a lawyer of their preference to represent them, and they may go to any *bufete*

---

[32] Interview with Emiliano Manresa. Dr. Manresa reported in 1989 that one lawyer had earned upwards of 1,000 pesos in one month, although that was unusual. Since the economic crisis hit in 1990, the purchasing power of the peso declined substantially. Thus, unskilled workers in the tourist industry have higher effective earnings than professionals because they receive tips in hard currency. Although the government has raised the salaries of some professionals, the economy is still too weak to elevate them to their former earning power.

[33] Decreto-Ley 81(1984), Art. 1.

[34] Ibid.

[35] Ibid., Art. 16(c).

[36] Ibid., Art. 3. Lawyers wishing to join the ONBC make application to the corresponding Provincial Director where they want to practice. The application is sent by the Provincial Director, along with his recommendation, to the National Board of Directors (JDN). Ibid., Art. 17.

[37] The Ministry of Justice gave special permission to a retired lawyer whom Elizardo Sánchez, leader of the Comité Cubano Pro Derechos Humanos, had requested to defend him at his trial in the fall of 1989.

[38] Decreto-Ley 81(1984), Art. 16.

[39] Both the ONBC and the UNJC organize courses and seminars for lawyers on legal developments.

they wish. The lawyer, however, is not obligated to take the case if there is a justifiable reason to reject it,[40] and in the event the lawyer does refuse, the director of the *bufete* will appoint another lawyer to represent the client.

The ONBC is governed by rules of ethics[41] and lawyers may be disciplined by the ONBC for violations. The first Code of Ethics, adopted in 1978, set forth grounds for discipline which included: gross negligence, intervening in a case or substituting for another lawyer without his or her prior knowledge and consent; breach of confidential relationship; violation of regulations governing the *bufetes* or any violation of law; impeding justice; resorting to false testimony or evidence; and being disrespectful to officials and judges of the courts, prosecutors, other lawyers and persons involved in legal procedures.[42] Discipline may consist of a warning, a fine, transfer or even dismissal. In most cases the disciplinary measure is a private or public warning, but in cases of serious violation, the lawyer could be suspended or dismissed.[43] In each case the disciplinary decision could be appealed to the National Board, the decision of which is final except in cases of dismissal or denial of admission. In such cases appeal could be made to the Ministry of Justice.[44] In contrast, the Soviet advokatura never adopted a code of ethics.[45]

In 1982 and 1983 a number of lawyers and judges were tried for corruption. Apparently, lawyers had been taking money under the table from clients and using some of it to pay off judges in return for acquittals. Lawyers involved in this scandal, known as *toga sucia* (the dirty toga), were dismissed from legal practice and sentenced to jail.[46] Although there are occasional reports of isolated incidents of corruption, primarily asking clients for unauthorized payments, it is not perceived to be a systemic problem as it was prior to 1959.

---

[40] The regulations governing the practice of law specify justifications for refusing to take a case. These generally include situations where there is a conflict of interest by virtue of blood relationship, friendship or other compromising relationship with the opposing party. Resolución No. 142-84 (Ministry of Justice), Art. 50. Although the regulation does not address situations where the lawyer simply has too many cases already to be able to attend to another, this often happens, and he or she is excused from taking the case.

[41] This code seems to have been subsumed by Resolución No. 142-84 which sets forth not only the infractions for which a lawyer may be disciplined but also the procedure for such discipline and the appeal process. Resolución No.142-84 (Ministry of Justice), Arts. 59-70.

[42] Ibid., Art. 59.

[43] Decreto-Ley 81 (1984), Art. 27.

[44] Ibid., Art. 29.

[45] Michael Burrage, "Advokatura: In Search of Professionalism and Pluralism in Moscow and Leningrad," *Law and Social Inquiry,* Summer 1990, p. 462.

[46] Interview with Emiliano Manresa Porto, December 20, 1988, Havana, Cuba.

Socialist Legality and the Practice of Law

The law guarantees every lawyer the right to practice with independence[47] and with all the legal rights and guarantees to initiate proceedings and make statements related to the rights he or she defends.[48] The law also obliges lawyers to observe and contribute to the strengthening of socialist legality.[49] In a sense, this obligation is not very different from the obligations imposed on lawyers in the United States, who as officers of the court, are expected to scrupulously obey the law. It differs, however, in that Cuban lawyers are expected to support socialist ideology and to work for the perfection of socialist law, whereas U.S. lawyers have no obligation to support any particular ideology or legal philosophy. The question that might be asked with respect to Cuba, where the collective good generally takes precedence over the individual, is to what extent does the socialist system, particularly its political dynamic, limit a lawyer's ability to freely defend his or her client's interests against the state.

The 1977 revision of the law of judicial organization stipulated that legal representation be conducted in a manner that would "avoid abusing the legal guarantees of defense in ways that would impede the social functions of justice."[50] In addition, one of the violations listed in the Code of Ethics is conduct by an attorney that "impedes justice from fulfilling its social function."[51] The meaning is unclear, but regardless of whether the 1977 statutory provision was interpreted to mean anything other than that lawyers were obligated to obey the law and not obstruct justice, there is no evidence to suggest that Cuban lawyers have been pressured not to vigorously represent their clients.[52] In fact, the new law and regulations governing the practice of law that were adopted in 1984 emphasize the independence of the attorney and the obligation to defend his or her client's interests with maximum diligence.[53] For example, the regulations specifically state:

---

[47] Decreto-Ley No. 81 (1984), Art. 2(a).
[48] Ibid., Art. 2(b).
[49] Ibid., Art. 2(c).
[50] Ley No. 4 (Ley de Organización del Sistema Judicial), Art. 143, *Gaceta Oficial*, August 25, 1977.
[51] Código de Ética, Art. 2 (10), *Gaceta Oficial*, December 27, 1978.
[52] Some jurists have noted, however, that during the 1970s lawyers in general were not very competent and frequently acted passively in encounters with state agencies Interview with Emiliano Manresa Porto, December 20, 1988. According to Manresa, in the 1970s the best lawyers joined the judiciary or the Fiscalia. This pattern has changed considerably in recent years.
[53] Resolución No. 142-84 (Ministry of Justice), Art. 34 (b).

> In the practice of law attorneys enjoy the guarantees established in the law, by virtue of which no one can interfere with the decisions of a technical character made pursuant to their responsibility.[54]

This emphasis on diligence, independence and competence is consistent with the general concern and policy of strengthening the *bufetes* and the quality of legal services. It appears to be having a positive effect.

Moreover, in the area of criminal defense there is much anecdotal evidence of Cuban lawyers having worked with great dedication and diligence on their clients' behalf, even in sensitive cases. In one case related by a young criminal defense lawyer, the prosecution tried to raise the homosexuality of the accused as being material to guilt. The lawyer, who admitted to being homophobic himself, nevertheless successfully blocked admission of such evidence and won a reduced sentence for his client against whom there was evidence of guilt.[55] In another case, a lawyer gained acquittal, on grounds of insufficient evidence, for a client accused of writing anti-government slogans on a wall.[56]

In 1989, the then national director of the ONBC argued that "the revolutionary lawyer is the one who provides his client the best defense he can."[57] Yet despite repeated encouragement as well as examples of highly motivated and capable defense lawyers, there remained lawyers who did not actively defend their clients, a fact that drew the attention of their colleagues within the *bufetes*. In a paper delivered at the National Juridical Conference of the ONBC in 1989, the proponent criticized lawyers for not actively participating in the preparatory phase of criminal prosecutions.[58] Even today, many defense lawyers do not take advantage of the opportunities provided in the current Code of Criminal Procedure to propose proofs during the preparatory phase.

The role of defense counsel in the trials resulting from the drug trafficking scandal of 1989 drew strong criticism from some members of the Cuban legal community. The trial of the military personnel, including decorated

---

[54] Ibid., Art. 2.

[55] Interview with Prof. Jorge Arránz, June 11, 1990, Havana, Cuba.

[56] Interview with Menelao Mora, January 7, 1992, Havana, Cuba. In contrast, Soviet lawyers were far less vigorous in defense of their clients. See, e.g., Peter Solomon, "The Case of the Vanishing Acquittal: Informal Norms and the Practice of Soviet Criminal Justice," *Soviet Studies*, vol. 39, No. 4, 1987, p. 547. See also, Solomon, "The Role of Defence Counsel in the USSR," p. 84.

[57] Interview with Emiliano Manresa, December 29, 1989, Havana, Cuba.

[58] Mariano Mieres Martí, "Los Abogados en el Fase Preparatorio," published in a collection of papers entitled *Ponencias Derecho Penal* (Havana: Organización Nacional de Bufetes Colectivos, 1989), pp. 55-77.

General Arnaldo Ochoa, was televised nationally almost in its entirety.[59] The broadcasts provoked daily commentary among Cuban lawyers who debated the evidence and the merits of the defense counsel in informal conversations.[60] Among the lawyers with whom I spoke, none thought the defendants were innocent or that the evidence against them was insufficient for convictions, though some questioned the legal justification for the death penalty. In general, however, the consensus was that the defense counsel, with few exceptions, had been unduly passive in the face of the aggressive prosecutor.

In contrast, a second trial, that of former Minister of the Interior José Abrantes and members of his staff, which took place a month later, inspired praise for the quality of the defense counsel. The trial was video taped and shown fairly widely to groups of lawyers as well as to some Party members. Unlike the former trial, where the government had appointed military lawyers to defend the accused, the defendants in the Abrantes trial exercised their legal right to appoint their own counsel and chose from among the best criminal defense lawyers in Havana's *bufetes*. Although none of the defendants was acquitted, the defense counsel did manage to obtain reduced sentences and drew rave reviews from their peers for their performance. In fact, their energetic and intelligent defense was held up by some as a standard for all criminal lawyers.

The impact of increasing professionalism is felt in the area of civil law as well. In cases challenging administrative decisions, such as those made by the Housing Institute, lawyers have improved as advocates for their clients.[61] They have also become advocates for reform in aspects of civil law.[62]

Thus, the obligation to support socialist legality, does not require compromising the diligent representation of their clients' interests under the law. One area, however, in which lawyers are called upon specifically to contribute to the strengthening of socialist law is in the education of both their clients and other citizens with respect to their legal rights.[63]

---

[59] Although it is impossible to know exactly what portions were omitted from broadcast, several persons who were present at the trials commented to me that they were quite surprised at the extensiveness of the television broadcasts.

[60] I was in Cuba during the trials. This information is based on conversations with Cuban lawyers during that period.

[61] Interview with Rodolfo Dávalos Fernández, Legal Director of the National Housing Institute of Cuba, Havana, March 24, 1989.

[62] See papers collected in *Ponencias Derecho Civil* and *Ponencias Derecho Penal*, both published by the ONBC in 1989.

[63] Decreto-Ley 81 (1984), Art. 2(ch).

The ONBC Today

Since 1984, the ONBC has expanded significantly in size and importance. The number of *bufetes* has grown to more than 250 nationwide, some of which are staffed by as many as 50 or more lawyers.[64] Likewise, the number of lawyers working in the *bufetes* increased from 634 in 1965 to approximately 2,000 by 1992 and has remained at that number since.[65] There are also two types of special *bufetes*: those that handle criminal cases for defendants who cannot afford to pay the fee for an attorney (*de oficio*), and those that handle appeals (*Bufete Especializado de Casación*). In addition, in 1994, the ONBC established the Bufete Internacional to handle matters and cases for foreign visitors and residents. This *bufete* is a source of hard currency for the ONBC as it charges its clients higher fees than those charged Cuban citizens and the fees are valued in U.S. dollars.

The number of cases handled by the ONBC increased by more than 50 percent in the 1980s, from 114,675 in 1980 to 177,015 in 1989.[66] Today, cases exceed 200,000 annually. In Havana a single *bufete* may handle 8-9,000 cases a year.[67] The most common cases concern divorce, inheritance, housing matters and criminal defense. The growth in the number of cases particularly civil, stems from several factors. First, the new civil code and housing law provided the basis for an increased number of civil actions. Second, the ONBC itself embarked on a promotion campaign using weekly television spots that provided citizens with legal advice and answered questions about legal problems. The program was part of a concerted effort to get citizens to seek the assistance of the *bufetes* to resolve legal and administrative problems, as opposed to going to local or national Party units, which, as already mentioned, had taken a major role in dispute resolution in the 1960s and 1970s. In the 1980s authorities tried to reverse this habit because it undermined efforts to strengthen the legal system. Newspapers also carry regular columns discussing legal issues, particularly those related to housing and workers' rights. The effort appears to have met with success.

In order to meet the growing demand for legal services, the Ministry of Justice approved a program in 1982 of obligatory social service for recent law graduates. Under this program, law graduates were required to work at a *bufete colectivo* for three years. While at the *bufete*, the young lawyers

---

64 Ibid.

65 Mosak, p. 38; interview with Raúl S. Mantilla Ramírez, president of the ONBC, Havana, Cuba, June 16, 1999.

66 "Principales Indicadores de la Prestación de Servicios Jurídicos," mimeograph (ONBC 1989).

67 Mosak, p. 39.

received additional training and were exposed to a range of practice, including civil, labor and criminal law. They received a set salary of 198 pesos in the first and second years.[68] In their third year, they were treated as full members of the *bufete* and received the same remuneration as other lawyers. They also received an annual evaluation which was a prerequisite to remain working at the *bufete*. Upon completion of three years' service, they could decide to continue working at the *bufete* or to seek employment in other legal areas, such as counsel to commercial enterprises or government agencies, the procurator's office, etc. As a result of this program, the number of lawyers working in the *bufetes* increased by about 250 each year from 1988 to 1992.[69] This program has been eliminated allowing law graduates to fulfill their social service obligations in a wide variety of jobs, including entry level judiciary posts, in the office of the attorney general,and in enterprises as well as in the *bufetes*.

The profile of lawyers working in the *bufetes* has changed considerably since 1980. In 1989, fewer than 21 percent of the lawyers were over 45, and almost 60 percent were under 30 years of age, reflecting the number of recent graduates who are joining the profession.[70] According to a 1989 report, of the young lawyers who entered between 1983 and 1986, almost 60 percent remained working in the *bufetes* after completing their three-year social service commitment.[71] By the end of the 1990s the vast majority of the *bufete* lawyers belonged to the generation that graduated from law school after 1985.

The evolution of the ONBC in the 1990s also reflects reforms taking place in Cuba. Thus, since 1993, the ONBC moved into new areas of representation. For example, since the early 1990s, many large state farms have been broken up and the land given over to cooperatives and to private farmers, particularly for coffee and tobacco growing. This growing privatization in agriculture produced new clients for the ONBC which now provides legal assistance in the area of agrarian law. The ONBC has also developed specialists in the areas of finance, commercial and intellectual property law enabling lawyers from the *bufetes colectivos* to provide legal assistance to state enterprises. A special unit of labor law specialists not provide legal advice and representation to the Cuban Workers Central and its member unions.

---

[68] Interview with Emiliano Manresa, December 20, 1992.

[69] Ibid.

[70] "Composición por Grupos de Edades de los Abogados Miembros y Jóvenes Juristas que Cumplen el Servicio Social en la ONBC," mimeograph (ONBC, 1989).

[71] "Promoción de Jóvenes Juristas Que Han Cumplido el Servicio Social en la ONBC," mimeograph (ONBC, 1989).

The organization has also become much more actively involved in the debate over legal reform, particularly in civil and criminal law. The ONBC sponsors national and regional conferences on legal issues at which lawyers not only engage in discussion of technical issues, such as resolving certain inheritance or divorce problems, but also present papers exploring theoretical issues and proposals for reform of both law and legal practice. For example, one paper presented in 1989 called for greater diligence among criminal defense lawyers during the preparatory phase of the criminal procedure;[72] others critiqued the provision of the Criminal Code entitled "social dangerousness."[73] These papers are often published by the ONBC, thus adding to the growing body of legal literature in Cuba. In 1998, the ONBC co-sponsored an international seminar in Havana on alternative dispute resolution. Such exchanges have had a positive impact on professional expertise and morale among the lawyers.

In addition, the ONBC participates actively in the development and critique of legislation. It organizes special commissions to study or to make legislative proposals and to draft reports that will be submitted to the appropriate commission of the National Assembly or other institutions responsible for drafting legislation. Members of the *bufetes* also participate in the National Union of Cuban Jurists (UNJC), the national bar association. Some are active members of the various law societies organized by the UNJC, particularly the Civil and Family Law Society and the Criminal Law Society, and many attend other lectures and events sponsored by the UNJC. They also have increasing contact with lawyers and legal service organizations in other countries resulting in important exchanges of experience and materials.

Practice in a Bufete Colectivo

In many ways, Cuba's lawyers resemble their counterparts in U.S. legal service and public defender offices which have faced severe budgetary restraints in recent years. Despite the increase in the number of lawyers at Cuba's *bufetes colectivos*, lawyers carry large case loads and work under

---

[72] Mieres Martí, pp. 55-77.

[73] For example, see Mario Alberto Taglo y Babé, "Contribución para el Perfeccionamiento del Vigente Código Penal Cubano," in *Enfoques Jurídicos de Abogados Cubanos*, (Havana: ONBC, 1989), pp. 202-264; Carmen López González, et al., "Algunas Consideraciones Sobre el Estado Peligroso en Cuba," published in a collection of papers entitled *Ponencias Derecho Penal* (Havana: Organización Nacional de Bufetes Colectivos, 1989), pp. 153-178.

very difficult physical conditions, particularly in the early 1990s with the shrinkage of hard currency and imports. These problems seem to have been more acute in Havana than elsewhere because of the density of Havana's population.

Until recently, the economic crisis made it very difficult for the ONBC to obtain necessary supplies and equipment. Secretaries typed legal documents on a manual typewriter, generally with a well-worn ribbon. Cuba's telephone system dated to the 1950s and frequently the one or two telephones that a *bufete* had was out of order.[74] The *bufete* offices, like everyone else, suffered the black outs caused by power shortages. Moreover, the scarcity of gasoline in the early 1990s crippled the public transportation system and posed enormous obstacles to adequate client contact and delivery of service. One lawyer told me that his colleagues often peddled more than thirty kilometers from Havana to visit clients who were held in detention. It is a tribute to the dedication of many of these lawyers that they persevered under such conditions to diligently represent their clients.

The appeals process was also reportedly plagued by inefficiencies in telegram and mail service, sometimes delaying delivery of petitions for appeal until after the expiration of the appeal date. The *bufete* specializing in appeals submitted a special report to the General Assembly at its meeting in June 1990, in which it detailed the difficulties and published a series of communications to the president of the Supreme Court in which the lawyers described the seriousness of the problem and solicited assistance in finding a solution that would preserve the rights of the appellants.[75] The report demonstrates not only the difficulties caused by inefficiencies in the postal service, but also the diligence of the lawyers in protecting the rights of their clients.

There have been subjective impediments as well. As in many other countries, Cuban lawyers frequently have to contend with delay, inefficiency and ineptness in the court system, and often, it is the lawyer who is blamed by the client for the delay or unfavorable outcome. As one young lawyer complained:

> People consider us to be professionals and come to us to solve their problems. But we are not like doctors who can give a consultation and then a cure. To solve a problem, we have to depend on the efficient work of others like police instructors, administra-

---

[74] The telephone system is gradually improving as a result of foreign capital investment and technology.

[75] Bufete Especializado de Casación, *Información*, mimeographed report distributed at the General Assembly of the *Bufetes Colectivos*, Havana, June 8, 1990. According to the report, the *bufete* handled 2,564 appeals in the first five months of 1990. Ibid., p. 29.

> tors and the courts. But we cannot solve a legal problem if others are not doing their job, and the clients sometimes think it is our fault.[76]

At the General Assembly of the ONBC, held in June 1990, before the full impact of the impending economic crisis was felt, young lawyers in particular were highly critical of the courts and the lack of professionalism among judges in the trial courts.[77] They also had harsh words for inefficiencies in the prosecutor's office as well as for police instructors who do not produce required reports and files necessary for the defense of criminal defendants. Responses to these criticisms by representatives of the courts and the Ministry of Interior were honest and candid, producing a consensus that the quality of personnel in these institutions was not acceptable and had to be improved if the legal system was to work properly.

Today, material conditions in the *bufetes* have improved substantially, although still far from ideal. Almost all offices are computerized and linked by systems of electronic communications. New digital telephone lines are being installed throughout the country, facilitating communications. In addition, the leadership of the ONBC has introduced innovative programs to train lawyers in new fields of law relevant to Cuba's economic reforms. Lawyers are given the opportunity to take a sabatical and to study abroad.

However, even though salaries are high in comparison with other Cuban workers, the Cuban peso has lost much of its purchasing power. As a result many lawyers seek employment in commercial sectors where the economic rewards are greater because, in addition to their peso salary, they may receive goods or even a portion of their salary in hard currency. There may be other perks as well, such as transportation to and from work and meals may be provided at the workplace.[78]

Despite problems, Cuban lawyers have reclaimed a place of importance in society and have developed considerable pride in their profession. Very different than the lawyers practicing in the 1950s, both in attitude and training, they display a deep understanding of the everyday problems of the Cuban population, whose interests they represent on a daily basis. For many, this experience influences their personal sense of justice.

---

[76] Interview with Avelino González González, June 10, 1990, Havana, Cuba.

[77] I attended this General Assembly meeting, June 8-9, 1990, and this information is based on my observations and notes.

[78] Such perks are common in enterprises in the export sector, joint ventures with foreign investors and in enterprises which deal with tourism.

III. NEW INDEPENDENT LAW OFFICES

Although Cuba does not permit independent legal practice, since the early 1990s when the government began to court foreign investment, it has permitted the formation of new law offices which provide legal assistance to foreign nationals, be they investors, workers or tourists.[79] These services include the legal work connected with commercial dealings such as gaining approval of an investment deal, compliance with Cuban commercial regulations and registration of foreign firms, contract disputes, protection of intellectual property as well as immigration issues of foreign workers and residents. Services also include personal assistance such as criminal defense of foreigners, questions of inheritance, matrimony and divorce. There are now more than half a dozen such offices, most of which are located in Havana. Services are charged for in hard currency at rates substantially higher than those paid by Cuban citizens.

Each of these *bufetes* or offices has an institutional link to a ministry or other Cuban entity. For example, the Consultoría Jurídica Internacional belongs to the company CIMEX; the Bufete Internacional is an entity of the tourism enterprise Cubanacan; LEX, S.A., which handles intellectual property registrations and claims, is affiliated with the Cuban Chamber of Commerce; Rado y Asociados is a law office connected with Habaguanex, S.A., the enterprise belonging to the Office of the Historian of the City of Havana responsible for the restoration and revitalization of the historic district of Old Havana. As noted, the ONBC has also established such services for foreigners and has the advantage of having offices nationwide. Foreign lawyers are permitted to establish branch offices in Cuba, but these are exclusively confined to the Duty Free Zones.[80] Foreign lawyers, however, may not practice before the courts, tribunals or administrative bodies in Cuba.

---

[79] The formation of these law offices was permitted in Decreto-Ley No.77 (Sobre las Sociedades Civiles de Servicio), *Gaceta Oficial Esp.*, No.1, January 25, 1984, but this provision was not utilized until the economic changes of the 1990s necessitated the formation of such specialized services for foreign companies, individuals and joint ventures.

[80] In the Berroa duty free zone of Havana, there are three foreign law offices operating, two Spanish and one Dutch. Their services are limited to providing legal assistance to the enterprises which operate in the duty free zones and they cannot represent their clients before the courts or other tribunals in Cuba.

IV. LEGAL ADVISORS TO STATE INSTITUTIONS AND ENTERPRISES

For those not working at a *bufete*, one of their career options is to become a legal advisor to state agencies, ministries and commercial enterprises, whether or not state owned. In 1999, about 30% of the lawyers in Cuba worked as legal advisors.[81] As a kind of in-house counsel, these lawyers provide legal services and advice, particularly with respect to commercial relationships and contracts.[82] They also represent these institutions in arbitration and court proceedings, although the institution or enterprise may also choose to contract for a lawyer from one of the *bufetes* to do so. Unlike lawyers who work for *bufetes*, legal advisors receive a set salary established by the State Committee on Prices. The salaries are generally lower than those of many lawyers who work in the *bufetes colectivos*, but they often receive other perks and bonuses from their employer.

Little has been written about these legal advisors. Prior to the economic reforms of the 1990s, their primary importance was to assist the management of commercial enterprises in fulfilling their legal obligations under the highly centralized economic system:

> It corresponds to the legal advisor to assist in the perfection of economic contracts, in the first place, advising the chief of the enterprise and the enterprise council about the obligatory nature of contracts, its legal force and the economic and political consequences resulting from disregard for the economic legislation.[83]

Under the system of a centrally planned and managed economy where even international trade was negotiated by centralized government agencies, the lawyer was relegated to a minor role in which he or she reviewed contracts solely for their technical compliance with regulatory norms. However, the process of decentralization and restructuring of the state enterprises since the mid-1990s both augments and changes the role of the legal advisor.

Now that the economy is increasingly decentralized and economic relationships are more dynamic, the legal advisors must take a more active role in protecting the interests of the enterprise. In addition to getting current in

---

[81] Documents prepared for the Fifth Congress of the UNJC held January 19-21, 2000.

[82] The functions of legal advisors are governed by Decreto No. 138 (Normas para el Trabajo de Asesoramiento Jjurídico en las Entidades Estatales), *Gaceta Oficial Ext.*, No.5, March 23, 1987.

[83] Pablo Prendes Lima, "Algunos Apuntes Acerca del Contenido Político-Ideológico en la Actividad de la Asesoría Jurídica de las Empresas Estatales," in *Política Ideología y Derecho* (Havana: Editorial de Ciencias Sociales, 1985), p. 212.

new areas of substantive law, lawyers must now adapt to the adversarial, competitive nature of market-based transactions. Considerable effort is needed to prepare them to be advocates, to be participants in negotiations, to draft and analyze contracts and not just to be the passive technicians they were in the past. Given the critical importance of commercial law and international trade to Cuba's future, one can expect greater attention will be paid to improving the skills of this sector of the legal profession.

Undoubtedly in-house counsel are extremely important to the current process of reorganizing state enterprises as independent, self-financing businesses.[84] Thus, the legal institutions have recognized the need to prioritize the development of this sector, providing both continued legal education, opportunities to participate in international events and exchanges and increases in salaries and benefits. Improvements in the law school curriculum have also provided a stronger base of knowledge among recent graduates. Most lawyers working in these enterprises are young and continue to be given special courses in areas related to commercial and intellectual property law. At the same time, however, management must change its perception of its legal staff as passive subordinates and incorporate their legal expertise and analysis into enterprise decision-making.

V. LEGAL EDUCATION

Recovery of legal education took a long time. After almost two decades of experimentation in search of a curriculum adequate to form lawyers capable of fulfilling their role in a socialist system based on the Soviet model, the law faculties today have been transformed into vigorous, modern academic centers which attract the brightest among Cuba's university students. Post-graduate education has been expanded, including the development of masters and doctoral programs. Many young professors have studied abroad since the early 1990s. In fact, Cuban law professors today are contracted by law faculties in Latin American countries to impart classes.

---

[84] See, Chapter 9.

Evolution of the Curriculum

It was not until 1976 that the Ministry of Higher Education reestablished the Faculty of Law as an independent faculty within the university. Although fewer than 50 students matriculated in the day school during most of the 1970s, many more attended law school at night through a special program initiated in 1969.[85] At the same time the curriculum was reviewed and redesigned to meet the needs of the evolving legal system.

A new plan of study was adopted, called Plan A, which included 3,500 hours of study over a five-year period in four areas of specialty: penal, civil, international and legal advisor to enterprises. Students chose a specialty area upon entering. The plan also introduced practice as a part of study, and students were given the opportunity, albeit limited, to spend time as interns at various institutions. In 1980, this plan was criticized as insufficient to produce the quality of lawyers and legal advisors needed. The curriculum was considered still too narrow. A new curriculum was introduced, but within two years it, too, came under review for modifications. So discouraged were some of the leadership with the quality of legal training, that the Minister of Justice once remarked that most lawyers who graduated before 1984 were useless.[86]

In 1982-83 a new plan was proposed to improve the quality of lawyers. Implemented in 1984, this plan increased required study to 4,500 hours, adding a semester to the program. It also broadened the subject areas from four to eight: Roman law, mercantile law, financial law, agrarian law, civil and criminal procedure, general civil, economic contract law and private property law. Practical education was expanded, and students were also were required to present two major research papers (trabajos de cursos): one in the first two years and a more specialized investigation in the third and fourth years.

Although Plan B represented a marked improvement, in 1989 a committee of professors and experienced lawyers began yet another study of the curriculum with the goal of developing a new plan to be instituted in 1990-91. According to then Dean Julio Fernández Bulté, the starting point of the new plan was its conceptual basis: the definition of the legal profession and a model of the professional in socialism.[87] The plan took into account the various activities of the different institutions and the specific challenges that

---

[85] Interview with Julio Fernández Bulté, former Dean of the Faculty of Law at the University of Havana, December 21, 1988.

[86] Interview with Juan Escalona Reguera, former Minister of Justice, December 19, 1988, Havana, Cuba.

[87] Interview with Julio Fernández Bulté.

lawyers faced in Cuba. It, therefore, emphasized basic theory and history. Substantive subjects were organized in four areas of study: penal, civil, international (both public and private) and commercial enterprise law (including economic law, labor law, finance, etc.). Students were required to take courses in all areas. Practical experience increased to a total of twenty-four weeks.

The dramatic changes in Cuba after the collapse of the Soviet model led to further reconsideration of the curriculum. As a result, new courses have been added, particularly those previously abandoned or given secondary importance, such as corporate and commercial law, international trade law, intellectual property law and environmental law. The expansion of the curriculum into these areas of commercial law required intense preparation of the faculty. Foreign lawyers and academics, primarily from Spain and Latin America, came to Cuba to offer seminars and post graduate courses. A number of Cuban law professors went abroad to study, many earning masters and doctorate degrees.

At the same time that the curriculum was being revised, professors at the law faculties began to experiment with methodology, setting aside the rigid lecture format that traditionally characterized university classes. Younger faculty, in particular, seek to engage students in discussion in class and work with students in special research projects. Many older jurists who complained bitterly in the past of the poor quality of Cuba's law graduates are now enthusiastic about the quality of recent graduates, who are viewed as more skilled, dynamic and dedicated.

A grant from the Canadian government enabled the law faculties to establish computer laboratories for students and faculty. At the Law Faculty of the University of Havana, five computers are available 24 hours a day, plus an additional 20 computers available during school hours, all permanently connected to the internet. The university also has a web page. In addition to expanding their research capabilities, this network facilitates faculty communication of assignments and notices to students and sharing of research.

Admission and Enrollment

Over the years, the number of law students has increased substantially. In 1984, law faculties were created at the universities in Camagüey, Santiago de Cuba and Villa Clara. Enrollment increased steadily and, since 1988, there have been over 1,100 law students at the University of Havana and approximately 3,500 in the entire country in all five years of school.[88] In addition, independent law faculties have been created in all provinces with limited specialties. At first, the study of law did not attract the most qualified students, who continued to pursue more prestigious careers in science and medicine. As the legal profession has become more respected and independent—as well as better paid—admission to law school has become increasingly competitive. More and more women have also entered the profession and now make up between 60 and 70 percent of all law students as well as more than half of the lawyers in the *bufetes*.[89]

Entrance requirements are now even more rigorous as competition for admission to university has intensified. In 1987, 35,000 applicants were refused entrance into the university.[90] There are two ways in which students are selected: 40 percent are chosen solely on the basis of pre-university scores; and 60 percent are admitted by special exam. The exam consists of mathematics, Spanish language (writing and grammar) and history. Many of those applying by way of special exam are students seeking admission after doing their military service or who wish to change careers. Applicants for law school must also submit to an interview by the National Union of Cuban Jurists to assure their moral aptitude.

Those denied entry as full-time students may, however, still pursue a degree in almost all areas of study through a system known as *enseñanza libre*, a kind of correspondence course. Students in this program buy books and follow a program of study worked out with the faculty. They do not attend classes, but may view classes on videotapes. They take three exams a year. More than one thousand students have enrolled in this program in 2002 and hundreds more are studying law in university extension programs established in cities throughout the country.[91]

Although professionalism can also breed elitism, several factors may slow, if not prevent, its happening in the legal profession in Cuba. First, education from grade school through post-graduate degrees is free in Cuba. Thus, tuition to law school is free for Cuban residents, as is room and board. Students must pay for books, but the price of books in Cuba is very modest as production is subsidized by the government. As a result, university students come from a broad range of backgrounds, and it is not unusual to find the daughter of a small farmer or a hotel floor sweeper is a law student.

[88] Ibid.

[89] Ibid. Women are also well represented in other areas of legal work. One-third of the judges of the Supreme Court were female in 1990.

[90] Ibid.

[91] Interview with Juan Mendoza, Vice Dean, Faculty of Law, University of Havana, May 15, 2002.

Further, as already mentioned, upon graduation, all students are required to do social service as a way of repaying society for its investment in their education.[92] Until recently, for most law graduates this meant three years' service in a *bufete colectivo* after which time they may choose to apply to stay or seek other employment. Today, there are other sectors which claim the services of recent graduates legal advisor offices and state enterprises, the Office of the Attorney General and the judiciary.

Post-Graduate Education

Substantial attention is paid to post-graduate education, both for faculty and law graduates, including judges, lawyers, prosecutors, notaries and legal advisors. Concern for upgrading skills in areas of law hitherto ignored as well as bringing Cuban lawyers up to date on legislative developments in Cuba led to the organization of a Post Graduate School, directed by a board composed of the director of the ONBC, the Attorney General, the president of the Supreme Court, the Minister of Justice, the Director of the UNJC and the Minister of Higher Education. Although there is no formal requirement that legal professionals enroll in such courses, most do at one time or another. Time off from their regular work duties is given so that they may attend these courses. In addition to the courses offered by this program, the ONBC has established its own post-graduate course program for its members.

In addition, Masters programs are available both in Cuba and at universities abroad. Since 1999, through cooperation with faculty from the Universities of Valencia and Barcelona, more than 400 Cuban lawyers and academics have received masters degrees in a variety of specialties related to business law, including intellectual property, commercial law and finance.[93] In addition, the board organizing post-graduate education instituted programs to accredit jurists as Specialists, a title which has the same academic standing as a Masters Degree but is oriented toward practice as opposed to research. In 2002, Specialist titles were offered in three areas: criminal law, civil law and legal advisors. The two-year program is open to all lawyers,

[92] This requirement was established for law graduates and other graduates of technical schools by law in 1973. Ley No. 1254 (Sobre el Servicio Social de Egresados) *Gaceta Oficial*, No.18,} August 2, 1973.

[93] Interview with Juan Mendoza, Vice-Dean of the Faculty of Law, University of Havana, May 15, 2002. In January 2002, 152 Cuban lawyers received a Masters Degree in Commercial Law and Finance through a collaborative program with the Univesity of Barcelona.

judges, prosecutors and legal advisors. In the first year, 680 jurists enrolled. The faculty for this program comes from the university as well as from ministries and other centers.

VI. THE NATIONAL UNION OF CUBAN JURISTS

The taking over of the Havana Bar Association in 1960 by revolutionary militants did not signal the establishment of a new professional association of any permanence. There is no mention in the literature of the association's activities after the early 1960s. Its dissipation is not surprising given the general demise of the profession. The restructuring of the judicial system and the renewed attention given to the legal profession in the mid-1970s, however, gave impetus to the establishment of the National Union of Cuban Jurists (UNJC), in 1977.

Approximately 85 percent of jurists in Cuba belong to this association, although membership is not obligatory. Membership includes lawyers, legal advisors, judges, prosecutors, law professors and notaries. It is headquartered in an elegant house formerly occupied by one of Havana's elite. Small offices and meeting rooms open onto a central courtyard. The upstairs is occupied by a modest law library. Like other non-governmental associations, the UNJC is now self-financed from membership dues, sale of publications and conference fees. The UNJC has chapters throughout the country in all cities.

During a short period after the death of its first president, Francisco Varona Duque Estrada, in 1986, the UNJC's professional activities declined, and it was criticized as being little more than a social club. Since then, however, it has become extremely important as a professional association which brings together jurists working in the many areas of law. The UNJC plays a major role in organizing national and international legal conferences and programs for continuing legal education. It also has established relations with bar organizations in other countries and contributes to the exchange of information between Cuban lawyers and those in other countries.

Law societies organized by the UNJC meet regularly to debate legal issues. The societies bring together specialists in the areas of family law, criminal law, civil and administrative law, commercial and economic law, labor law, constitutional law, environmental law and international law. Members of the societies come from all sectors of the legal profession, including the *bufetes*, legal advisors, notaries, the ministries, the judiciary, the attorney general's office, and the law faculty. Because of the breadth of participation and experience, the societies often review and present commentaries on proposed legislation on matters in their area of expertise.

The UNJC also publishes a law review, *Revista Cubana de Derecho*,[94] and a bi-monthly bulletin. In addition, it produces videotapes on various aspects of the law that are sent to branches of the UNJC around the country. Lawyers frequently visit the UNJC to use its library or to purchase legal books and literature at the small bookstand on the front porch.

As a measure of its importance, jurists increasingly look to the UNJC as a center for holding activities and discussions. A series of forums sponsored in 1992 on the law of joint ventures drew a large audience that overflowed the main hall, which seats about one hundred. Similarly, registration for an interdisciplinary forum on abortion law had to be closed several days in advance because of lack of space.

The UNJC has also been instrumental in organizing numerous important national and international legal conferences in Cuba. In 1984, it sponsored the first national legal symposium on socialist law. The symposium, which was primarily for Cuban jurists, included papers on all major areas of Cuban law. In 1987, the UNJC hosted the first in a series of Inter American conferences on labor law co-sponsored by the American Association of Jurists. Together with the Ministry of Justice and the Office of the Attorney General, the UNJC hosted the United Nations Conference on Criminal Law in August of 1990. Even in the midst of economic difficulties, Cuba continues to be the forum for important legal conferences. For example, in the fall of 1992, Cuba organized an international conference on environmental protection, and in September 2002, Cuba hosted the 12th International Congress of Family Law. It has also sponsored other smaller conferences on such subjects as forensic medicine, the use of computers in legal practice and criminology.

VII. CONCLUSION

Once denigrated, the legal profession is today an important sector in Cuban socialist society. Along with the elevation of status, lawyers and legal academics are playing an increasingly prominent role in shaping and drafting of legislation. Their growing influence is evident in all areas of law and legal procedure.

---

[94] This law review was published quarterly, but shortages and economic difficulties since the early 1990s have reduced publication to sporadic issues.

With respect to commercial and business law, the current situation poses particular challenges to the legal profession. Lawyers must deal with the complex legal issues raised by the collapse of the socialist community and the demands of the economic transformation of Cuba. In supporting the reshaping of Cuban socialism, the Cuban legal profession along with economists and other specialists must develop a new legal framework. Cuban lawyers working in enterprises must evolve from their status as passive technicians to skilled and knowledgeable advocates. In addition, they will have to sharpen their ability to represent Cuban interests in the world of international competition. Development of these skills requires not only improved academic training, but hands on experience.

At the same time, the population has come to expect relatively easy access to legal services in a system that has substantially diminished, if not eliminated altogether, inequality in its law and legal process. Legal representation is no longer a privilege of class. The expansion and improvement of services provided by the *bufetes colectivos* has strengthened the functioning of the legal system and the rights of Cuban citizens. Similar efforts need to be made to improve the quality of the prosecutors and police instructors as well as the judiciary. Access to justice is an important right, and despite its imperfections and failings, Cuba is closer to guaranteeing that right to all of its people than most countries in the world.

Chapter 5

LAW AND EQUALITY

Equality is one of the principal goals of Cuba's socialist system. In large measure, the Cuban revolution has achieved an egalitarian distribution of goods and services. Everyone in Cuba is assured at least a minimally adequate diet, access to education, health care, shelter and employment. Moreover, opportunities have been opened to large numbers of people who were excluded previously from everything but the most menial work. Visitors to Cuba in the 1980s who had occasion to ask a factory worker or a chamber maid what the revolution meant to him or her generally received some variation of this answer: "My child is studying to be an engineer (or a doctor), which could never have happened before the revolution." Although the reforms enacted to confront the economic crisis of the 1990s introduced a measure of economic inequality,[1] Cubans fare well under indices of human development and equity established by the United Nations Development Program, ranking among the top three countries in Latin America.[2]

In addition to correcting social and economic inequities, the revolution took specific initiatives to remedy gender and racial discrimination. Women, who constituted the largest class of persons suffering from inequality before the revolution, were the recipients of concerted efforts to make them full participants in the new political and economic order. Cubans of African descent[3] also benefited from the revolution's express policy of eradicating racial discrimination and providing equal access to services as well as economic and educational opportunities previously closed to them. Despite impressive advances, however, neither women nor Cubans of mixed race have achieved full equality in Cuba.

---

[1] For an explanation of these measures and their economic impact, see Chapter 9.

[2] *Investigación sobre desarrollo humano y equidad en Cuba 1999*, (Havana: UNDP 2000). This index measures life expectancy, education and cultural development as well as equitable distribution of resources and services. See also, Jim Lobe, "Learn from Cuba, says World Bank," Inter Press Service, April 30, 2001.

[3] As a result of a long history of interracial marriage, Cuba's population is very mixed racially; Cubans may identify themselves as black, mulatto, white or somewhere in between.

Moreover, in the early 1990s, the Cuban Communist Party and government began to remedy some forms of religious discrimination as well as discrimination against homosexuals. Religious groups in general have not suffered persecution or denial of their right to exercise their religious beliefs,[4] a right protected by the Constitution, but until 1991 the established atheist character of the Cuban government excluded from full participation individuals who professed a religious belief.[5] Repression of homosexuals, at its worst in the 1960s and 1970s, is no longer official policy. Tolerance now visible in both societal and governmental attitudes is promoted by public education, health and cultural agencies.

This chapter describes and analyzes the issues of gender and racial equality as well as religious freedom and their evolution since 1959. The rights of homosexuals are discussed in other chapters. Fuller treatment is given to gender rather than racial equality, not because of its greater importance, but because it has received considerably more attention in Cuba and, therefore, more information is available. Recently, however, the issues of racial bias and stereotyping have become an increasingly important subject of public concern and reflection.

I. WOMEN AND THE LAW

> The day must come when we have a Party of men and women, and a leadership of men and women, and a State of men and women, and a Government of men and women.
>
> —Fidel Castro[6]

The advancement toward women's equality in Cuba has often been referred to as the "revolution within a revolution."[7] In fact, women's incorpo-

[4] See, Aurelio Alonso Tejada, "Catolicismo, política y cambio en la realidad cubana actual," *TEMAS*, No. 4, 1995. The exception is the followers of Jehovah's Witness who have not been permitted to practice freely because their beliefs oppose service to the state, particularly military service.

[5] The limitations on participation included exclusion from membership in the Party, and, thus, high ranking positions in government. In addition, until December 1998 no religious holidays were observed in Cuba, and workers were expected to work whenever a holiday, such as Christmas, fell on a work day. Since then, December 25th has been declared a national work holiday. Outside of Christmas, although workers can be excused from work for religious purposes, they do not receive pay for the time off.

[6] Speech by Fidel Castro at the Second Congress of the Federation of Cuban Women (November 19, 1974), in *Second Congress of the Federation of Cuban Women, Central Report* (1975), p. 276. [Hereinafter cited as *Second Congress FMC.*]

ration into the economic, political and social life of the country has been impressive. Further, the revolution has provided significant advances for women in health care and education. Reproductive choice is secure as a right, available to all women as part of universal health services.

In the revolutionary context, law is far from "neutral." As discussed earlier, it is an instrument of social change, intended to be both a vehicle for shaping new values and attitudes and a mechanism for enforcing societal norms. For the most part, legislation has promoted progress for women, and recent modifications to the Constitution have strengthened the concept of equality. However, on occasion regulations have indirectly perpetuated inequality. For the most part these inadvertent barriers have been removed.

Advances in gender equality in Cuba (or anywhere), however, cannot be simply brought about by writing equality into the law. Although the revolution's project has included affirmative efforts that go far beyond insuring parity in work and pay, social norms and attitudes have changed more slowly and remain a barrier to women. Women still bear most of the burden of household and childcare duties which discourages them from taking on more responsibilities outside the home. Despite Party and government support for and a steady rise in the number of women in decision-making positions, Cuban women have yet to share authority equally with men. The reasons Cuban women have still not reached this goal can be understood from the historical and social context of women in Cuba before and since the Cuban Revolution. Forty years—the span of one generation—is not a very long time for such a radical social transformation.

Further, without doubt, the economic crisis that began in 1989 has had a particularly negative impact on women. Power blackouts, cooking fuel shortages and deficits in public transportation made domestic life ever more difficult and vastly increased the amount of time women, still the primary caretakers, had to spend on household chores. Although these conditions have improved significantly, most Cuban families continue to be severely affected by the economic crisis, and it generally falls on women to budget and manage the scarce supplies within the home. Moreover, the stagnation of the economy and shrinkage in many sectors temporarily halted advancement for many women as well as men. Yet despite these setbacks, and, although machismo continues to dominate sexual politics, the policies of the

[7] The phrase was first used by Fidel Castro in a speech given at the Fifth National Plenary of the Federation of Cuban Women (FMC) in 1966. Fidel Castro, "The Revolution within the Revolution," in *Women and the Cuban Revolution* (New York: Pathfinder Press, 1981), Elizabeth Stone, ed., p. 48. It has since been repeated in the literature of the FMC and has even appeared on billboards and posters in Cuba.

last four decades have engendered a national consciousness of gender equality in Cuban public life that is firmly established and that provides a solid basis for progress.

Beginning the Revolution: The First Decade

Although Cuban women won the right to vote in 1934, and middle- and upper-class feminists had left a mark prior to the revolution,[8] women constituted only about 15 percent of the work force in 1959.[9] For most of those women, work was an absolute necessity that provided no opportunity for development or self-fulfillment: Well over half were maids or domestic servants,[10] and a substantial number were exploited by the hundreds of notorious brothels of pre-revolutionary Cuba.[11] The remainder were primarily teachers, clerks and factory workers. Economic and educational opportunities were available only to women of the middle and upper classes. Even among these advantaged classes, the vast majority of women did not depart from their socially assigned function of housewife and caretaker. Coupled with the mores of a patriarchal culture that impeded women from participating in political and economic activity, high unemployment and underemployment among men also limited possibilities for women.[12]

---

[8] Several groups of feminist activists in the 1920s and 1930s worked for the right to vote and employment benefits. In addition to suffrage, activists won very progressive statement on women's equality inserted in the 1940 Constitution. The latter, however, was primarily a paper victory since the rights won were minimally enforced. Nor was any effort made to provide opportunities for poor and working class women who did not have access to education or employment. See K. Lynn Stoner, *From the House to the Streets* (Durham, N.C.: Duke University Press, 1991).

[9] The reports on the percentage of women employed in the late 1950s vary from 13 percent to 17 percent, representing 200,000 to 260,000 women. Alfred Padula and Lois Smith, "Women in Socialist Cuba, 1959-84," in *Cuba: Twenty-Five Years of Revolution, 1959-1984* (New York: Praeger, 1985), Sandor Halebsky and John M. Kirk, eds., p. 80 (report that 17 percent of women were employed in 1959); Carmelo Mesa-Lago, *The Economy of Socialist Cuba* (Albuquerque, N.M.: University of New Mexico Press, 1981), p. 188 (reports 13 percent in 1958).

[10] Some authorities estimate the percentage of women working as domestic servants at 70 percent. Padula and Smith, p. 80; Margaret Randall, *Women in Cuba: Twenty Years Later* (New York: Smyrna Press, 1981), p. 23.

[11] Padula and Smith, pp. 80-81. The open practice of prostitution reemerged in Cuba in the early 1990s in the wake of the economic crisis. The increase in foreign tourists and businessmen visiting the island provided a ready market for young women seeking material goods in exchange for sexual relations.

[12] In 1958, 28 percent of the labor force, more than 600,000, were either unemployed or underemployed. Carollee Benglesdorf and Alice Hageman, "Emerging from

A number of women, however, did play an active role in the revolution. Women helped organize demonstrations to protest the repression of the Batista regime and the jailing of opposition leaders. During the armed struggle, women acted as couriers, raised funds, and transported guns and supplies to the guerrillas fighting in the mountains. A small number of women also participated in combat. One platoon, the Mariana Grajales Platoon, consisted entirely of women.

Although women in general constituted an oppressed class, and women actively participated in the liberation movement, women's rights per se were not on the agenda of the armed revolutionaries. Equality for women was not mentioned once in Fidel Castro's famous 1953 trial defense, known as "History Will Absolve Me," setting forth the vision of the just society for which the revolutionaries fought;[13] nor was women's equality included in the Manifesto of the Sierra Maestra.[14] Thus, there was little to suggest in 1959 that the revolution would radically change the position of women in Cuban society. Even in the United States a broad movement against sex discrimination did not emerge until after the civil rights struggle of the mid-1960s.

However, the decade following the triumph of the revolution transformed women's lives. Concerted efforts were made to integrate women into the economic and political life of the country. To do so required an abrupt departure from the dictates of patriarchal tradition which dictated that the identity and life of women revolved completely around home, marriage, and family. However, the revolutionary process and the new social organizations it spawned awakened women's consciousness to new possibilities offered by education, volunteer service, work outside the home, and control over reproductive choices. From this awakening would emerge more clearly defined goals of self-realization and full equality for women in Cuba.

Within one year of the fall of the Batista regime and the takeover of political control by the revolutionary movements, a national organization of Cuban women was founded—the Federation of Cuban Women (Federación de Mujeres Cubanas, or FMC). The FMC was created not by women to secure equal rights, but rather by the revolutionary government seeking to mobilize women to take on emergency tasks at a time of great urgency.

Underdevelopment: Women and Work," *Cuba Review* (September 1974), p. 4. This entire issue of *Cuba Review* is devoted to women in Cuba.

[13] Fidel Castro, *History Will Absolve Me* (New York: Center for Cuban Studies, undated).

[14] "Manifesto No. 1 del 26 de Julio al pueblo de Cuba." The manifesto is printed in English translation in *Revolutionary Struggle* (Cambridge, Mass: The MIT Press, 1972), Rolando E. Bonachea and Nelson P. Valdés, eds., pp. 259-271.

Vilma Espín, a founding member and FMC president since 1960,[15] recounts that, although she and other Cuban women fought in the revolution, they never once considered the idea of creating a distinctly women's organization.[16] According to Espín, who was a leader of the Santiago de Cuba underground, it was Fidel Castro who convinced her and other women active in the revolutionary movement that a women's organization was necessary to incorporate women into the revolution.[17]

At the founding meeting of the FMC on August 23, 1960, Fidel Castro, while paying homage to the women who fought in the revolution, spoke primarily of the grave economic and military situation confronting the nation.[18] Growing hostility in the middle and upper classes, pockets of armed opposition and incidents of sabotage threatened consolidation of the revolution. In addition, the new leadership was faced with the staggering implications of the emerging U.S. economic sanctions.[19] Strong support for the revolution among the population was essential in order to develop an independent economy and to diffuse counter-revolutionary activity.

Thus, the sole agenda of the FMC at its founding was to strengthen support for the revolution by organizing women into the social programs and productive forces of the new society. The governing statutes adopted by the FMC at its first congress in 1962 do not even mention women's equality as one of its goals:

> The Federation of Cuban Women, founded in 1960 with the objective of uniting all women and incorporating them in the process of transformation begun with the triumph of the revolution, . . . confronts a new and great objective: the effective and full incorpora-

---

[15] Vilma Espín, who married Raúl Castro in the year before Batista's defeat, became the first president of the FMC and remains its president today.
[16] Randall, p. 125.
[17] Ibid. Details of the origin and conception of the FMC are scarce and hardly mentioned in the literature. Apparently the founding members came primarily from the same groups which joined to overthrow Batista. The Cuban Revolution was fought by a loose coalition of political groups which included the 26th of July Movement headed by Fidel Castro, the Revolutionary Directorate (primarily a student movement), and the Popular Socialist Party (PSP), which was the old Communist Party. William LeoGrande, "Party Development in Revolutionary Cuba," *Journal of InterAmerican Studies & World Affairs* 21 (1979), pp. 457-458.
[18] Randall, p. 130.
[19] For an analysis of the United States economic sanctions against Cuba, see, Michael Krinsky and David Golove, *United States Economic Measures Against Cuba*, (Northampton, MA: Aletheia Press, 1993).

> tion of the Cuban woman from all sectors of the population in the construction of the socialist state.[20]

A great many tasks needed to be done, and women were an enormous untapped resource that could serve the revolution.

The FMC was up to the challenge. It quickly launched a major campaign to get women out of the house and into productive work. The first activities into which women were recruited related to health and education. FMC members went from house to house to persuade women to undertake these tasks. Women were given first-aid training and organized into health brigades that carried out the first nationwide vaccination programs against tetanus and polio.[21] They were also mobilized to help repel the Bay of Pigs invasion in 1961.[22] As a result of FMC organizing, young women, including adolescents, ventured away from their homes for the first time and joined the tens of thousands of youth who carried out the famous literacy campaign of 1961.[23] In addition, the FMC was instrumental in providing training programs and social services that enabled thousands of former prostitutes to find new jobs.[24]

---

[20] *Primer Congreso Nacional de la Federación de Mujeres Cubanas, Memoria* (1962), p. 52. [hereinafter cited as *First Congress FMC*]. All the mass organizations, like the FMC and the Central Organization of Cuban Workers (CTC), as well as the Communist Party of Cuba, hold national congresses of their members. Since 1975, the interval between congresses has been regularized to every five years. The FMC generally holds its congress in the year preceding the Party congress.

[21] Leo Huberman and Paul M. Sweezy, *Socialism in Cuba* (New York: Monthly Review Press, 1969), pp. 62-63. In 1964, almost 2.5 million children under age fourteen were vaccinated against polio. An additional 1.4 million children under age six were vaccinated in 1966.

[22] On April 15, 1961, an invasion force of Cuban ex-patriots landed at the Bay of Pigs. The invasion was planned by the CIA and approved by President Kennedy, who was misinformed by some of his advisors about the potential for success. It was believed that large numbers of people in Cuba would quickly join the invading forces to overthrow the revolutionary government. The invasion was defeated within a few days. For a thorough account of the planning, execution, and defeat of the Bay of Pigs invasion, see Peter Wyden, *Bay of Pigs* (New York: Simon and Schuster, 1979). Many women went to the battlefront to carry supplies to the troops and to care for the wounded. Vilma Espín, "The Early Years," in Elizabeth Stone, ed., pp. 43-45.

[23] Padula and Smith, p. 82. As a result of the campaign, a little over 700,000 people were taught to read and write. The illiteracy rate in Cuba dropped from 23.6 percent to about four percent. Huberman and Sweezy, p. 27. Fifty-five percent of those taught to read and write were women. *Second Congress FMC*, p. 101. For an account of the literacy campaign, see generally Jonathan Kozol, *Children of the Revolution* (New York: Delacorte Press, 1978).

[24] See Padula and Smith, pp. 80-81; Randall, p. 24.

To expand women's participation in the revolution, particularly in rural areas, the FMC also organized educational programs that had both an ideological and skill-oriented content. Rural women were encouraged to attend special sewing classes. Traditionally a female-identified skill, sewing appealed to women who had never worked outside the home and was an acceptable activity to reluctant parents and spouses.[25] Among the first such schools were the Ana Betancourt Escuelas Campesinas for rural women. Thousands of campesinas were brought from rural areas into the city of Havana to attend these schools.[26] In addition, approximately 20,000 former domestic servants attended special schools for the Advancement of Domestic Servants established in Havana in 1960. Many of these women were trained to staff the child-care centers established the following year.[27] Once in classes, however, they were not only taught to sew but were given an elementary education, including basic hygiene, and were exposed to the social and political ideas and goals of the revolution.[28]

At the same time, the government provided material support for women to enter the work force: the first day-care centers were created in 1961;[29] a maternity law providing liberal paid leave for pregnant women was enacted in 1963;[30] and educational opportunities were created that helped women advance into new areas of work.[31] Provided free of charge, these programs

---

[25] *Women and Revolution*, p. 11; Isabel Larguia and John Dumoulin, "Women's Equality and the Cuban Revolution," in *Women and Change in Latin America* (South Hadley, Mass.: Bergin and Garvey, 1985), June Nash and Helen Safa, eds., pp. 344, 348. The authors report that many of these women came from homes where their parents "would often frown on their even learning to read and write."

[26] Heidi Steffens, "FMC: Feminine, Not Feminist," *Cuba Review* (September 1974), p. 22.

[27] Benglesdorf and Hageman, p. 5.

[28] Women and Revolution, pp. 11, 41-42.

[29] Day-care centers (*círculos infantiles*) were first started by the FMC in 1961. The FMC trained former domestic servants to work in the centers. *Second Congress FMC*, p. 104. The number has grown slowly since then due to economic constraints; as of 1984, 838 day-care centers existed. *Cuarto Congreso de la Federación de Mujeres Cubanas, Informe Central* (1984), p. 53 [hereinafter *Fourth Congress FMC*]. In 1998-99, the number had grown to 1,113. *La Seguridad Social en Cuba* (Mexico: Editorial Piensa, S.V., 1998), p. 25. Day care was initially free, but by 1970 the government began charging a maximum of 25 pesos per month for day-care services dependent on ability to pay. The actual cost for one child at the time was about 100 pesos a month. Padula and Smith, p. 85.

[30] Ley No. 1100 (Ley de Seguridad Social), March 27, 1963. The Working Woman Maternity Law of 1974 expanded the benefits provided by this earlier law. Ley No. 1263 (Ley de Maternidad de la Trabajadora), *Gaceta Oficial*, No. 3, January 16, 1974.

[31] *Second Congress FMC*, pp. 104-105. During the first fifteen years of the revolution, the number of students enrolled in schools of higher education increased more than five-fold from 15,000 to 83,800. Marvin Leiner, "Cuba's Schools: 25 Years Later," in *Cuba: Twenty-Five Years,* pp. 27, 31. Education at all levels in Cuba is free, even adult education programs, and students receive additional support in the way of room and board. By 1983, Cuba ranked 20th among 142 countries in the percentage of women enrolled in university programs.

enabled the FMC to encourage significant numbers of women to obtain employment. In 1964, a Secretariat of Production was created within the FMC to examine the issues concerning the incorporation of women into the work force and to develop additional strategies for incorporation. Slow, steady progress was achieved in the 1960s, largely as a result of incorporating into new jobs women who had previously worked as domestic servants.

A surge in women's employment resulted from the great "ten ton sugar harvest" planned for 1970, which required a massive mobilization of the entire population, both men and women, into productive work.[32] In the late 1960s the Central Organization of Cuban Workers (CTC), the national trade union organization,[33] and the Ministry of Labor and Social Security (MTSS) responded to the need to incorporate more women into the work force to reduce the labor shortage. In 1968, the Ministry of Labor adopted a preferential hiring program for women under which certain jobs, particularly in the textile industry, were set aside for women.[34] In 1969 and 1970, more than 100,000 women entered the production forces in both paid and voluntary work.[35] For the majority of women, this was to be their first work experience outside the home.

The following year the Frente Feminino, or Women's Front, was organized as a secretariat within the CTC to monitor the progress and address the needs of women in the workplace.[36] The Front, renamed the Department of Women's Affairs in the early 1980s,[37] became one of the most active groups within the CTC and a powerful voice for women. Each work center elected a delegate to the Front. Delegates were elected not just by women, but by all workers in the work center, resulting in the election of a small number of men as delegates. The rationale for not keeping the Front exclusively fe-

---

[32] Benglesdorf and Hageman, p. 3.

[33] For an analysis of the trade union movement in Cuba since the revolution, see Debra Evenson, *Workers in Cuba: Unions and Labor Relations*, (Detroit, MI: Guild Law Center, 2001). See, also, Marifeli Pérez-Stable, "Class, Organization, and Conciencia: The Cuban Working Class After 1970," in *Cuba: Twenty-Five Years*, p. 291.

[34] *Women and Revolution*, pp. 13-14. Resolution 47, which set forth the program, was repealed after the CTC voted in 1973 to end it. It had become clear that despite educational and training programs there were still not enough women in the work force to fill all the jobs set aside.

[35] Padula and Smith, p. 84.

[36] Very little literature on the Women's Front exists. For a brief description, see Carollee Benglesdorf, "The Frente Feminino," *Cuba Review* , September 1974), p. 27.

[37] Interview with Esther Lidia Chinea, National Director of the Department of Women's Affairs of the CTC, Havana, December 27, 1985. According to Chinea, the change was made because the name "Front" was too confrontational in tone and inconsistent with the principle of women's solidarity with the revolution.

male was that the goal of women's equality was to be shared by society as a whole. Although the Department of Women's Affairs no longer exists, the subject of women's equality in the workplace and the unions is a permanent item on the agenda of the CTC.

Moreover, the national priority given to free education and the expansion of women's participation yielded dramatic results in the 1960s. Illiteracy in Cuba dropped from 23 percent to less than 5 percent. By 1970 young women made up 55 percent of high school students and 40 percent of those attending institutions of higher education.[38] The professions were immediately opened to women who took advantage of the opportunities. Nearly one-half of Cuban medical students in the mid-1960s were women.[39] By 1971, the percentage of women in the labor force had reached twenty-three percent nationwide with even greater increases in rural areas.[40]

Some observers argue that the advances in providing day-care and liberal maternity benefits were promoted not to help women but rather to push them into unfilled jobs.[41] This criticism is unfair. Although socialism, as well as capitalism, requires a productive work force, Cuban women were never forced to work nor penalized for not working. Moreover, the changes in Cuba went far beyond what was necessary simply to get women into assembly lines. Although the majority entered jobs traditionally held by women,[42] Cuban women were given opportunities to and did enter a wide variety of professions. Indeed, the revolution gave Cuban women unprecedented financial independence and options.

This progress, however, was not reflected in the representation of women in leadership. Women remained barely visible in the ranks of leadership outside their own organizations. Nevertheless, the first steps in the

---

[38] Benglesdorf and Hageman, p. 5. Almost half of the 15,000 students enrolled in state-funded universities were women in 1956-57. Marcia Dolores Ortiz, *Cuban Women in Higher Education* (Havana, 1985), pp. 20-21. Fewer than 20 of these, however, were enrolled in engineering or the sciences. During the 1984-85 school year, of more than 240,000 students enrolled in Cuba's universities, approximately half were women. Ibid., p. 22. Moreover, approximately half of the students enrolled in schools of technology, sciences, economics, and medicine were women. Ibid., p. 23.

[39] *Women and Revolution*, p. 11. As of 1984, women comprised well over half of Cuba's medical students. Ortiz, p. 23.

[40] Benglesdorf and Hageman, p. 8, note 7. The figure is even more impressive when one considers the difficult challenge of expanding production and absorbing the large numbers of unemployed men in an underdeveloped country faced with an almost total hemispheric economic blockade imposed by the United States and its Latin American allies in 1961.

[41] See, e.g., " 'La Silenciada,' Cuba: Paradise Gained, Paradise Lost—The Price of 'Integration,' " in *Sisterhood Is Global* (Garden City, N.Y.: Anchor Press/Doubleday, 1984), Robin Morgan, ed., p. 169.

[42] Benglesdorf and Hageman, p. 7 (chart showing large percentages of women who worked in textile production [80 percent], health services [60 percent], and education [55 percent]).

process through which advancement into leadership positions could be achieved had been taken. Moreover, Cuban women now had national organizations supported by the revolution through which they could address their concerns in society and in the workplace.

The FMC

A creation of the revolution, the FMC was recognized in the 1976 Constitution as one of the mass organizations charged with "fulfill[ing] the state functions . . . according to the Constitution and the law."[43] These "state functions" were not specified, but the FMC, because it traditionally worked with the family, took on a significant role in the implementation of state policies, such as crime prevention and efforts to increase school attendance. From 1960 to 1975, the Party leadership exercised considerable guidance over and gave direction to the activities of the FMC. Since then, the Party has continued to provide general political direction, but the content of Party policy with respect to women's issues has become increasingly influenced by the FMC. In 1997, the FMC established the Center for Women's Studies which has undertaken research on various aspects of women's lives and gender equality in Cuba. Other centers also engage in gender research and development of policy concerning women, such as the Cuban Society of Civil Law, the National Center for Sex Education and various academic research institutions.

Membership in the FMC is voluntary and in 2000 included 82.5 percent of Cuban women over age fourteen.[44] The organization grew rapidly. In 1961 there were approximately 17,000 members.[45] Within two years, by the date of its first congress, more than 350,000 Cuban women had joined.[46]

[43] Constitución (1976), Art. 7. In a step towards separating the mass organizations from the state, this article was amended in 1992 to eliminate any reference to state support of these organizations or their role in carrying out state functions.

[44] *Asi fue nuestro VII Congreso de la FMC* (Havana: Editorial de la Mujer, 2002), p. 16 [hereinafter cited as *Seventh Congress FMC*]. The percentage of membership has remained fairly constant over the years. In 1985 is was 83.5% *Fourth Congress FMC*, p. 9

[45] *First Congress FMC*, p. 6.

[46] Ibid.

Though initially supported financially by the state, it is now self-financed, mainly from membership dues.[47]

The FMC came under considerable attack during the public discussions leading up to the Fourth Party Congress held in 1991. Although no one questioned the need to continue to advance women's equality, some posited that it was no longer necessary to have a separate organization because the FMC's work was duplicative of the CDRs and the trade unions. There were also suggestions that it had lost touch with the new generation of women. Many of the most dynamic young women work within the Union of Communist Youth (UJC) or in other spheres. The FMC, however, continues work on family, employment and community issues and to represent Cuban women in international institutions and networks of women's organizations.

Defining Goals and Confronting Obstacles

From the outset, both the FMC and the Department of Women's Affairs concerned themselves with women from all sectors of society—the well educated as well as the newly literate, professionals as well as production workers. This equal concern is consistent with the socialist content of the women's movement and underscores the attention given to the elimination of class bias in the search for women's equality in Cuba.

The FMC's efforts during the 1960s to get women out of the house and into some kind of participation—into educational programs, into voluntary service, and into the work force—caused direct confrontation with entrenched notions of the traditional role of women as circumscribed by home and family. Success in breaking down these social and psychological barriers generated a new consciousness among many women, who began to seek not just opportunities for participation but conditions that would lead to equality. Although Cuban women rapidly gained equal access to higher education and the professions after the revolution, equality in the workplace and in leadership were not as readily achievable. The gains made by women were not permanent as long as they were not accompanied by a transformation of social norms.

---

[47] Similar to other mass organizations, the structure of the FMC parallels the pyramidal scheme of the national political institutions. The base level consists of small delegations that are grouped into *bloques* roughly corresponding to a neighborhood. These *bloques* elect delegates to municipal, provincial, and national committees. Issues may be raised at all levels for discussion and action, but policy is made at the national level. Although the full congress, which is attended by several thousand women, only meets every five years, the national plenary meets annually to discuss issues and to direct the work of the organization.

One indication of the problem was the large number of women who left the work force in the 1970s. Although more than 700,000 women joined the labor force from 1969 to 1974, more than 500,000 simultaneously dropped out.[48] Concern over the impermanence of female workers was heightened by the economy's growing demand for workers.[49] The FMC and the Department of Women's Affairs studied the problem to find out why the female labor force was so unstable. The major problems were not difficult to identify and were listed by the Second Congress of the FMC: "[p]ressure of home and family, [inadequate] services, lack of economic incentive, lack of minimal conditions of hygiene and protection at work sites, lack of political work with the newly incorporated women on the job, [and] a lack of understanding concerning women's role in society."[50]

Women's participation in social and economic activities outside the home did not relieve them of responsibility for all the household chores and care of their children. In Cuba, as elsewhere, housework was traditionally women's work exclusively. A survey of 251 working women in 1975 showed that they spent "an average of 13 hours a day on job-related or household activities, and eleven and a half hours on weekends, due to the accumulation of housework."[51] This double duty has been called the "second shift."

The popular Cuban film Portrait of Teresa, made in 1976, vividly portrays the pain and frustration of a young woman trying to respond to the multiple demands of job, family and self.[52] There is no happy ending.

---

48 Thus, the net increase during these years was fewer than 200,000. *Tesis y Resolución: Sobre el Pleno Ejercicio de la Igualdad de la Mujer* (Havana: Instituto Cubano del Libro, 1976), p. 16 [hereinafter cited as *Tesis*]. This thesis on women's equality was presented to and adopted by the First Congress of the Party in December 1975.

49 Benglesdorf and Hageman, p. 6. A vagrancy law went into effect in March of 1971. Although the statute states in article 2 that "[a]ll citizens who are physically and mentally fit have the social duty to work," and includes all such women between the ages of seventeen and fifty-five, only men were ever legally accountable for not working. The law stops short of making it a crime if women do not work. But its direction is clear. The discussions it provoked made this obvious. *Granma* of March 14, 1971, reported that during the discussions of the law, one of the changes proposed, but not adopted, was 'that it be applied to single women who neither work nor study.' Some work centers recommended that the full weight of the law be applied to women. Generally, however, it was recognized that the material conditions did not yet permit such an application." The vagrancy laws have since been repealed.

50 *Second Congress FMC*, p. 116.

51 *Tesis*, pp. 15-16.

52 Cuban film has consistently played an important role in heightening societal consciousness of women's burdens and frustrations in the Cuban Revolution. Examples of such films

Teresa's struggle, universal to working women, is all the more difficult in an underdeveloped economy. Material conditions in Cuba had not advanced to the extent that services, convenience goods and foods, or electric appliances such as washing machines were readily available. Teresa is shown rising at dawn to hand wash the family laundry, prepare breakfast for husband and children, dress the children and get them off to school before she goes to work. More housework awaits her return from work. She has little time for her husband, who does not do any household chores and courts the attention of a young, single woman.

In addition, because the economy was struggling to provide basic goods, there were few consumer items to buy with excess income. Therefore, if the husband worked, the wife had little economic incentive to work as well. Equally important, attitudes about the role of women in society had not advanced very far. Most men, as well as women, continued to hold "old-fashioned" beliefs about women as participants in economic and political activity.[53]

In large measure, the failure of the FMC and other institutions early on to articulate and define the goal of women's equality impeded progress in the steady advancement of women. Continued economic growth could ameliorate the material conditions that hindered women's participation, but only a full-scale assault on subjective attitudes involving the commitment of the entire society could bring about the radical change necessary. That commitment did not originate with the population; rather, it was initiated by the governing leadership, which marshaled the nation's institutions to support the goal of women's equality.

In the mid-1970s, critical years in the political and economic development of the revolution, the FMC, the CTC and the Party each addressed the question of women's equality and the necessity of eradicating the conditions that kept women in an unequal status. The central theme of the Second Congress of the FMC, held in March 1974, was not simply the incorporation of more women into productive service but the "struggle for women's equality." The First Congress of the Cuban Communist Party in 1975 took up this theme and embraced women's equality as an objective of the Cuban Revolu-

---

include *De Cierta Manera,* directed by Sara Gómez, which candidly portrays the frustration of a schoolteacher whose consciousness and aspirations have advanced beyond the people she serves. The film also deals with manifestations of machismo among Cuban men. A 1983 film, *Hasta Cierto Punto*, is a painfully honest look at the complexity of the male/female relationship. A popular film in Cuba and winner of first prize at the Latin American Film Festival in Havana, the film demonstrates a perceptive and sophisticated consciousness of the issues.

53 *Women and Revolution*, p. 15. Stories abound from the 1960s and 1970s of husbands appearing at job sites or FMC or CDR meetings and demanding that their wives return home.

tion: "[T]he participation of women in society must be in absolute equality with men, and so long as any vestige of inequality remains, it is necessary to continue working to achieve this objective of the revolution."[54] Recognizing the historical double exploitation of women, the Thirteenth Congress of the CTC in 1973 also approved a resolution on the full equality of women.[55]

Rhetoric was translated into far-reaching legislation, which the FMC had a role in shaping by initiating proposals, reviewing drafts, and recommending changes. Both the Family Code[56] and Constitution, enacted in 1975 and 1976 respectively, declare the equal status of men and women in Cuban society. Although the direct impact of these laws on the achievement of gender equality has been mixed, yielding both advances and disappointments for women, the laws not only codified the commitment to equality but, most importantly, articulated an ideal against which progress could be measured.

The Constitution

The Constitution of 1976 specifically prohibited discrimination on the basis of sex.[57] In addition to prohibiting discrimination, the Constitution expressly granted women "the same rights as men in the economic, political and social fields as well as in the family,"[58] and incorporated as law the equal relationship of men and women in marriage previously codified in the

---

[54] *Tesis*, p. 9. This thesis as well as other reports presented at the Congress were discussed at length in the year preceding the Congress at workplaces, schools, military units, and mass organizations. Randall, p. 33.

[55] "Resolución Sobre la Mujer Trabajadora" in *Trece Congreso de la CTC* (Havana: Editorial de Ciencias Sociales, 1973), pp. 152-54. The CTC Congress resolved to (1) contribute to women's full and dignified access to whatever type of work as a right and duty conferred by the socialist society; and (2) realize the incorporation of women into work with full equality with men.

[56] Código de Familia (1975), *Gaceta Oficial*, No. 6, February 15, 1975. The Family Code was approved by popular referendum in November 1974. It was officially enacted by the Council of Ministers on February 14, 1975, and became effective on International Women's Day, March 8, 1975.

[57] Constitución de la República de Cuba (1976), Art. 41.

[58] Ibid., Art. 43.

Family Code.[59] Further, the Constitution set out the state's obligation to support women's integration into the work force:

> In order to assure the exercise of these rights and especially the incorporation of women into socially organized work, the state sees to it that they are given jobs in keeping with their physical makeup; they are given paid maternity leave before and after giving birth; the state organizes such institutions as children's day care centers, semi-boarding schools and boarding schools; and it strives to create all the conditions which help to make real the principle of equality.[60]

Although intended to be supportive of women's equality, the provision reflected paternalism which perpetuates unequal treatment based on physical capacity and child-rearing responsibilities.

After years of debate, this article was amended in July 1992 to eliminate explicit differentiation between men and women. The new provision states:

> Women and men enjoy the same economic, political, cultural, social and family rights. The State guarantees that women will be offered the same opportunities and possibilities as men to the end that women achieve full participation in the development of the country.[61]

The Constitution maintains the state's commitment to providing day care, but after 1992 expresses it in gender neutral terms:

> The state organizes institutions such as day care centers, boarding schools, homes for attention of the elderly and services which help the working family in carrying out their responsibilities.

---

[59] Ibid., Art. 35 of the Constitution states: "Marriage is the voluntary established union between a man and a woman . . . It is based on full equality of rights and duties for the partners, who must see to the support of the home and the integral education of their children through a joint effort."

[60] Ibid., Art. 41.

[61] Constitución de la República de Cuba (1992), Art. 44. This article further provides:

> To assure healthy births, the state grants women maternity leave, before and after birth, and insures that women may be given work positions compatible with her function as mother. The state makes an effort to create all the conditions which facilitate the realization of the principle of equality.

The 1992 constitutional modifications also explicitly grant both men and women equal employment opportunities.[62]

Cuba's Constitution designates the National Assembly, not the courts, as the arbiter of legislative constitutionality. Thus, to redress legislation that is discriminatory or contradictory to the Constitution, women must seek action from the National Assembly or from administrative bodies to which the National Assembly has delegated authority. Individual acts of discrimination, such as workplace discrimination, may be challenged in workplace assemblies or in the newly established base organs of labor justice, or in the courts.

In the few instances where the FMC has sought changes in discriminatory legislation or regulations it has been generally successful. In the 1980s, the FMC undertook a study of laws and customs that perpetuate inequality and reinforce attitudes about women's place in society as chief caretaker and homemaker. For example, in Cuba relatives or close friends assist hospital staff in caring for sick family members. However, hospital regulations permitted only women to undertake this care.[63] Consequently, in the case of prolonged illness, a woman could be absent from work for substantial periods of time. These absences, forced on women by discriminatory practices and rules, diminished their chances of being hired or promoted.[64] The FMC successfully urged that these hospital rules be changed and pressed for more equitable application of work rules to eliminate discrimination.

The Social Sphere: Home, Marriage, and Family

Since household work remained women's responsibility, the FMC and the Party initially sought to ameliorate the burden by expanding day care services, increasing the availability of washing machines, and making food shopping more convenient. These measures, however, did not address the real problem: Men did not share child-care responsibilities or the housework. In 1975, the husband's obligation to share household responsibilities became law with the enactment of the Family Code. Although this obliga-

---

[62] Ibid., Art. 8(b).

[63] In Cuba, relatives are required to assist hospital staff in caring for sick family members. They carry out such non medical tasks as bathing and feeding. Wald, pp. 12-13.

[64] This problem was specifically noted at the 1984 FMC Congress. *Draft Thesis IV*, pp. 13-15.

tion was not legally enforceable, making divorce the only legal recourse, the adoption of the Family Code did focus attention on the problem.

Changes in family law since the revolution, a subject more fully discussed in Chapter Six, has had a significant impact on domestic relations. The Family Code establishes equality in the marital relationship with respect to property and provides for alimony only on the basis of objective need. Both parents are responsible for child support. Yet old habits are difficult to shed. With little or no attention given to psychological and emotional factors that keep women in a subordinate relationship to men, only limited progress has been made in developing equality in the home.

The Economic Sphere: Employment

In 1999, women made up 43.6% of the work force,[65] faring well in many professions in which they constituted 49% of professional judges, 65% of prosecutors, and more than 60% of doctors.[66]

1. Affirmative Action Measures. Over the years, Cuba has implemented various preferential programs to advance the employment of women. These programs have had varying success. The preferential hiring program of the late 1960s was abandoned in 1973 when it was shown that few qualified women applied to fill the positions allotted. Pursuant to a second plan, approved in 1980,[67] women were given preference for almost 500,000 positions designated by the managers of enterprises with the approval of the workers' councils.[68] The FMC was to be consulted on the positions selected. Since many more women had received education and training in the interim years, there were more qualified women to take these positions than before. A special commission, composed of representatives from the State Committee on Labor and Social Security, the CTC, and the FMC, was established in 1981 to oversee implementation of this program.[69] According to the FMC, in 1985 women occupied the vast majority of the reserved positions.[70]

---

[65] *Seventh Congress FMC*, p. 12.

[66] Ibid.

[67] Resolución No. 511 (Comité Estatal de Trabajo y Seguridad Social), September 13, 1980.

[68] *Fourth Congress FMC*, p. 37.

[69] Ibid., p. 37. Expressing concern for the success of the program, the Main Report of the Fourth Congress declared it "absolutely necessary" that the FMC take a more active role in the Commission's activities in the future. *Draft Thesis IV*, p. 18.

[70] *Fourth Congress FMC*, p. 37.

A 1988 directive of the MTSS creates preferential employment opportunities for women today.[71] Management of each enterprise, together with the local union, designates certain positions in which an effort will be made to preferentially employ women.[72] In this endeavor management is also required to consider the opinion of the FMC as to the positions that will be set aside. The proposed positions to be designated as priority jobs for women are presented to the workers' general assembly for a vote. Further, provisions for setting aside certain jobs for women are included in the collective bargaining agreement. By law, when jobs designated for women become vacant, an attempt must be made to fill the position with another female employee.[73]

Women have not been the only beneficiaries of affirmative action measures. Faced with the growing dominance of women in some areas of higher education, Cuba has at times embarked on a preferential program for men. Women's success in gaining entrance to professional schools such as medicine and law had been so great that they constituted 60 to 70 percent of incoming students in 1984.[74] In 1985, medical schools instituted special quotas to maintain a proportional balance of men and women, though women continued to hold a slight edge.[75]

The "special period" created by the economic crisis that began in 1990 has taken its toll on employment opportunities and individual development for everyone in society. Women were particularly affected by the sharp decline in the textile and clothing industries where they comprise more than 60% of the workforce. Special efforts were made by the MTSS and the Commission on Women's Employment, jointly established by the MTSS, the CTC and the FMC, to prioritize jobs for women laid off during this period.[76] Moreover, there were fewer professional positions available and many university departments have shrunk, the major exceptions being in the sciences, law, and economics.

2. Pay equity. Although concentrated in some areas of traditional work, Cuban women have not been locked into "feminine" jobs and locked out of

---

[71] Resolución No. 51-88 (Reglamento para la Aplicacíon de la Política de Empleo) (Ministry of Labor and Social Security), December 20, 1988.

[72] Ibid., Art. 6.

[73] Ibid., Art. 28.

[74] Fidel Castro, "Speech given at the Fourth Congress of the FMC, March 8, 1985," in *Granma*, March 24, 1985, p. 4, col. 3.

[75] Ibid.

[76] See, *Seventh Congress FMC*, pp. 12-13; "Mujeres entre avances y pronósticos de empleo," *Granma,* May 1, 1999, p. 3.

nontraditional jobs as the result of preferential treatment. Women continue to break into new areas of work at both production and professional levels. Nor has the growing proportion of women in certain fields resulted in a devaluation of that profession in terms of wages.[77] For example, women now constitute more than half the lawyers in Cuba and are as likely to specialize in criminal law or economic law as they are to specialize in domestic relations law. Yet, salaries for lawyers have increased steadily and in legal services are currently based on productivity, not the area of specialty.[78] Similarly, traditional areas of women's work are not paid less, on the average, than nontraditional work. For example, women constitute a large proportion of health technicians. The entry-level salary for nurses is equal to that of all other skilled technicians.[79]

3. Benefits and paternalism. Cuba has one of the most advanced maternity leave laws in the world demonstrating extraordinary concern and care for pregnant women and their babies.[80] The Working Woman Maternity Law adopted in 1974, extended the fully paid maternity leave provided by the previous law of 1963 from twelve to eighteen weeks.[81] In 1992, paid leave was extended an additional twelve weeks at 60 percent pay; an additional non-paid leave up to one year after childbirth could be taken with a guarantee that the woman can return to her original position.[82] In May 2001, the government further extended maternity benefits guarantying of 60

---

[77] This is a common phenomenon in the United States, for example. See, e.g., *County of Washington* v. *Gunther*, 452 U.S. 161 (1981); *American Federation of State, County & Municipal Employees* v. *State of Washington*, 578 F. Supp. 846 (W.D. Wash. 1983). In Cuba, salary schedules covering broad categories of work are legislated by the State Committee on Social Security and Labor. Until 1999, salaries were not negotiated individually or by local trade unions with the management of a particular state enterprise. A new system of enterprise management introduced as part of present economic reforms gives greater autonomy to state enterprise management and greater flexibility in rewarding workers with higher salaries. The unions also have some say in salary schedules.

[78] "Informe de Rendición de Cuenta de la Junta Directiva Provisional a la Asamblea General de Bufetes Colectivos," in *Memorias de la Sesión Constitutiva de la Asamblea General* (Havana: Organización Nacional de Bufetes Colectivos, 1985), pp. 23-25.

[79] Compare Resolución 693 (April 15, 1981) (CETSS) with Resolución 741 (June 1, 1981) (CETSS) (salary schedules of technicians and nurses). In 1981, the starting salary for nurses, depending on classification and experience, ranged from 148 to 231 pesos. Starting salaries for technicians in 1981 ranged from 111 to 198 pesos monthly. For medical school graduates the starting salary for the first two years was 231 pesos a month. Although salaries have increased, the same concepts of equity continue to be applied.

[80] Cuban women received maternity benefits by law as early as 1934, but these benefits were limited and the law largely not enforced. Perreira interview; Ministry of Justice, "Forward" to *Working Woman Maternity Law* (Havana: Editorial Orbe, 1975), p. 3.

[81] Ley No. 1263 (1974), Arts. 12-13.

[82] Resolución No. 2 (1974), Art. 14 (Ministry of Labor and Social Security). This resolution

percent pay for a full year after childbirth.[83] Women are also given one day of paid leave a month to visit a clinic for prenatal care before birth and one day of paid leave a month during the child's first year for pediatric checkups.

Maternity benefits, however, were initially coupled with paternalistic attitudes that affected women's opportunities. Because of their reproductive capacity, women were excluded from many kinds of work considered dangerous to female reproductive organs. The first such regulation, Resolution 48, adopted in the late 1960s, was overly inclusive and applied to all women whether they were of childbearing age or not.[84] Under this regulation women were prohibited from all jobs requiring heavy lifting, excluding women from many nontraditional jobs. As a result of women's complaints about the discriminatory nature of the regulation, Resolution 48 was replaced in 1976 by Resolution 40 which perpetuated paternalism, but the list of exclusions was substantially reduced.[85]

Finally, in 1977, the National Assembly approved a new occupational health and safety law that permitted a woman to choose to work at jobs from which she was previously excluded, provided she obtained a certificate from her doctor indicating she was fit.[86] The Women's Affairs Department was particularly aggressive in scaling back the number of positions not recommended for women and in protecting a woman's right to reject the recommendation.[87] As noted above, the 1992 constitutional modifications have eliminated language that limits the access of women to certain jobs on the basis of gender related health factors.

---

[83] Resolución No. 11(2001) (Ministry of Labor and Social Security), as published in *Trabajadores*, May 1, 2001, p. 2.

[84] *Women and Revolution*, pp. 13-14.

[85] Resolución 40 (1976) (Ministry of Labor). The list was still shockingly long and overly inclusive, barring women from such jobs as all work below water or more than five meters above ground on scaffolds, and all work operating offset machines in book factories. It drew criticism from the FMC at its Third Congress in 1980: "Resolution 40 still suffers from many of the defects of the previous regulations which are presently being revised to correspond to the reality of women today in our country." *Third Congress FMC*, p. 78.

[86] Ley No.13 (Ley de Protección e Higiene del Trabajo), *Gaceta Oficial*, No..48, December 29, 1977. This law was incorporated in the Código de Trabajo (1985), Chapters 7-8, *Gaceta Oficial Ext.*, April 24, 1985.

[87] Chinea interview; Ora Schub, unpublished notes of interview with Digna Cires, Director of Women's Department of the CTC, Havana, September 14, 1985.

Reproductive Rights

Even before the Cuban revolution, abortion was legal in some instances in Cuba. The former Social Defense Code exempted abortion from criminal sanction when it was necessary "to save the life of the mother or to avoid serious damage to her health" as well as in cases of rape or to prevent the transmission of a serious hereditary or contagious disease.[88] This relatively liberal law, given loose interpretation by doctors for women who could afford their services, did not help low-income and poor women who did not have access to such services and often suffered at the hands of unskilled abortionists.

Outrage at the number of women who died or suffered serious physical harm from illegal abortions prompted Dr. Celestino Alvarez Lajonchere to campaign for the opening of free abortion services in Cuba in the early 1960s. His concern that women not die from illegal abortions led to an interpretation of the law that no woman be denied an abortion since illegal abortions posed potential "serious damage to her health" and were life threatening. In 1965, abortions were made available in the Calixto García Hospital in Havana to all who desired them, and in 1979, all criminal penalties for abortion were eliminated from the Cuban Criminal Code. Abortion services are available at all hospitals and clinics.

There is one area, however, in which inconsistency persists in the law: parental involvement in the case of minors. Ministry of Health regulations require parental consent where the young woman is under 16, but this is rarely required in fact. On the other hand, health workers report that at times it is the parents who insist on the abortion contrary to the wishes of the young woman. No consistent approach has been developed to deal with such cases.[89]

Since 1965, when abortion services were first made freely accessible in Cuba, the number of abortions has grown to almost match the number of live births. Statistics from 1992 show that for ten births there were nine abortions and that almost one-third of abortions involved women under the age of twenty.[90] Although there has been a decline since 1989, studies suggest that the decline is only apparent as more and more women who believe they are pregnant seek a menstrual "regularization," a procedure by which

[88] Código de Defensa Social (1936), Art. 443.

[89] This information is based on the author's participation in discussions held at the First Interdisciplinary Forum on Abortion, held at the National Union of Cuban Jurists in Havana, Cuba, May 30, 1992.

[90] Luisa Alvarez Vázquez and Sonia Catasus, "Consideraciones Sociodemográficas sobre el Aborto," paper presented at the First Interdisciplinary Forum on Abortion, Havana, Cuba, May 30, 1992 (photocopy).

menstruation is brought on by extraction. This procedure is not technically considered an abortion, but it seems to be used frequently for the purpose of ending an unwanted pregnancy when detected very early.

The birth rate in Cuba has declined to below replacement levels and in 1996 stood at 1.44 children per female,[91] the lowest in Latin America. This low birth rate is not due to increased infertility, but rather to the choice of Cuban women to have fewer children. For many, this choice means terminating unwanted pregnancies. Abortion is not a substitute for contraception, but abortion has become so commonplace that its availability may impede greater use of other forms of pregnancy prevention.

According to one joint study by Dr. Sonia Catasus of the Center for Demographic Studies and Dr. Luisa Alvarez of the Ministry of Public Health, there are many social and economic factors that influence a woman's choice to terminate a pregnancy.[92] Changes in sexual behavior have led to increased sexual activity outside of wedlock or stable relationships, particularly for adolescent women. Women who become pregnant in such circumstances are more likely to terminate the pregnancy than women in stable relationships. Moreover, the likelihood of a pregnancy being terminated is higher when the family unit living together is a nuclear family as opposed to an extended family, suggesting that women who have greater family support networks are more likely to bring a pregnancy to term. Poor housing conditions and lower income are also linked to higher abortion rates.

As in most societies, the prevention of pregnancy is still generally viewed as the woman's responsibility. Although use of condoms is increasing as the result of educational efforts concerning venereal disease and AIDS, unfortunately, there is continued resistance among the population to the use of condoms which the Ministry of Public Health is working to overcome. Further, for most of the 1990s condoms as well as birth control pills depended on imports curtailed by hard currency shortages as well as by the effects of the U.S. trade embargo, which makes finding sources more circuitous and expensive.[93]

Although Cuban women no longer suffer the harm of illegal abortion, abortions themselves, and multiple abortions in particular, pose health risks.

---

[91] Maria Elena Benitez Pérez, "Familia y Cambio Social en Cuba," in *Diversidad y Complejidad Familiar en Cuba* (1999, University of the Havana), p. 27.

[92] Luisa Alvarez Vázquez and Sonia Catasus, 1992.

[93] G. Reed and M. Frank, *Denial of Food and Medicine: The Impact of the US Embargo on Health and Nutrition in Cuba.* 1997: American Association for World Health, Washington, D.C., pp. 138-39.

The growth in the number of abortions has alarmed many doctors and specialists. Yet the focus in Cuba is not to limit access to abortions but to find ways to reduce the number of unwanted pregnancies. The Cubans present at an interdisciplinary forum held at the National Union of Cuban Jurists in May 1992 unanimously agreed that abortion is foremost a health issue requiring that abortion services be available to all women exercising their right to choose to terminate an unwanted pregnancy.

Integration into Leadership

In addition to establishing women's rights to equality, the 1976 Constitution established a new political structure and institutions that opened opportunities for women, as well as men, to participate in decision making by electing and being elected delegates to the Popular Assemblies. In the 1985 elections, women took 11.5 percent of the delegate positions in the municipal, 21.4 percent in the provincial, and 22.6 percent in the national assemblies.[94] Although these figures represent an increase over the previous elections,[95] women did not advance in the first direct elections of members of the National Assembly held on February 24, 1993, receiving only 22.75 percent of the delegate positions; only five women (16%) were elected to the thirty-one member Council of State. The 1998 elections resulted in a slight increase in women's participation to 27.6% of delegates, but the percentage of women elected in the Council of State remained the same.[96] National elections will again be held in early 2003, and the media has placed significant attention on the increasing numbers of women who have been nominated for the local and national assemblies.

In addition, although the number of members of the Cuban Communist Party more than doubled between 1975 and 1980 as a result of its reorganization,[97] and membership among workers expanded,[98] women's membership in the Party, increased very slowly during the same period from 14.1 percent

---

[94] *Fourth Congress FMC*, p. 48.

[95] Arnold August, *Democracy in Cuba and the 1997-98 Elections* (Havana: Editorial José Martí, 1999), pp. 365-367.

[96] Mayda Alvarez Suárez, "Mujer y Poder en Cuba", *Temas*, No. 14. April-June 1998, p. 16.

[97] William LeoGrande, "Party Development in Revolutionary Cuba," *Journal of Inter American Studies & World Affairs*, Vol. 21, 1979, pp. 473-477.

[98] In December 1975 Party membership totaled 211,642 compared to 434,143 in 1980. *Second Congress PCC*, p. 77. The percentage of production and service worker members in the Party rose from 36.3 percent to 47.3 percent during the same period. Ibid. p. 78.

in 1974 to 21.9 percent in 1984.[99] By 1998, the percentage of women members of the Party had grown to 30.1%, the percentages roughly mirroring growth in women's representation in the National Assembly.[100]

Clearly, the advance of women in employment and education has not been reflected in the nation's leadership. Progress has been frustratingly slow in the area of upper-level management and national leadership positions. In 1999, women occupied the top position in only three of the nineteen ministries: the Ministry of Science, Technology and Environment, the Ministry of Domestic Commerce and the Ministry of Foreign Investment and Economic Cooperation. Women faired slightly better at middle level positions, occupying 17 posts as vice ministers and 30 percent of the directorships of economic enterprises.[101] Similarly, in the CTC as of 2001, women held only 26.1 percent of leadership positions on the national level, but more than 50 percent of middle level leadership positions.[102] It is interesting that fellow workers have more confidence in women's ability to provide leadership than do the national labor leaders.

Further advancement of women in leadership was not on the agenda of the Fourth or Fifth Party Congresses in 1985 and 1991. Other issues, specifically economic and political reform, critical to the very survival of the revolution, took precedence. Despite the elevation of many younger members to leadership in the Party in 1991, the percentage of women in the Central Committee did not change. Three women now sit on the Political Bureau which numbers twenty-five. Of significance, the FMC no longer has a representative on the Political Bureau. Vilma Espín, the only woman previously a full member, was removed. Espín still retains her seat in the Central Committee as does Yolanda Ferrer, who is also in national leadership of the FMC. The need to elevate more women into leadership has received increasing attention in the national press and is a high priority of the FMC.

---

[99] *Fourth Congress FMC*, p. 51.

[100] Alvarez Suárez, p. 16. Party membership is not a requirement for election to the National Assembly although most delegates are also party members.

[101] Ibid.

[102] Resolución: La Mujer Trabajadora, adopted at the 18th Congress of the CTC in April 2001. This is a slight increase from the previous decade.

Rejection of "Feminism"

Although disappointed with the pace of change, the FMC has never adopted a separatist approach to women's rights; instead, it maintains the view that women's equality is inseparable from the advancement of the society as a whole. At its Fourth Congress in 1985, the FMC concluded:

> All the advances which we report here are the result of a certain conception that, in an underdeveloped country like ours, women must fight for their own liberation at the same time they fight for the liberation of the nation and society, and that later, when transformations have been produced in the socioeconomic structures, it will be necessary to continue struggling for equality between women and men in all aspects of life.[103]

In fact, members sometimes state that it is a "female" not a "feminist" organization, meaning that they do not concern themselves with women's rights divorced from comprehensive social change. This is a recurrent refrain heard by visitors to the FMC's headquarters in Havana. The phrase is used often to distinguish their approach from what they perceive to be the pervasive approach among North American feminist groups: a struggle for women's rights separate from advancement of the socialist project.[104]

Conclusion

Cuban women have found their voice within the revolution. Constitutional guarantees expanded since 1959 have enhanced equality. The representation of women in policy making positions, although not proportional, is substantial and slowly increasing. Cuban women could not have come so far, however, without a national commitment to women's equality—a commitment which, thus far, has not sacrificed equality on the altar of "economic efficiency." Yet neither equality of opportunity, supportive legislation nor further democratization guarantees the revolution in consciousness essential to full realization of equality. Paternalism and machismo persist as barriers to change. The day is yet to come when Cuba has a party, leadership and government of men and women.

---

[103] *Fourth Congress FMC.*
[104] Perreira interview; Steffens, p. 22.

II. RACIAL EQUALITY

Although it is not within the objectives or competency of this book to explore the complexities of racial identity in Cuba, it is essential keep in mind that the Cuban population is very diverse making identification or affiliation by skin color very complex and elusive. The understanding of the social and historical origins of race in Cuba is fundamental to an understanding of the roots of racial bias and its reproduction in Cuban society today.[105] In the following discussion concerning the issue of advancement towards racial equality I use the terms "black," "mulatto" and "white" acknowledging that such terminology is superficial and ignores the nuances of the racial mix of Cuban society. Yet, it is undeniable that, historically, it has been Cubans of dark complexion who have suffered the most discrimination and whites who have enjoyed the greatest economic advantage as a group.

There is a paucity of literature on race, race relations and racial discrimination in Cuba, both pre- and post-revolution. Nor are there recent published studies which measure the depth of racial cleavage or the progress toward equality that has actually been achieved as a result of the revolution. Only since the mid-1990s have Cuban researchers and institutions begun to pay significant attention to these issues.[106] According to the last census on the racial composition of Cuban society in 1981, 66 percent of the population was defined as "white," 22 percent as "mixed," and 12 percent as "black,"[107] but there were no published statistics on the racial composition of political institutions, professions or other sectors. The 2002 census is underway as this book goes to press and will yield new data on the racial composition of the Cuban population.

What can be stated unequivocally, however, is that the revolution did not merely pay lip service to the goal of racial equality as previous governments had done. The socialist government immediately set about to dismantle institutional racism and actively pursued a policy of racial equality. For a variety of reasons, however, it has not been able to eradicate the vestiges of historic racial stereotypes and bias. Further, the economic crisis which began in 1990 and some of the measures introduced in response to that cri-

---

105 For a discussion of these issues see, Juan Antonio Alvarado Ramos, "Relaciones raciales en Cuba. Notas de investigación;" María Magdalena Pérez Alvarez, "Los prejuicios raciales sus mecanismos de reproducción;" and María del Carmen Caño Secade, "Relaciones raciales, proceso de ajuste y política social;" in *Temas*, No. 7, July-Sept. 1996.

106 See, for example the journal *Temas*, No. 7, July-Sept. 1996 which contains a number of articles on race and race relations in Cuba.

107 Jean Stubbs, *The Test of Time* (London: Latin American Bureau, 1989), p. v.

sis[108] have brought social consequences that could threaten the gains towards racial equality previously achieved.

Race Relations prior to 1959

Cuba did not abolish slavery until 1886, placing it second to Brazil as the last countries in the hemisphere to do so. Although Cuba never experienced the persistent, virulent racism that is so much a part of U.S. history, black Cubans did suffer violent repression in the early years of the Republic. Despite their substantial role in the war for independence, blacks suffered discrimination at the hands of, first, the U.S. military government[109] and, then, the elected government which deprived them of equal participation in the political and economic life of the new republic.[110] In fact, some commentators observed that blacks were better treated during the colonial period than in the early years of independence.[111]

As a result, Cubans of African descent organized an association of voters in 1907 that became the Party of the Independents of Color in 1910. This movement was frustrated by legislation outlawing political parties of racial identity. The party was banned as were its newspapers. Lourdes Casal has described the devastating impact of government response to the movement:

> [T]he Morúa Amendments to the Electoral Reform Law of 1910 closed the door of legality to the organization of parties along race lines and eventually led the Independientes to take arms against the José Miguel Gómez Administration. The ensuing racial war, still insufficiently studied, led to a nationwide extermination of blacks of quasi-genocidal proportions.[112]

More than 3,000 black Cubans were killed. According to Casal, "[The] black Cuban community never recovered from the heavy losses inflicted

---

[108] For example, the legalization of the use of the US dollar parallel to the Cuban peso has advantaged those who receive remittances from relatives abroad, the majority of whom are white.

[109] Louis A. Pérez, *Cuba Under the Platt Amendment* (Pittsburgh, Penna.: University of Pittsburgh Press, 1986), p. 149; Lisa Brock and Otis Cunningham, "Race and the Cuban Revolution," *Cuban Studies*, Vol. 21, Winter 1991-1992, p. 175.

[110] Pérez, pp. 149-50.

[111] Ibid.

[112] Lourdes Casal, "Race Relations in Contemporary Cuba," in *The Cuba Reader* (New York: Grove Press, 1989), Philip Brenner, et al, eds., p. 474

upon its most race-conscious male leadership."[113] Since then, the affirmation of black racial identity has found no expression in organized politics. Moreover, in general, blacks were increasingly excluded from opportunities in the higher-paid trades and continued to constitute the poorest sector in Cuba, particularly in urban areas.[114]

Although early constitutions each contained a general provision declaring all citizens equal before the law, none specifically proscribed racial discrimination until the 1940 Constitution was adopted. The 1940 Constitution contained two sections specifically relevant to race. Article 10 declared that

> the citizen has the right....[t]o reside in his country without being the object of any discrimination...on basis of race, class, political opinions or religious belief.

Article 20 stated, in addition to repeating former provisions concerning equality of citizens before the law, that

> [a]ll discrimination based on sex, race, color or class, and any other motive harmful to human dignity is declared illegal and punishable.

To enforce this provision, a 1955 amendment to the Social Defense Code of 1936 made acts of discrimination on the basis of "sex, race, color or class" punishable by fine.[115]

None of these provisions, however, was enforced. Racial discrimination was so openly practiced right up to 1959 that even Batista was denied admission to some of Havana's exclusive clubs because he was mulatto. Many recreational facilities as well as jobs were known to be closed to blacks. Moreover, the Social Defense Code itself contained provisions which expressly discriminated on the basis of race. For example, Article 571 (Violations of the Public Order) punished as a misdemeanor the practice of certain religious cults of African origin. Also, anyone who went out on the street, without special permission to form part of a comparsa, or conga or other "dance of an African character," was chargeable with a misdemeanor.

---

[113] Ibid.

[114] Ibid. pp. 476-477; Jorge I. Domínguez, *Cuba: Order and Revolution*, (Cambridge, Mass.: Harvard University Press, 1978), pp. 75-76 and Appendix B.

[115] Código de Defensa Social (1936), Art. 213(Bis), added by Decreto-Ley No. 1933, Art.1, *Gaceta Oficial,* January 24, 1955.

These provisions were not repealed until the Criminal Code of 1979 was adopted.

Racial Equality after 1959

As was the case with respect to gender equality, racial equality was not expressly included among the goals for which the revolutionaries fought. It, too, went unmentioned in Castro's speech in his defense after the assault on the Moncada Garrison in which he detailed the injustices that prompted rebellion. However, elimination of racial discrimination quickly became a permanent part of the program for the new society. In the early months after the defeat of Batista, Castro openly and directly denounced racial discrimination in unequivocal terms. In March 1959, he declared:

> One of the battles we must prioritize more and more every day . . . is the battle to end racial discrimination at the work place. . . . There are two types of racial discrimination: One is the discrimination in recreation centers or cultural centers; the other, which is the worst and the first one we must fight, is racial discrimination in jobs.[116]

The closing of private schools in 1961 and the public investment in education were extremely important to the process of rectifying racial inequality. Even in special secondary schools set up by the new government for the brightest students, a policy of regional representation helped increase the number of black youths attending. Numerous programs were designed, to assure that children attended school, and many of the families that received this attention were among the poorest and therefore more likely to be black or mulatto. However, although race has not been taken into account as a factor in admission to schools at any level and educational opportunities have been available on an equal basis, social factors rooted in the vestiges of past discrimination continue to impede black youth.

Despite these obstacles, there is clear evidence of progress. Increasing numbers of blacks and mulattos enter university and the professions and have become increasingly prominent in high-level positions in governmental and non-governmental institutions. At the 1990 General Assembly of the *bufetes colectivos*, for example, black and mulatto lawyers made up nearly

---

[116] Fidel Castro, "Discurso del 22 marzo de 1959," *Revolución,* March 23, 1959, pp. 24-27.

half the delegates elected to the assembly.[117] Moreover, there is an increasing number of black judges at all levels of the judiciary. Similar advancement is visible in other professions, such as medicine and the sciences.

Black Cubans also benefited from the elimination of the private rental of housing and efforts to improve housing conditions. Immunization projects, sanitation services and the development of a national health service have substantially improved health conditions. Thus, since the black population as a whole was among the most disadvantaged in pre-revolutionary Cuba, it benefited disproportionately to other sectors. It is not surprising, therefore, that support for the revolution among blacks was reportedly higher than among whites. Maurice Zeitlin reports in a 1962 survey that 80 percent of black industrial workers as compared to 67 percent of white workers expressed support for the revolution.[118]

The government policy of non-racialism also had an influence on social attitudes. While the persistent and acute housing shortage has not enabled the eradication of run-down, marginal neighborhoods in Havana (which are primarily black and mulatto), most neighborhoods have become increasingly integrated with respect to both race and profession.[119] Inter-racial marriage, which was never a rarity in Cuba, began to increase markedly after 1959[120] and has become widely accepted among most Cubans, although the norm continues to be marriage within ones own racial group.[121]

The 1976 Constitution, like the 1940 Constitution, contained a provision prohibiting discrimination on the basis of race, color or national origin. In addition, however, it also imposed an affirmative duty on the state to educate "everyone, from the earliest possible age, in the principle of equality among human beings."[122] Also, the Constitution enumerated certain specific rights of all without respect to race, color or national origin.[123] Among these rights are equal pay for equal work, access to jobs based on merit and abil-

---

117 This assessment was made by personal observation. Such statistics are not compiled or reported.

118 Maurice Zeitlin, *Revolutionary Politics and the Cuban Working Class* (Princeton, N.J.: Princeton University Press, 1967), p. 77. See also, Brock and Cunningham, p. 175.

119 Indeed, in the face of increasing differences in family income since 1990, one of the reasons why the government has prohibited the private sale of residencies outside of the method of "permuta" or exchange is that to do so would create social stratification in neighborhoods. See, Chapter Eight.

120 Casal, p. 479.

121 See, Juan Antonio Alvarado Ramos, "Relaciones raciales en Cuba. Notas de investigación," in *Temas*, No. 7, July-Sept. 1996, pp. 37-43.

122 Constitución (1976), Art. 41.

123 Ibid., Art. 42.

ity, access to all educational institutions and medical care. These rights are maintained in the 1992 amendments to the Constitution, the protected categories being modified only to replace the word "color" with "color of skin," and to add religious beliefs.[124]

With the adoption of the 1979 Criminal Code, the criminal penalties for racial discrimination were broadened and strengthened. Article 349.1 imposes sanctions of six months to three years and/or a fine on "anyone who discriminates or promotes or incites discrimination, with expression or offensive intent against one's sex, race, color or national origin or who obstructs or impedes enjoyment of rights of equality." The same sanction is imposed against anyone who disseminates ideas based on racial superiority or hatred or commits acts of violence or incites commission of such acts.[125] These provisions are consistent with Cuba's ratification of the United Nations Convention on the Discrimination of Apartheid and All Forms of Racism.

There is no information available regarding any individual complaints of race discrimination or enforcement of these laws. Unlike gender, where individual cases of job discrimination have been prosecuted or reported in the press, often leading to redress of the discriminatory conduct, complaints based on race have not been publicized. Because the issue of race is rarely discussed in public, incidents of race discrimination may be less likely to be reported by the victim himself. However, consciousness of the issue surfaced with the introduction of foreign investment accompanied by a perceived bias in the tourist industry. In the early 1990s, the appearance of racial bias in the hiring practices of foreign hotel managers created such concern that the issue was aired in the public media. Some years later, a foreign hotel manager was forced to resign as a result of complaints of racial discrimination by the hotel workers union. Concern about racial discrimination in employment was also raised by members of the FMC in meetings preceding the Seventh FMC Congress in 2000.

Although black and mulatto Cubans have increasingly integrated into the political and economic life of the country, disparities have persisted. In an unprecedented recognition that correction of "historic injustices cannot be left to spontaneity," Castro exhorted the Party at its 1985 Congress to undertake affirmative measures to promote youth, women and blacks. The acknowledgment of racial disparities came as quite a surprise. Unlike gender equality, which was always the focus of public attention, this was the first time that Castro, or any other leader, publicly acknowledged the need

[124] Constitución (1992), Art. 43.
[125] Código Penal (1979), Art. 349.2.

for affirmative measures to eradicate the vestiges of Cuba's long history of racial discrimination.

Although black Cubans had the same educational and employment opportunities as all Cubans and entered in increasing proportion all professions and economic sectors, observers could not help but notice the small numbers of blacks and mulattos in leadership posts. It was not readily apparent how such an affirmative action program would work as an increasingly large proportion of the Cuban population is racially mixed. No explicit program of implementation was announced. From conversations with members of local CDRs and trade unions, however, it seemed that the pronouncement had some effect in sensitizing awareness of the problem. Elections to offices in these organizations at the time reflected greater consciousness of race, at least in the short run. For example, in one CDR election, an active member was nominated for president. After the nominator presented a lengthy list of his many qualifications, she added, "Also, he is a black!" which was greeted with laughter. He was elected.

In 1989, membership of the Central Committee of the Party was 28.4 percent black or mulatto (self-defined).[126] Because there were no statistics available by race it is not possible to give an accurate account of the ethnic makeup of the National Assembly, but, according to Casal, the combined black and mulatto representation in 1978 was approximately 38 percent, compared to 9 percent in the 1943 Congress.[127] Nevertheless, the number of blacks among the very top cadres is disproportionately small compared to the population. For example, after the 1991 Party Congress which elevated more women and young party members to the Political Bureau, non-whites continued to make up less than 15 percent.

Moreover, although black and mulatto Cubans have had great success in entering the professions, high-level management in both the enterprises and the bureaucracy remain disproportionately white. A variety of factors converge today to compel re-examination of racial equality in Cuba to promote advances and prevent the re-emergence of a social divide. Despite impressive progress, the vestiges of deep historic discrimination have left substantial numbers of black Cubans among the poorest sectors of the population. Recent research suggests that negative racial stereotyping still exists among a significant portion of the population.[128] As the government increasingly decentralizes decision-making in order to meet the challenges of entering

---

[126] Nelson Valdés, "The Changing Face of Cuba's Communist Party," in *The Cuba Reader* (New York: Grove Press, 1989), Philip Brenner, et al., eds., p. 176.
[127] Casal, p. 483; Domínguez, p. 226.
[128] See, Pérez Alvarez, p. 46-47.

the global economy, biases that may persist among the managerial sector could resurface with negative repercussions. Some anecdotal evidence suggests that this has been the case on occasion.

Moreover, criminal activity, such as theft, increased dramatically in the 1990s parallel to the economic crisis. Although many Cubans have resorted to illegal activity to "resolve" their individual economic needs, blacks have been and continue to be over represented in the prison population. There is a general perception among the population, that street crime is primarily committed by blacks. The stereotype of the "jinetera" or prostitute in Cuba today is black or mulatta. The unfortunate result of these phenomena is the perpetuation of negative stereotyping of black youths who are much more likely to be stopped by police in the street for routine identity checks.[129]

The perpetuation of such stereotyping is not the result of a system that denies equal opportunity or that fails to encourage full participation. Rather, it reflects failure to recognize and address the profound social impact of past inequities as well as persisting biases among many Cubans. The severe economic crisis of the early 1990s only exacerbated the situation. Despite government efforts to distribute goods equitably, a thriving black market offered scarce goods to those who had more money. For the lowest-paid workers and the growing numbers living on pensions as a result of lay-offs, such goods were only obtainable by receiving money from family abroad or participating in illegal activities. Although the modest economic recovery and the re-opening of the farmers markets have substantially reduced the black market, the price of food and basic consumer items at such markets remain quite high in relation to salaries.

Regrettably, measures taken to confront the economic hardships that descended on the Cuban population in the past decade have had a unintentional but disparate racial impact. In order to increase the inflow of hard currency, the Cuban government legalized the use of the U.S. dollar among the Cuban population and, thus, encouraged relatives abroad to send money to their families.[130] However, it is generally acknowledged that since Cuban emigrants were predominantly white, the remittances could widen economic differences between white and black Cubans on the island. Further, as a measure to absorb growing unemployment, the Cuban government permitted growth of self-employment into a broader area of services than previ-

---

[129] "Cuba Begins to Answer Its Race Question," *The Washington Post*, November 12, 2000, p. A1.

[130] United States law permits Cuban emigrants to send up to $300 every three months to single households in Cuba. 31 CFR 515.570. Although, this special exemption to the US embargo was temporarily suspended from September 1994 until1999, Cubans in the United States frequently ignored US government prohibitions and continued to send funds to their relatives in Cuba, often exceeding legal limits.

ously permitted including small family restaurants. To some extent, since whites have greater access to resources to engage in such activities, often receiving assistance from relatives abroad, this measure might also contribute to increasing economic differences although many self-employed laborers such as plumbers, carpenters, locksmiths, etc., are non-white.

Further, subtle forms of bias linger in the national culture and are apparent in the way in which the visual media portray black and mulatto Cubans. In general, the main characters in movies are white, and while blacks and mulattos are not relegated to stereotypes, they infrequently appear as the protagonist. Moreover, couples in movies are almost always of the same race, which is at odds with Cuban society where intermarriage is not unusual. This portrayal appears to reflect an attitude in which "blackness" continues to be undervalued. In Cuban idiom, the term "negrito" or "negrita" is widely used to describe a person with affection whether white or black, but it also may be used disparagingly to identify those who commit petty crimes. There is no comparable term to identify a white person. These remnants of prejudice and bias impede the full realization of a non-racial society. Yet, until the 1990s, they remained unacknowledged in public discourse. Issues of racial bias and racial equality are rarely, if at all, mentioned in the media or in public forums. Despite these negative factors and tendencies, social cohesion in Cuba is still quite strong. Impressive progress in economic and racial integration is still a hallmark of Cuba's achievements.

The issue of racial identity as a differentiating characteristic in Cuban society is fraught with contradictions. Cuban culture and national identity are bound up with the intertwining of its Spanish and African origins. Although Afro-Cuban religions were repressed to different degrees throughout Cuban history prior to 1979, Afro-Cuban music, art and other cultural manifestations have been infused in the Cuban cultural identity for more than a centry as have Spanish culture and traditions. Castro himself gave recognition to this dual heritage when he described Cubans as a "latino-african people." As Casal noted, Cuba after the revolution has evolved into a "true mestizaje of the complex interactions of two powerful cultural traditions."[131] This fusion, as well as the socialist ethic of collectivity, prevents fragmentation and the political expression of separate racial identity.

It has been the silence on the issue of race in Cuban society that has differentiated it from the issue of gender equality. There is continuing public discussion about the affects of gender differentiation and considerable

---

[131] Casal, p. 484.

public dialogue on the struggle against machismo. However, once the government dismantled institutional racism, racial bias and inequality were expected to disappear and any discussion of their continued existence, even in subtle forms, touched a sensitive nerve.

Only since the late 1990's have Cuba's cultural and social organizations begun to discuss publicly the issue of race in Cuba. Research on racial identity and the reproduction of prejudices was published in *Temas*, a popular journal of social commentary, in 1996. In 2001, the National Union of Cuban Artists and Writers held a forum on racial images in Cuban culture. Such public discussions are a critical starting point in facing the persistence of racial biases and its negative social consequences. The span of a generation is a short time to uproot such deeply held social biases, but until Cubans are able to publicly recognize the issue and discuss it openly, Cuban society will not overcome the vestiges of its past.

III. RELIGIOUS FREEDOM

Although the 1976 Constitution declared Cuba an atheist state, the Cuban revolutionary government never banned religious organizations or persecuted religious believers. No churches or houses of worship were closed or expropriated. Nevertheless, religious practice was discouraged and the influence of religion over social affairs diminished. Religious believers could not be members of the Communist Party. Christian holidays previously observed as national holidays, no longer were so observed.[132] Yet, religious believers were not denied employment and many achieved important positions of respect,[133] even if not members of the Communist Party. Religious schools were permitted for purposes of religious instruction, but they were not licensed to replace public education. As the numbers of people attending churches and synagogues declined, the resources necessary to maintain the buildings and facilities also diminished. Thus, by the early 1990s many were in considerable disrepair.

Throughout the last 40 years the Protestant churches and the Jewish community maintained cordial relations with the government, cooperating with the government in social programs and participating in the Cuban

---

[132] Christmas was observed as a national holiday until December 1969 when it was overriden by the exigencies of the 10 ton sugar harvest. It was restored again in 1998.

[133] For example, nationally lauded poet Eliseo Diego was a practicing Catholic as is Cintio Vitier, who served as a deputy in the National Assembly from 1993 to 1998; lawyer Raúl Gomez Treto, active in the Catholic laity, held an important position in the Ministry of Justice.

Ecumenical Council. The members of the Jewish population who followed kosher traditions were able to get special rations of kosher meat. Matzoh and other products for special holidays were imported, generally from Canada.

Santería, perhaps always the majority religion in Cuba, the public practices of which were outlawed before 1959, has remained strong throughout the revolution. Considered a part of AfroCuban culture as much as a religious sect, santería touched almost everyone in some way or another. Afrocuban music finds its rhythms rooted in the yoruba traditions underlying santería.

At the outset of the revolution the Catholic Church maintained an antagonistic attitude toward the new government, frequently aligning itself with the armed counter-revolutionary insurgents in the 1960s. It also cooperated with U.S. inspired maneuvers such as Operation Peter Pan the objective of which was to increase opposition from within Cuba by convincing parents to send their children unaccompanied to the United States to spare them the horrors of communism. The Catholic diocese in Miami received the children and placed them in homes and institutions.

The path to improved relations between the government and the religious community was perhaps opened by the 1984 interview of Fidel Castro by Brazilian priest Frei Betto published in a book widely distributed in Cuba entitled "Fidel and Religion."[134] In 1991, at the urging of many of its members during public meetings, the Cuban Communist Party publicly acknowledged that exclusion of religious believers was discriminatory and opened its membership to religious believers. The following year, the National Assembly of Peoples Power adopted modifications to the Cuban Constitution that explicitly forbade discrimination on the basis of religious belief[135] and eliminated the statement that the socialist state is based on the concept of "scientific materialism."[136] Moreover, a new article expressly recognizes freedom of religion and the separation of religion and the state as fundamental principles of the Cuban constitution.[137]

As a result of these measures, churches and synagogues began to attract new members to their dwindling and aging congregations. Santaría experienced a resurgence of followers as well. December 25 was restored as a

[134] Frei Betto, *Fidel y Religión* (Havana: Consejo del Estado, 1985).
[135] Constitución (1992), Art. 42.
[136] Compare Art. 54 of the 1976 Constitution with Article 55 of the Constitution as amended in 1992.
[137] Ibid. Art. 8. "The state recognizes, respects and guarantees religious freedom. In the Republic of Cuba, religious institutions are separate from the State."

national holiday in 1998 and makeshift trees with ornaments and lights appeared in many homes (even of those who are not Christian or church goers). As a demonstration of the new respect afforded religious institutions, Fidel Castro attended the Hanukah celebration at one of a Jewish synagogue in Havana in 1998. Masses and other church ceremonies are occasionally broadcast on Cuban TV or given newspaper coverage.

Preparations for Pope's visit to Cuba in February 1998 laid the basis for improved dialogue between the government and the Catholic Church. The Pope's visit was greeted with great enthusiasm by both the Cuban government and the population and given broad media coverage. The Pope performed four public masses while in Cuba, all of which were televised and broadcast by radio. Cubans were encouraged, and in some cases even organized, to attend. Important cultural institutions participated in concerts and choral accompaniments to the masses.

Despite the apparent thaw shown by a new level of dialogue and tolerance, relations between the government and the Catholic Church, remain distant. The Pope asked for concessions the Cuban government is not willing to make: he urged the government to permit the church to organize schools parallel to public schools, the establish a catholic university and to grant the church broad access to the mass media. None of these requests has been received positively.

One of the first actions of the Cuban revolution was to ban private schools and guarantee universal free public education. Church run programs of religious education were permitted outside of the public schools. The government was not now about to reverse the deeply held belief that education should be equally available and free of charge to all. Nor did the Catholic Church find allies for its proposal among other religious orders which maintained strong support for public education and opposed any form of privatization. Further, it was implicit that the church that would most benefit from such a change in policy would be the Catholic Church, the resources of which could be rivaled by none.

While the media has given some coverage to religious ceremonies and the activities of religious leaders, the churches have no general access to either the mass print or electronic media. They may, and do, however, distribute newsletters and other written material to their congregations. Such limitations impede the church's ability to proselytize beyond the members of their congregations.

Nevertheless, the opening since 1991 has fomented renewed interest in religion and growth in the followers of all religious sects. Although still not as large as the Catholic Church, the protestant church congregations are growing at a faster pace. Santería, always more extensive that other religions, appears to be growing the fastest. In 1999, Protestant churches celebrated a festival throughout the country culminating in a public ceremony in the Plaza de la Revolución. The activities were reminiscent of the Pope's four masses celebrated in four cities across Cuba. The crowds were smaller, to a large extent because of the absence of the historic figure of the Pope who attracted many more persons who were curious rather than believers. The Protestant ceremonies largely attracted the faithful. Their message was also one of harmony and embrace of the revolution's humanitarian values.

As another indication of the new importance given to the various religions in Cuba, religious leaders frequently participate in public events. Reverend Raúl Suárez, a deputy to the National Assembly accompanied the Cuban delegation to the opening session of the United Nations in fall 1999. In addition, in winter of 2002, clerics of all religions were invited to speak to the mass demonstrations organized to protest the refusal of the extreme anti-Cuba lobby in Miami to permit the return of six year old Elián González to Cuba to live with his father.[138] The prominent role of the Cuban Council of Churches together with the United States National Council of Churches to help return the boy further highlighted the social role of religious groups in Cuba.

However, the new opening and increased guaranty of religious belief has not satisfied critics. The Vatican continues to call for further concessions that would broaden the role of the Catholic church in Cuban society. Further, U.S. State Department Human Rights Reports continue to criticize Cuba for lack of religious freedom, particularly impediments to the expansion of the role of churches in social and political life. In an odd statement, the 1999 report on Cuba criticizes the Cuban government for not permitting nativity scenes in public buildings although similar religious displays in public buildings are also unlawful in the United States.

As a matter of law, the question raised by the demands of the Catholic Church is whether the concept of religious freedom must include 1) private, religious based schools in the place of public education and 2) access to the mass media for religious programs. What the Catholic Church seeks, with respect to religion, is the right to proselytize beyond its congregation using public resources or vehicles of mass communication. It further seeks a greater role in the social life of the country by offering services to the general population parallel to those provided by the state. These demands raise interesting questions of separation of church and state and whether Cuba's policies discriminate against or suppress religious beliefs. Church sponsored

---

[138] Conspicuously absent from participation were representatives of the Cuban Catholic Church.

religious classes are not impeded by a state policy that denies private secular education. Moreover, no religion is given any greater access to the media than another.

If there are no impediments to the organization of religious institutions and religious belief is a matter of individual choice and conscience, does Cuban policy interfere with the free practice of religion or with the establishment of religious organizations? Is there a legal basis for insisting that religious institutions have social and political rights that go beyond tending to the faith and religious education of their adherents? A question has been raised concerning use of available land and the ability to erect new religious buildings. In a context of severe housing shortages and the need for building and renovating hospitals and schools, what priority should be given to religious groups to obtain land and materials for building new houses of worship?

Chapter 6

FAMILY LAW

Like the former Marxist regimes of Europe, the Cuban government has not attempted to socialize family functions significantly. To have done so would have been totally at odds with the deeply rooted culture of patriarchy and so socially disruptive as to endanger other goals of the revolution. Although measures were taken early on to assist families economically and to formalize consensual unions, it was not until the mid-1970s, that the government undertook to define the socialist family, its role in society and the rights of its members. Rather than weaken the nuclear family, the revolution aspired to support and strengthen it as the basic unit of the new socialist society.

The socialist Family Code adopted in 1975 was conceived as an instrument to cultivate an ideal family based on mutual affection and "absolute equality" between spouses and among children.[1] Explicitly rejecting the bourgeois family norms that maintained patriarchy and the subordination of women, the government attempted to transform the marital relationship into one of true equality. Under the new concept of marriage, men and women not only have equal rights with respect to property, but they each undertake obligations to contribute equally to the maintenance of the home and the care of children. The express goal of establishing gender equality in the family is distinctly feminist in approach and distinguishes Cuban law and policy from that of other contemporary socialist countries.

Although the "model" socialist family required a stable base, the event of the revolution itself and the ensuing economic and social transformations as well as the persistence of patriarchal customs opposed that stability and frustrated the project. Thus, a variety of complex social forces have affected the structure of the Cuban family. Yet, family bonds in Cuba remains strong and find support in the social policies of the revolution.

As the revolutionary agenda unfolded, Cuban families were strained by the trauma of radical social transformation. The former social and political

---

[1]Código de Familia (Ley No. 1289), Preamble, *Gaceta Oficial*, February 15, 1975. The Code eliminated all previous legal discrimination applied to children, natural or adopted or whether born in wedlock or not.

influence derived from family ties among the propertied classes evaporated with the nationalization of most private enterprise. Deep ideological divisions splintered family relations. Many families were torn apart as members of the upper and middle classes emigrated in vast numbers in response to the socialization of the economy, the new political order and the hardships created by the impact of the U.S. trade embargo.[2] In addition, although the marriage rate increased in the first decade after the revolution as a result of eased regulations to formalize consensual unions,[3] the divorce rate soared as adjustments to radical social changes shook family bonds.[4]

Adding to family tensions, in the early 1960s, the Cuban Roman Catholic Church together with help from both governmental and non-governmental agencies in the United States spread fear among the middle and upper classes that the new government was going to interfere with guardianship of children and destroy the family.[5] Parents were urged to send their children unaccompanied to the United States to prevent the revolutionary government from sending them off to the godless Soviet Union for indoctrination. As a result of this project, dubbed Operation Peter Pan, thousands of parents were convinced by such propaganda to separate from their children for what they believed would be a short time, assuming the regime would be toppled in a matter of months. In the United States, these children were housed, fed and sent to schools. Separated for months or years, most families reunited only when the parents finally emigrated to the United States. For many children the separation was a traumatic experience, causing deep wounds within the family.[6]

Political and economic changes affected the families that stayed as well. Although the government lifted some economic burdens from families by providing important services in the areas of health care, day care and education, it also recognized that the state could not replace the family in the primary role of raising children, looking after their everyday needs as well as ethical and intellectual development. Some measure of responsibility is borne by educational institutions, but these are not viewed as an adequate substitute for parental affection and guidance. However, having lifted some

---

[2] Margaret Randall, *Women in Cuba: Twenty Years Later* (New York: Smyrna Press, 1981), pp. 87-89.
[3] Olga Mesa Castillo, "El Divorcio: Otro Angulo de Análisis," *Revista Cubana de Derecho*, No. 38, July-September 1989, p. 114.
[4] Ibid.
[5] Raúl Gómez Treto, *The Church and Socialism in Cuba* (New York: Orbis Books, 1988), p. 37.
[6] In a powerful video documentary, eight women who came to the United States through this program detail their experiences. "The Other Side of the Glass" (1996), produced by ICAIC and directed by Mercedes Arce, Guillermo Sentena and Marina Ochoa.

burdens, the government has imposed others by encouraging volunteer work as well as political participation, taking parents away from the home and limiting their time with their children. Moreover, the integration of women into political and social activities forced re-examination of the traditional role of women in the family and put strains on emotional bonds still shaped by inequality in sexual relations.

I. THE PRE-REVOLUTIONARY FAMILY

There has never been a "typical family" in Cuba. Ever since the colonial era, family characteristics varied by both class and race, and rural family patterns differed from those of urban families.[7] Upper-class families before the revolution most closely mirrored the traditional patriarchal family of the colonial period,[8] but even the bourgeois family did not conform to traditional religious teaching. Married men frequently formed extra-marital relationships with women with whom they maintained a household and had children. Informal marriages, or consensual unions, were common among both the urban and rural poor. Regardless of class, however, household membership extended beyond the "nuclear" unit to include grandparents and other relatives. In the case of the upper class, the extended family included resident servants as well.

Pre-revolutionary Cuban family law, derived from the strongly patriarchal Spanish Civil Code that governed domestic relations in Cuba from 1868 until 1950,[9] bore little relation to the complex reality of sexual relations and affiliation. The legal institution of marriage was really a small enterprise run by men to serve their everyday needs and to produce heirs. In fact, the law prohibited anyone not capable of procreation from marrying.[10] Moreover, the law provided for financial support for married women and their children, but afforded them no rights, conserving their dependence on fathers and husbands. Wives served both as the reproductive vessel and as managers of the household. Although upper- and middle-class families were likely to employ servants, these advantages did not permit women to

---

[7] Raúl Gómez Treto, "Hacia un Nuevo Código de la Familia?" *Revista Cubana del Derecho*, Vol. 34, 1988, pp. 32-33; see also, Lisandro Pérez, "The Family in Cuba," in *The Family in Latin America*, Man Singh Das and Clinton J. Jesser, eds. (New Delhi: Vikas Publishing, 1980), pp. 238-39.

[8] Pérez, p. 238.

[9] Ibid.

[10] Código Civil (1889), Art. 83(3).

freely engage in social, economic or political activities that would take them outside the home. They were expected either to do the household chores or to supervise the servants who did them. A small number of women, however, did receive higher education and became teachers and professionals.[11]

Under the 1889 Civil Code, a married woman was completely subordinated and obligated to obey her husband, who was designated the sole administrator of the marital property as well as the protector and legal representative of the wife.[12] A double standard of sexual morality was strictly applied. Social norms dictated that women be virgins until marriage and remain absolutely faithful to their husbands. Female virginity was so prized and protected that an unmarried woman was prohibited by law from leaving her family's home until she reached the age of twenty-three except for purposes of marriage, even though the legal age of majority for both men and woman was twenty-one.[13] A young man, on the other hand, was expected to prove his manhood immediately upon reaching puberty and to reaffirm it in subsequent "conquests" regardless of his marital status or that of the woman involved.[14] Although divorce was not legally recognized until 1918,[15] the Civil Code provided that couples could separate for cause. Pursuant to these provisions, the wife's adultery was always legitimate cause for legal separation, but the husband's adultery was cause only if it resulted in public scandal or neglect of the wife.[16] Thus, the law gave tacit approval to extramarital relationships of men.

Changes in the law affecting traditional family relations began to occur well before the revolution. The first law providing for a legal divorce, enacted in 1918, permitted divorce on specific grounds, including proof of incompatibility.[17] Further, the Cuban Constitution of 1940, considered one of the most progressive in the hemisphere at the time, contained a provision

---

[11] Elizabeth Stone, *Women and the Cuban Revolution* (New York: Pathfinder Press, 1981), p. 6. The reports on the percentage of women employed in the late 1950s vary from 13 to 17 percent, representing 200,000 to 260,000 women. Carmelo Mesa-Lago, *The Economy of Socialist Cuba* (Albuquerque, N.M.: University of New Mexico, 1981) (13.1 percent in 1958); Padula and Smith, "Women in Socialist Cuba," in *Cuba*, Sandor Halebsky and John Kirk, eds. (New York: Praeger, 1985), p. 80.

[12] Código Civil (1889), Arts. 57-59.

[13] Código Civil (1889), Art. 321 (as modified by Law of June 18, 1916, Art. 2).

[14] Interview with Monika Krause, Director of the Cuban Institute of Sex Education, Havana, Cuba, December 27, 1985.

[15] Ley de 29 de Julio 1918 (Sobre Divorcio con Disolución del Vínculo Matrimonial), *Gaceta Oficial*, July 30, 1918, Art. 104.

[16] Código Civil (1889), Art. 105.

[17] Ley de 29 de Julio (1918), Art. 3(13). The divorce law was modified several times, but maintained the list of grounds which had to be proven in court. See, for example, Decreto-Ley No. 206, Art. 3, May 10, 1934.

prohibiting sex discrimination. Ten years later, the domestic relations provisions of the Civil Code, which had denied women even the semblance of equality in the marital relationship, were modified to eliminate some of the more blatant inconsistencies between the code and the equality provisions of the Constitution.[18] As a result, married women were specifically granted the right to administer property and to be their own representatives.[19]

However, these changes produced virtually no improvement in women's status since they lacked societal support for their implementation.[20] Rather, social values and custom kept most women in the same situation as before. Further, the law was not only male- but class-biased; it only recognized rights and responsibilities within that minority of families consisting of husband, wife and children born in the marriage, which described primarily middle- and upper-class families. Women in the lower classes frequently did not have the benefit of formalized marriage or the resources to enforce their rights if they did. Many of the children born to lower-class women were fathered by married men from the upper classes, since it was dishonorable to "spoil" unmarried women of their own class.[21] Despite the large number of such children born out of wedlock, they were not protected by family or inheritance law. Informal unions were also patriarchal and generally unstable, placing heavy burdens on women who labored under both the oppressiveness of machismo in domestic relations as well as social and legal discrimination. Poor and rural women worked outside the home out of necessity, most frequently as factory workers, domestic servants and farm laborers.

Thus, the revolution inherited deeply entrenched patterns of patriarchy in family relations. The first effort the revolutionary government undertook in the early 1960s with respect to family structure was conservative in nature and centered on legitimizing the thousands of consensual unions. Teams of workers canvassed the cities and rural areas attempting to register births and to encourage formalization of informal marriages. Despite the embrace of socialism and the promotion of women's equality in education

---

[18] Ley No. 9 (Sobre la capacidad civil de la mujer), *Gaceta Oficial,* No. 302, December 28, 1950.

[19] Ibid. Article 1 replaced Article 57 of the Civil Code and read: "The spouses must provide mutual protection and observe the considerations owed each other." Article 11 repealed the provision granting to the husband the right to administer the marital property. Article 12 revoked, without specification, all existing legislation that diminished equality between the sexes.

[20] Interview with Raúl Gómez Treto, Legal Advisor to the Archbishop of Havana, Cuba, December 20, 1986. Gómez Treto was one of the authors of the Cuban Family Code and later drafted amendments to its adoption provisions.

[21] Pérez, p. 240.

and employment in the early 1960s, nothing was done to overcome the patriarchal values so connected with women's subordination until 1975. It was not until women themselves began to react to the weight of having to shoulder both social and domestic responsibilities that attention was paid to the oppressive nature of the traditional family structure.

II. THE 1975 FAMILY CODE

The Family Code, adopted in 1975, was far-reaching in its purpose to redefine the Cuban family and transform it into the "elementary cell" of society that would contribute to the development of new generations of socialists.[22] The socialist concept of the family rejects the idea of the family as a private contractual union, implicit in the former Civil Code. Consistent with Engels' argument in The Origin of the Family, Private Property and the State, in he posited that only with the destruction of the bourgeois family structure, which was based on economic dependency, would true monogamous unions founded solely on love be possible, the Family Code defines marriage as a union based solely on mutual affection and "absolute equality."[23]

The primary role of the family in socialist Cuba—and hence the goal of family law—is to contribute to the development and upbringing of children in accordance with socialist values and to provide for the emotional and material needs of individuals.[24] Thus, by eliminating inequality and subordination in the marital relationship, the objective of the Code was not to destroy the nuclear family but to strengthen it so that it could better contribute to the moral and educational development of children.[25] The Code also establishes equality for all children, eliminating all distinctions in the rights of "legitimate" and "illegitimate" children imposed under previous law. The principles set forth in the Code were reinforced and incorporated a year later in the Cuban Constitution.[26]

Although they studied other socialist experiences, the drafters of the 1975 Code felt no compunction to copy the legislation of other countries.

---

[22] Código de Familia (1975), Preamble.
[23] Ibid., Art. 1.
[24] The preamble of the Family Code must be read together with Article 16, which states the duty of parents to educate and guide their children "according to the principles of socialist morality."
[25] Ibid., Art. 1.
[26] Constitución de la República de Cuba, Arts. 35-38. *Gaceta Oficial,* No.7, February 24, 1976.

The Commission on Juridical Studies, which had a hand in drafting the Family Code, reviewed the laws of the European socialist countries published in Spanish translation in the late 1960s. Although these laws also characterized the family as the elementary unit of society based on mutual affection in which the spouses enjoyed equal rights and duties, none made women's equality a centerpiece of family law.[27] In contrast, the equality provisions of the Cuban Family Code are both more explicit and far-reaching, starting with the preliminary statement that all legal norms must be in "full conformity" with the principle of equality for women.[28]

Because provisions supporting women's equality were central to the Code, the FMC took a major role in its drafting. As with many pieces of major legislation in revolutionary Cuba, hundreds of thousands of tabloid copies of the draft were circulated among the population for discussion in the mass organizations: the Committees for the Defense of the Revolution, the Central Organization of Cuban Workers, the Federation of Cuban Women, the National Association of Small Farmers, the Federation of University Students, the Federation of Students of Intermediate Education and a number of state and social agencies.[29] Recommendations for modifications were sent from these groups to the drafters for consideration for incorporation.

The process not only allowed for popular participation in the drafting of legislation, even if resulting modifications were minimal, but it also stimulated mass discussion of major policy decisions. In the case of the Family Code, broad public discussion was of particular importance because the concept of equality between men and women in domestic relations was completely contrary to tradition and not one easily accepted by the general population. The final draft of the Code was adopted by popular referendum in 1974 and made effective on International Women's Day, March 8, 1975.

In addition to its focus on equality in the marital relationship, the Code includes other important innovations. It gives legal recognition to informal unions under certain circumstances, facilitates adoption procedures and extends family responsibilities with respect to financial support beyond the nuclear family. Although the Code has not fulfilled its objective of creating the new socialist family, Cuban lawyers and policy makers continue to engage in active debate on ways to improve its effectiveness, and there are

[27] See, for example, the codes of Poland (Law No. 25, 1964), Bulgaria (Decree No. 225, 1968), Czechoslovakia (Law No. 94, 1963) and the Soviet Union (Bases of Legislation on Matrimony and the Family, 1964). See also, Peter Juviler, "Soviet Marxism and Family Law," *Columbia Journal of Transnational Law*, Vol. 23, 1985, p. 385.

[28] Código de Familia (1975), Preamble. The section also refers to equality among children.

[29] Ibid.

numerous proposals for both modifications as well enactment of a new code.[30]

Equality in Marriage

Where the 1975 Code diverges most from the past is in its express promotion of equality in the family relationship, a departure compelled both by ideology and practice. The growth of women's participation in the economic and political life of the country after the revolution represented an abrupt change from their established role as housewife and imposed enormous strains on family relations for women who chose to participate. Of course, poor women generally had always worked outside the home to feed their children and constituted the thousands of domestic workers. Rural women also engaged in productive farm work. At the same time, however, all women continued to be bound by traditional household and child-care responsibilities. The weight of these pressures kept many women from participation in the work force, and many who took salaried jobs in the late 1960s and early 1970s quickly left them and returned to the kitchen.[31]

Since Cuba did not socialize household tasks, the continued feminization of household responsibilities remained a formidable barrier to women's advancement as it has in most other countries, socialist or capitalist. A survey conducted by the Cuban Communist Party in 1975 found that employed women worked an average of thirteen hours a day from Monday through Friday and eleven-and-one-half hours a day on the weekends in order to fulfill the obligations of both job and home.[32] The initial government response to the double burdens of working women was to find ways to make housework easier. For example, in the early 1970s, working women were allocated special times to shop and were given priority in shopping lines to make grocery shopping more convenient and faster.[33] But improved material conditions could not and did not provide an adequate solution. If women were to be fully integrated into productive work as well as leadership roles,

---

[30] Interview with Dr. Olga Mesa Castillo, President of the Cuban Society of Civil Law, July 10, 2000.

[31] Although more than 700,000 women joined the labor force from 1969 to 1974, more than 500,000 simultaneously dropped out. *Sobre el Pleno Ejercicio de la Igualdad de la Mujer, Tesis y Resolución*, (Havana: Empresa de Medios de Propaganda, 1976), p. 16.

[32] Ibid., pp. 15-16.

[33] Carollee Benglesdorf, "Emerging From Underdevelopment: Women and Work," *Cuba Review*, No. 4, 1974, p. 9.

family relationships would have to be restructured and family responsibilities shared.

The Family Code of 1975 attempted that reordering. While continuing to reflect the traditional value placed on the nuclear family as the norm for society, the Code eliminated features of the past patriarchal model that reinforced the subordination of women. Its major provisions declare the equality of men and women in marriage and the duty of both husband and wife to share in household chores and in the raising and support of their children. Equality between husband and wife in marriage became a constant theme in the media, in educational materials and in popular discussion.

Although the 1950 amendments to the Civil Code had given women and men the same rights in marriage, the Family Code of 1975 affirmatively expressed and established both equal rights and duties between the marriage partners. This equality extends not only to the right to own personal property and to administer marital property, to seek divorce and to exercise *patria potestad* (parental rights and duties) over children, but also to the equal legal obligation to care collectively for the home and children.

The heart of the civil marriage ceremony consists of the reading of Articles 24-28 of the Family Code, which establish equality between the parties. The mutual obligation to share housework is one of the most important issues related to women's equality and, not surprisingly, it was the most controversial provision in the Code. Article 26 explicitly states:

> Both parties must care for the family they have created and each must cooperate with the other in the education, upbringing and guidance of the children. . . . They must participate, to the extent of their capacity or possibilities, in the running of the home and cooperate so that it will develop in the best possible way.

Moreover, the fact that a woman may not be employed does not relieve the husband of his duty to cooperate with housework. As provided in Article 27:

> The parties must help meet the needs of the family they have created with their marriage, each according to his or her ability and financial status. However, if one of them only contributes by working at home and caring for the children, the other must contribute to this support alone, without prejudice to his duty of cooperating in the above-mentioned work and care. (emphasis added)

Articulation of this collective family obligation to share household duties is explicit recognition of the fact that if women truly were to have opportunities to be fully integrated into productive work and leadership, men had to be integrated into housework.

The significance of these provisions is not that they create a legally enforceable duty to share housework. Enforceability of Articles 26 and 27 is doubtful. Rather, the Code codifies a desired societal norm and has become a tool for education and social change. The adoption of the Family Code and the discussion it fostered began to alter the way many Cubans viewed domestic relations. Although men did not pitch in with the laundry and cooking immediately, and the majority still resist, particularly among older generations,[34] the message was clear that the correct, revolutionary thing for a man to do is to share in housework.

This ideal of equality in the marital relationship is promoted in education and through the mass media. By the mid 1980s, it began to be an accepted way of life among younger couples, according to Rita Perreira, a member of the national staff of the FMC.[35] If the evolution of humor is any indicator of a trend, men's attitudes toward household responsibilities was evolving. Perreira recounted that when the Family Code was first passed, men poked fun at others who helped in household chores such as washing dishes and laundry. A decade later, many jokes were pointed at the men who did not do their share.[36]

Yet old habits die hard. Practices and customs persist that undermine equal sharing of household responsibilities. Women themselves often are accomplices in the perpetuation of sexist customs by not socializing children, particularly male children, into sharing household chores.[37] A number of Cuban observers have pointed out that in many cases, even if the woman resented the unshared burdens of housework, she lacks the will to demand her rights.[38] As a result, even today, women may decline promotion or public office because they cannot bear more responsibilities.[39] Even women in high positions may not challenge tradition and try to both excel in their career and shoulder all the housework.

Other social factors conspire against change in traditional attitudes. Many women who work outside the home entrust primary care of their children when not in day care to grandparents or other elderly family members

---

[34] Interview with Rita Perreira, Federation of Cuban Women, Havana, Cuba, June 4, 1984.

[35] Ibid.

[36] Ibid.

[37] Monika Krause, *Algunos Temas Fundamentales sobre Educación Sexual* (Havana: Editorial Científico-Técnica, 1988), pp. 34-35.

[38] Raúl Gómez Treto, p. 31; interview with Monika Krause.

[39] The problem recognized by the FMC in 1984 persists today. See, *Draft Thesis: Cuban Women: 25 Years of Revolution*, IV Congress of the FMC (1984), p. 27. Mayda Alvarez Suárez, "Mujer y Poder en Cuba," in *Temas, No.* 14, April-June 1998.

or to neighbors who reinforce the behavioral patterns of past generations. In addition, because of the housing shortage, several generations frequently share the same dwelling. The mother-in-law, be it the wife's or the husband's mother, may not encourage male children or the husband to do housework and may even insist that they not do it.

The economic crisis of the 1990s exacerbated the burdens of this traditional role for women. Meals became harder to plan and prepare because of shortages. A lot of time was spent just finding and obtaining necessary supplies. Power blackouts, which were frequent and long until recently, limited time to do ironing and cleaning chores; transportation difficulties lengthened commuting time to and from work. In addition, women workers were particularly affected by the closure of factories, particularly widespread in the textile industry.[40] Although these conditions have improved and the economy shows signs of modest recovery, most Cuban families' incomes are barely sufficient and the burden of carefully supervising the family food budget and planning falls on women who must make sure food is on the table each day.[41]

Other aspects of the Code do not depart significantly from prior law and perpetuate differences based on gender. For example, the legal age for marriage without special consent is eighteen for both men and women,[42] but boys may marry at age sixteen and girls at fourteen with the consent of their parents, their guardian or a court.[43] The legal age for marriage was an issue of great discussion in mass discussions prior to the adoption of the Code. Many argued that the minimum age should be even lower. Previous law permitted boys and girls to marry at ages fourteen and twelve respectively with consent of parents,[44] reflecting deeply held social beliefs that girls, in particular, were eligible for marriage at puberty. The new Code, however, maintains similar sex-based distinctions that are clearly less favorable to young girls, who are more likely to be pressured into marriage at an earlier age than boys because of persistent attitudes toward female sexuality.[45]

---

[40] For a description of the effect of "special period" on women's employment, see Debra Evenson, *Workers in Cuba: Unions & Labor Relations*, (Detroit: Sugar Law Center, 2001), p. 35.

[41] For a discussion of the problem, see Mayda Alvarez Suárez, "Género y familia en Cuba", in *Diversidad y Complejidad Familiar en Cuba* (Universidad de la Havana, 1999), pp. 137-142.

[42] Ibid., Art. 3.

[43] Ibid.

[44] Código Civil (1889), Art. 83(1).

[45] In the United States, state laws frequently specify a lower permissible marriage age for girls than boys. Yet, statutes which differentiate the age of majority based on gender have been held unconstitutional as a violation of equal protection. See, *Stanton* v. *Stanton*, 429 U.S. 501 (1977).

Further, although the Family Code eliminated the provisions of the Civil Code that reinforced the double standard of sexual morality so strictly adhered to in pre-revolutionary Cuba, other legislation maintained old prejudices. For example, the Criminal Code provides for imprisonment for three to nine months for anyone who has sexual relations with a single woman between the ages of twelve and sixteen if sexual relations are obtained by fraud, promise to marry or abuse of authority.[46] However, until 1987, if the offender married the woman he would not be subject to prosecution. Thus, the law perpetuated patriarchal concern for injury to family honor resulting from the young woman's pre-marital sexual relations. The 1987 Criminal Code eliminated the defense.[47]

Similar to the requirement imposed under the former Civil Code, a marriage must be performed by a state official in a civil ceremony to be legally recognized.[48] Although civil, the marriage ceremony is not necessarily a cold, perfunctory affair. Brides often wear traditional white gowns accompanied by a wedding party. Civil ceremonies are performed at *palacios de matrimonio*, splendid old buildings which formerly were private clubs or residences of the upper classes. The government provides the newly-weds with beer and other refreshments for the wedding party, as well as hotel accommodations for a short honeymoon. Couples may choose to have a religious ceremony as well, but only the civil ceremony will be given legal recognition.

Divorce

The 1975 Family Code eliminated restrictions on divorce. The previous Civil Code permitted divorce only when sufficient cause was proven to the court.[49] Even mutual incompatibility as grounds for divorce had to be proven to the court. Today, a couple may mutually decide to divorce without having to show any cause to the court: "Divorce will take effect by common agreement or when the court determines that there are factors which have led the marriage to lose its meaning for the couple and for the children and, thus, for society as a whole."[50] The divorce procedure is regu-

---

[46] Código Penal (Ley No.21), Art. 361, *Gaceta Oficial*, No.3, March 1, 1979.
[47] Código Penal (1987), Art. 305
[48] Código de Familia (1975), Art. 16.
[49] Mesa Castillo, pp. 112-114.
[50] Código de Familia (1975), Art. 51.

lated by the Law of Civil, Administrative and Labor Procedure,[51] which permits either party to initiate the divorce process.[52] In non-contested cases, the court issues a judicial decree dissolving the marriage within about a month from the time the demand is filed.

The vast majority of divorces are non-contested or by mutual agreement. Prior to 1994, when the law was modified to enable couples without children to obtain non-contested divorces through a notary, procedures required judicial process and, generally, the services of a lawyer in every instance. However, in cases where the divorce was by mutual agreement and there was no dispute over property or custody, the parties could be represented by the same lawyer before the court. Conceptual difficulties arose, however, in the situation in which one party sought a divorce for cause and the other party denied the allegations. The very fact that one party wanted to dissolve the union itself suggested that the marriage had "lost its meaning for the couple." In such cases, the courts converted the process to one based on mutual agreement.[53] In 1977, the Cuban Supreme Court rejected this practice and issued instructions to lower courts requiring them to conduct a hearing in all contested divorces.[54] However, the instructions and decisions that are published do not illuminate how a court is to make the difficult determination of whether or not the marriage has lost its meaning for the couple and the children. At least one commentator has observed that the lower courts continue to treat most cases as divorce by mutual consent.[55]

The issue whether cause must be proven has sparked considerable debate among Cuban jurists. Several argue that marriage based on love cannot be regulated by law at all and that the state, in fact, exercises little influence through divorce laws.[56] Most of the debate centers on the nature of the legal process by which couples may obtain a divorce—that is, if it must be approved judicially. Whether a divorce is obtained for cause or by mutual consent has no effect on the rights of the parties established in the divorce decrees, except to the extent that the cause shown may be one relevant to issues of custody. Even in cases where divorce is by mutual consent, one party may argue for custody based on the best interests of the child. As two lawyers have noted, the debate perhaps becomes "theoretical" with respect

---

[51] Ley No. 7 (Ley de Procedimiento Civil, Administrativo y Laboral), Art. 381, *Gaceta Oficial*, No. 34, August 26, 1977.
[52] Ibid., Art. 53.
[53] Séfer Zárate, "El Código de Familia a la Luz de su Interpretación y Aplicación por el Tribunal Supremo Popular," *Revista Cubana de Derecho*, Vol. 19, 1983, pp. 82-85.
[54] Ibid.
[55] Mesa Castillo, pp. 118-119.
[56] Rigoberto Hernández León and Miguel Fernández Díaz, "Crítica de la Regulación Jurídica Estatal del Divorcio en Cuba," *Revista Jurídica*, No. 12, July-September, 1986, pp. 174, 177.

to the issue of divorce itself because the courts are not likely to deny a divorce where one party insists on dissolving the marriage.[57] The court cannot require one spouse to love the other. Yet, most jurists continue to believe that the courts have an important function to play in the divorce if there are minor children.[58]

The divorce rate in Cuba more than tripled in the first three decades after the revolution[59] and, in 1988, Cuba's divorce rate ranked third highest following the United States and the former Soviet Union.[60] Perhaps due to the stresses of the economic crisis, the divorce rate almost doubled again between 1990 and 1996[61] The increase in divorce has been attributed to a number of factors including changes in the law that make it relatively easy and inexpensive to obtain a divorce, changed societal conditions that give women more social and economic opportunities and the increasing number of marriages of couples under the age of nineteen.

The fact that women can enter the work force on virtually equal footing with men has profoundly changed women's attitudes toward marriage.[62] Women are no longer economically dependent on men, and this economic independence gives them the option to choose, decline or end a marriage.[63] According to Cuban researchers, in the 1990s women increasingly choose consensual relations instead of formal marriage bonds, and a growing number of Cuban households are headed by women.[64]

At the same time, however, the limited nature of alimony provisions encourage, if not necessitate, that women pursue a career. If the couple has lived together for more than a year or has children, the court may award alimony to the "party who does not have a job and lacks other means of support."[65] But this support is temporary, lasting only six months if there

---

[57] Ibid, p. 174.

[58] Mesa Castillo, p. 122.

[59] Ibid., p. 114.

[60] Ibid., p. 127, n. 4.

[61] Olga Mesa Castillo, "El Derecho de Familia en la Sociedad Cubana" in *Diversidad y Complejidad Familiar en Cuba* (Universidad de la Havana, 1999), n. 17. See also, Reinaldo Rojas Manresa, "Siglo XXI. ¿Qué Tipo de Pareja queremos y para qué pareja nos preparamos?", Ibid., p. 159.

[62] Both women and men have a constitutional right to a job: "The socialist state . . . guarantees that every man or woman who is able to work has the opportunity to have a job." Constitución (1992), Art. 9(b).

[63] In the mid-1980s, the vast majority of divorce petitions were filed by women. Interview with Raúl Gómez Treto.

[64] Sonia Catasús Cervera and Clotilde Proveyer Cervantes, "Genero y Jefatura del Núcleo Familiar en Cuba Hoy: Consideraciones Sociológicas y Demográficas" in *Diversidad y Complejidad Familiar en Cuba* (Universidad de la Havana, 1999), pp 143-155.

[65] Código de Familia (1975), Art. 56(1).

are no minor children and up to a year if there are.[66] Only in cases where a spouse is physically or mentally unable to work may alimony payments be extended beyond the statutory period. Thus, a woman who does not suffer a disability and who is of working age[67] must support herself financially after divorce, regardless of whether she worked during the marriage.

In other circumstances in which women have difficulty finding employment, particularly at wages comparable to those of men, such limitations on support payments might be considered unjust. That unfairness is blunted in Cuba by the accessibility of free education, the right to a job and the general equity in pay between women and men. However, if a man does not fulfill his obligations during the marriage and the woman shoulders all the housework and child-care, the marriage responsibilities will inevitably impede the woman's opportunities for development and advancement, and she will receive no compensation for her efforts upon divorce. Perhaps economic reality, if not higher consciousness, may push Cuban women to enforce the equal sharing provisions of Article 26.

In the event of divorce, custody of children can be arranged by agreement between the parents.[68] Similar to the practice in the United States, if the parents do not arrive at an agreement on custody, a court will decide on the basis of what is most beneficial to the child. In guiding that decision, the Code provides:

> Under equal conditions, the court will generally decide that the children be left under the care of the parent in whose company they have been until the disagreement arose. Preference is given to the mother in the case that the children lived with both father and mother, unless special reasons make another solution advisable.[69]

Thus, in practice, physical custody is granted in most instances to the mother. Some of the opinions issued by the Supreme Court indicate just how strong the presumption is in favor of the mother, particularly for children under three years old who are considered all but inseparable from their mothers even for periods as short as two weeks.[70] Visitation rights at regu-

---

[66] Ibid.

[67] Depending on the number of years worked, retirement age for women ranges from 55-60; for men it is 60-65. Ley No. 24 (Ley de Seguridad Social), Art. 31, *Gaceta Oficial*, No.27, August 29, 1979.

[68] Código de Familia (1975), Art. 88.

[69] Ibid., Art. 89.

[70] Zárate, pp. 98-99.

lar periods are awarded to the parent who does not have physical custody,[71] and both parents continue to exercise the right of *patria potestad*.

Child support remains the mutual and enforceable obligation of both parents regardless of marital status or who has custody.[72] Moreover, the obligation to provide support continues even if the parent has been legally stripped of the right of *patria potestad* as the result of criminal or grossly derelict behavior toward the child or other gross misconduct.[73] Criminal sanctions may also be brought against parents who abandon their legal duty to support their children.[74] As elsewhere, Cuban women often have a difficult time collecting child support payments,[75] although support payments can be enforced by garnishing the father's salary.[76]

The Code provides that child support be shared by the parents proportionate to their respective incomes,[77] but there is no provision apportioning child care responsibilities. Thus, although divorce does not inequitably shift the financial burden of child support to women, at least not as a matter of law, women in most instances assume the sole responsibility of child care after divorce. Access to day-care centers for a modest fee, extended family relationships and the availability of elderly women who seek to augment their pensions by caring for children help to lighten this burden. Yet the responsibility and additional household work that comes with care of children is an impediment to women's advancement. Presumably support payments contribute to the cost of child care services, but they do not compensate women for providing care or for lost opportunities resulting from being the sole caretaker.

Under the Family Code, marital property is held jointly and is to be divided equally at divorce.[78] This property generally consists of the house or apartment, furnishings, automobile, bank accounts and other personal property. If the couple does not come to an agreement on the division of property, a court will order liquidation or an appropriate division based on the needs of the party with custody of the children.[79] If no measures are taken within one year of divorce to resolve the division of property, the parties will be entitled to retain whatever property is in their possession.[80] This

---

[71] Código de Familia (1975), Art. 90.
[72] Ibid., Art. 59.
[73] Ibid., Arts. 95, 96.
[74] Código Penal (1987), Art. 373, *Gaceta Oficial Ext.*, December 30, 1987.
[75] *Draft Thesis IV*, p. 32.
[76] Ley No. 7 (1977), Arts. 460-463.
[77] Código de Familia (1975), Art. 60.
[78] Ibid., Art. 38.
[79] Ibid., Art. 41.
[80] Ibid., Art. 40.

last provision is significant in that the parties must quickly decide to bring a judicial proceeding against their spouse to claim property.

Recognition of Informal Unions

The 1940 Constitution permitted courts to treat a non-formalized marriage as comparable to formal marriage for reasons of equity in appropriate circumstances.[81] Although the legislature never enacted complimentary provisions to govern such situations, the courts did exercise their power to recognize property interests comparable to those of a formal marriage when the relationship between two people legally capable of contracting marriage was proved to be both stable and exclusive. The provision apparently was used exclusively in cases involving issues of inheritance.[82] Recognition gave the surviving member of the union rights to inheritance under intestacy laws.

Because the remedy was to be given only for reasons of equity, the mere existence of an informal marriage did not necessarily require recognition of rights, regardless of its stability or longevity. Despite its limited application, this provision was unique and quite progressive for its time. It transcended moral disapproval of cohabitation out of wedlock, providing special protection for women before married women even had the right to administer property.

The 1975 Code not only codified recognition of informal marriage, it substantially expanded the scope of its legal implications. Under the new Code, recognition is not based on requirements of equity as defined by the courts, but solely on the character of the relationship. Thus, the Code states:

> A matrimonial union between a man and a woman who are legally fit to establish it and which is in keeping with the standards of stability and singularity, will be just as binding as legally formalized marriages when recognized by a competent court.

The provision has implications not just for the division of property when one party dies, but for obligations to support and presumptions of paternity.

---

[81] Constitución (1940), Art. 43.

[82] María Elena Cobas Cobiella, Nancy de la C. Ojeda Rodríguez and Gisela María Pérez Fuentes, "Reconocimiento Judicial de Matrimonio. Problema que plantea la Interpretación y Aplicación del Articulado del Código de Familia," *Revista Cubana de Derecho*, Vol. 35, 1988, pp. 105, 110.

In essence, it grants the parties the same rights and duties as those formally married.

Couples who wish to formalize their marriage may seek to have the effect of formalization be retroactive to the date their union began.[83] Where the informal union has ended one party may seek legal recognition of the past relationship, and, in such circumstances, legal recognition will be given effect only from the date of the formation of the relationship to the date of its termination as established by judicial decision. Recognition of a past informal union does not affect the current marital status of either party.

Thus, although the law requires that both parties be "legally fit" to marry, the legal marriage of one of them to someone else will not prevent the other from seeking recognition of the informal union if he or she acted in good faith. Such equitable considerations for the party who has acted in good faith would not have been recognized in the past because under previous law the marriage of one party vitiated the requirement of exclusivity. In 1975, the Supreme Court overturned denial of recognition by the lower court where the woman found out that the man was already married but continued to remain in cohabitation with him. The Court ruled that the stability and length of the relationship were the determining factors in deciding her right to property the couple held in common.[84] Yet, it is not at all apparent what the legal effect would be respecting the conflicting claims and duties as between the various parties.

Clearly the purpose behind the statute is one of equity rather than encouragement of informal marriage. It is a significant advance and is consistent with the concept of family based on mutual affection as opposed to economic dependence. Informal marriage was not recognized in other socialist countries when the Cuban Family Code was enacted. Further, most states in the United States do not recognize common-law marriage,[85] and several still reject any recognition of rights derived from non-marital cohabitation.[86] Generally, in the United States, effect will be given to non-marital relationships only on the basis of express or implied contract or on the theory of unjust enrichment.[87] In such cases, the woman must demonstrate either evidence of an agreement or that she contributed quantifiable services for which compensation is deserved. Cuban law, on the other hand,

---

[83] Código de Familia (1975), Art. 19.
[84] Zárate, p. 73.
[85] William J. Wagner, "The Contractual Reallocation of Procreative Resources and Parental Rights: The Natural Endowment Critique," *Case Western Reserve Law Review,* Vol. 41, No 1, 1990, p. 64.
[86] Tammy L. Lewis, "Standing in the Shadows: Honoring the Contractual Obligations of Cohabitants for Support," *University of Puget Sound Law Review,* Vol. 75, 1991, p. 177.
[87] Ibid., pp. 181-193. See also *Marvin* v. *Marvin*, 557 P.2d 106 (Cal. 1976).

accords rights and interests based on the "marital" quality of the relationship as defined by its stability and faithfulness of both parties, not its economic character.

Adoption

Another innovation of the Cuban Family Code, the adoption provisions have contributed to the incorporation of orphaned and abandoned children into stable family situations. The new section on adoption greatly reduced the barriers to adoption posed by the former law that reflected irrational biases in favor of natural children. The pre-revolutionary law permitted adoption in very limited circumstances: when the couple had no legitimate children of their own and had reached the age of forty-five.[88] Such limitations were typical in Latin American countries, although Cuban law contained the highest age requirement.[89]

The primary goal of the new provisions is to promote the interest of the child to be nurtured and cared for in a family. The 1975 Code permits adoption both when the adoptive parent has other children or is childless, thus increasing both the numbers and varieties of potential families for children. Further, the age required of parents is now twenty-five,[90] but the adoptive parent must be at least fifteen years older than the adopted child.[91] This requirement is meant to assure that the parent will be sufficiently mature in comparison to the child.

All legal distinctions between adopted and natural children have been eliminated. Although the 1975 Code established that the relationship between the adoptive parents and the child shall be the same as between natural parents and children,[92] more recent legislation has extended the equality of legal relationship to include that which exists among all family members.[93] Thus, an adopted child may inherit by intestacy from a brother or sister or other blood relative of the adoptive parents. The converse is also

---

88 Raúl Gómez Treto, "La Adopción de Hijos en el Derecho Histórico, Comparado, Internacional y Cubano y la Protección a la Niñez y la Juventud," *Revista Jurídica*, No. 3, April-June, 1984, p. 87.

89 Mexico had the second highest age requirement (forty), but several others including Uruguay and Peru required adoptive parents to be at least thirty years of age. Ibid.

90 Código de Familia (1975), Art. 100.

91 Ibid., Art. 102.

92 Ibid., Art. 99.

93 Decreto-Ley 76 (De la adopción, los hogares y menores y las familias sustitutas), Special Provisions, *Gaceta Oficial Ext.*, No.1, January 21, 1984.

true. Likewise, such relatives may have the duty to provide support under certain conditions.

The law provides numerous avenues for adoption in addition to the case of a child whose parents are deceased.[94] A child may be adopted with the consent of the natural parent, which may be the situation where the parents are separated by divorce and the new spouse of one wishes to adopt the child. In addition, a child may be legally adopted if the parent has lost guardianship through a court process or has intentionally abandoned the child. The relationship between the child and natural parent are severed by adoption.

There is no legal requirement that adoption only be by one or both members of a heterosexual couple. In addition, a single person may adopt a child. However, adoption by more than one person can only be by a husband and wife.[95] Although homophobia has abated, Cuban society is not approaching acceptance of adoption by homosexual couples.

Unlike marriage, which is formalized by a notary, adoption requires court authorization. The court must find that the legislative requirements are met both with respect to the eligibility of the adoptive parent(s) and the legality of the severance of the relationship with the natural parent.[96] Adoption proceedings are initiated by the person or persons wishing to adopt the child. An adoption may be opposed not only by the natural parent, but also by grandparents, aunts or uncles and older siblings where one or both parents had been deprived of *patria potestad.*[97] Opposition must be filed at the time of the adoption procedure, or within six months of the adoption if just cause for the delay can be established.[98]

In 1984, Cuba created a network of national institutions including orphanages and day-care centers for children who did not have benefit of family either through abandonment, death or judicial action against the parents. Through these institutions the government saw that these children received adequate care and attended school. Decree Law No. 76 establishing these institutions also created a system of substitute families who would care for these children until they were either adopted or reached the age of majority.[99] According to family law specialist Raúl Gómez Treto there were 185 judicially approved adoptions in 1986, whereas during the same year the courts deprived 41 mothers and fathers of *patria potestad.*[100] Similar statis-

---

[94] Código de Familia (1975, as modified by Law No. 9, August 22, 1977), Art. 103.
[95] Ibid., Art. 101.
[96] Ibid., Art. 104.
[97] Ibid., Art. 108.
[98] Ibid., Arts. 109-110.
[99] Decreto-Ley 76 (1984), Arts. 11-15.
[100] Gómez Treto, "Hacia un Nuevo Código de la Familia," p. 43.

tics hold for 1984 and 1985. There are no studies available from which to evaluate how well the system functions.

Support Obligations of Children and Siblings

Although the primary object of the Family Code is the regulation of marriage and the parent-child relationship, Cuban law also recognizes duties of children to parents as well as duties among siblings. For example, the Housing Law grants such relatives protection from eviction if they have lived for a requisite period of time with the homeowner.[101] Similarly, the Family Code contains provisions regarding obligations of Cubans to support their parents and siblings.[102] Parents may demand support from their children, and siblings may demand support from each other when they are unable to support themselves due to age or disability. Although there are no statistics I am aware of that demonstrate how many, if any, do so, this provision as well as others reinforces the concept of obligation running to the extended family.

Because of the possibility of competing demands and the potential that more than one person may be obligated to contribute, the law provides for priorities among recipients. Spouses have first priority, followed by parents, children and siblings. Courts may also apportion the obligation according to ability to pay in cases where the obligation falls to more than one person, as in the case where a parent seeks support from more than one child. Inheritance laws are also consistent with the obligation to provide for those family members unable to support themselves. Thus, the only class for whom there is a "forced share" is that of close family members who have depended on the deceased for support and who are unable to support themselves.[103]

III. FAMILY PLANNING

Neither before or after 1959 has Cuba adopted any legislation or public policy regarding optimum numbers of children, nor incentives to have more

---

[101] Ley No. 65 (Ley General de la Vivienda), Art. 65, *Gaceta Oficial Ext.*, No.3, February 8, 1989. For a description and analysis of Cuban housing law, see Chapter 8.
[102] Código de Familia (1975), Arts. 121-136.
[103] Código Civil (1987), Arts. 806-822.

or fewer children. Rather, Cuban policy has been to give families choices regarding family size, not to regulate it in any way. However, special assistance may be provided to support families and children. Cuban law provides generous maternity benefits to working women and subsidized daycare. Further, in recognition of the special needs of families with children, they may be given priority for housing and amenities such as washing machines.

Since 1959, contraceptives have been distributed at low cost. In the early 1960s abortion was made available on demand. Unfortunately, the policy of making contraception readily available was not accompanied by sufficient educational efforts either by institutions or parents. As a result the numbers of unwanted pregnancies began to rise, particularly among adolescent mothers, leading to increasing numbers of abortions.[104]

Cuban youth, like their counterparts elsewhere, increasingly engage in sexual relations starting with puberty. Although sex education was introduced in schools, it was not adequate to instill a sense of responsibility for both the emotional or physical consequences of sexual relations. Since parents were often opposed to the new "liberation," girls either failed to get medical advice on contraception because of parents' disapproval or did not sufficiently understand their use. In fact, ignorance of their proper use abounded even among adults; in the case of birth control pills improper use increased the chances of unwanted pregnancy.

Moreover, by custom, responsibility is almost universally placed on females for preventing pregnancy either by abstention or use of birth control devices. Only recently have professionals and officials in Cuba begun to talk about the responsibility of males. Abstention or use of condoms by males is a hard sell, particularly in a country where male potency is revered with almost religious fervor. Although condoms have been recommended as the preferred contraceptive for more than three decades in Cuba, social bias against their use persists. Nevertheless, because of the presence of HIV, more and more Cubans are beginning to use them. However, despite continuing efforts to promote their use, current economic difficulties exacerbated by the tightening of the United States embargo made condoms and other contraceptives more difficult and expensive for Cuba to obtain or produce during most of the 1990s.[105]

Dramatic increases in teenage pregnancy in the early 1980s posed special strains on the family. In 1985, one-third of all births were to teenage

---

[104] Smith and Padula, p. 180.

[105] G. Reed and M. Frank, *Denial of Food and Medicine: The Impact of the US Embargo on Health and Nutrition in Cuba* (Washington, D.C.: American Association for World Health, 1997), pp. 138-39.

mothers.[106] Although teenage pregnancies began to decline in the 1990s,[107] it is still an issue of concern today since early motherhood creates health risks to the mother as well as the child and limits the education and employment opportunities of young girls. In addition, officials became increasingly concerned for the nurturing and development of the children of such young mothers who were frequently unmarried as well. In response, the issue has been one of concern within the FMC, the Ministry of Public Health, the youth organizations as well as those involved with family law. These groups have concerted their efforts in educational campaigns.

In the 1980s, some specialists looked to possible modifications of the Family Code as a partial solution to the problem. One recommendation was to establish the age of legal marriage as eighteen under all circumstances as a means of better assuring the emotional preparation of the couple for marriage.[108] Although it is hoped that such a change will instill greater responsibility to avoid unplanned pregnancies by youths, such a provision, is unlikely to reduce teenage pregnancy. The result is more to be either more children born out of wedlock or increasing numbers of abortions.

IV. FUTURE OF FAMILY LAW

Pre-revolutionary law regulated a family model not generally found among the majority of Cubans; where it did exist it was maintained by conditions that made women and children economically dependent on the stability of marriage. Once such economic dependence disappeared, without strong religious or social customs to maintain the family structure, the only basis for marriage became the emotional bond. Paradoxically, although the government strove to create optimum conditions for establishing marriages based on shared affection, some of the very provisions of the Code that were meant to nurture mutual relations put strains on emotional bonds still rooted in machismo. Nor could the government could predict the impact of other legislation on the family or shield the family from pressures arising from social change. Stability in the emotional relationship could not in fact be legislated because it is so intimately tied to psychological and social factors.

---

106 Smith and Padula, p. 180 and n. 18.

107 "Principales Indicadores de Salud, Cuba 1997," pamphlet of the Ministry of Public Health of Cuba. See also, "Características socio-culturales del aborto en Cuba," Ministry of Public Health of Cuba, 1995.

108 Gómez Treto, "Hacia un Nuevo Código de la Familia," p. 60.

Thus, in the more than 25 years since its passage, the Family Code has not succeeded in creating a new "socialist" nuclear family. Family structures in Cuba are as disparate today as before, and marriages are certainly not more stable as shown by the high rates of divorce. Since there never was a typical family, the diverse family patterns made it all that more difficult to establish a stable model for the socialist family Indeed, the ideal nuclear family exists even less today than it did before. As one Cuban scholar notes:

> It is no longer possible to speak of a single type of Cuban family, to the contrary, the structural changes and evolutions (divorce, second marriages), as well as difficulties with housing, have generated diverse forms of families. Thus, we find extended families (of various generations), families of multiple arrangements, single parents, families of second and third marriages.[109]

Some specialists continue to look to possible modifications of the Family Code to give recognition to the growing diversity of Cuban families as well as a response to family instability and the problems linked to dissolution. As noted previously, some have recommended raising the age of marriage as a way of curbing teenage marriages. Another concern focuses on the difficulties of inter-spousal communication and the need to instill greater commitment to marriage. It has been suggested that the government organize family counseling units to mediate family disputes with the aim of both reducing the numbers of divorces, increasing parental involvement with children during marriage and after divorce and resolving other family tensions.[110] Although submission to counseling would not be obligatory generally, it might be a prerequisite to filing a petition for divorce.

Several leading Cuban family law experts advocate the establishment of a court specializing in family matters.[111] One proposal suggests that such a process should be multi-disciplinary, recognizing that family disputes are not simply legal in nature but include social and psychological aspects as well.[112] Unlike other judicial procedures in Cuban courts, a family court would function to facilitate agreement among the parties rather than simply apply the law to the evidence submitted.

---

[109] Patricia Arés Muzio, "Familia actual: Realidades y Desafios", *Diversidad y Complejidad Familiar en Cuba* (Universidad de la Havana, 1999), p 20.
[110] Interview with Dr. Olga Mesa Castillo, July 10, 2000.
[111] Ibid.; See, also, Osvaldo M. Lavarez Torres, "Un procedimiento familiar en Cuba: una necesidad impostergable," *Revista Cubana de Derecho*, No. 18 (2001), pp. 66-79.
[112] Ibid., p. 75.

For many specialists the emphasis remains on widespread education and discussion of family issues in the schools, in the workplace, in social and mass organizations, and in the media. However, such proposals presuppose that there is a single model of the family that is not only widely accepted but also attainable. Recent research has shown that no such model exists. Indeed, some scholars call for recognition of the complexity of family relations and note that, despite the absence of stable unions, familial emotional bonds remain strong. Thus, the Cuban family is not described as in crisis; rather, it has evolved into a diverse set of relations that should be acknowledged in the Family Code.[113]

---

[113] See, e.g., Patricia Arés Muzo.

Chapter 7

CRIMINAL JUSTICE

Perhaps no other area of Cuban law has received as much attention in the foreign media as its criminal justice system. With some exceptions, most of this commentary has centered on the sensational aspects of the Revolutionary Courts that tried Batista collaborators and counter-revolutionaries in the 1960s, the trial of General Arnaldo Ochoa and three other military officials who were convicted and executed in 1989 for involvement in drug trafficking schemes and the trials of those accused of crimes against state security. Although these events and issues have importance, the development of criminal law and procedure in Cuba is far more complex and substantial than such a limited focus would reveal. It is not possible to describe fully the complexities of Cuban criminal law and procedure in a single chapter. Thus, the analysis offered here provides an overview of the evolution and most aspects of the contemporary criminal justice system.

From the time the revolutionaries established courts in the Sierras to prosecute "war criminals" during the armed rebellion to the present, those involved in the development of legal institutions have expressed commitment to creating a criminal justice system that is efficient, fair and devoid of its former class bias. In practice, criminal law and procedure have advanced toward the convergence of the societal interest in the prosecution of criminal activity and the right of the accused to a fair process. In this quest, Cuban jurists continue to address issues of both form and substance. Thus, reforms have focused not only on improving the law itself, but also on improving the quality of the personnel entrusted to effectuate the law and its objectives.

Among the first changes it introduced in the judicial process in 1959, the new government formally established special Revolutionary Courts under military control to prosecute the members of the Batista regime, including the hated secret police. These courts were similar to those that had been established in the guerrilla camps in the Sierras. By the end of 1959, the Revolutionary Courts also tried the cases of those accused of participating in counter-revolutionary activity. Among the reasons for usurping the jurisdiction of the existing courts over such crimes was that the existing criminal courts were not trusted by the new government. Many of the judges had been loyal to Batista and were unsympathetic to the revolution.

Because the Revolutionary Courts kept citizens from taking indiscriminate vengeance on former members of Batista's secret police force and army, Cuba did not experience a "bloodbath" in the aftermath of the revolution.[1] Although hundreds of people were sentenced to death during this period,[2] the Revolutionary Courts did not act arbitrarily; nor did they routinely impose death sentences. Many thousands were tried and sentenced to prison terms, the maximum term being twenty years except in cases where the death sentence had been commuted, in which case the term was thirty years. By 1967, the armed insurgency was quelled and relatively few cases were brought to the Revolutionary Courts after this period.[3]

Detractors disparaged the Revolutionary Courts for the summary procedures used and for the "public show" atmosphere that surrounded many of the trials of the more notorious Batista henchmen,[4] but the procedures have also been defended, even by those who later turned against the revolution. Twenty-five years after leaving Cuba for Miami, Raúl Chibas, who served as a judge in some of these trials at Castro's personal request, maintained that they were justifiable:

> Sincerely, I was in agreement with these trials. . . . I was in agreement beforehand, and I discussed with Fidel (in the Sierra) the need for carrying out justice after Batista's fall . . . on the grounds that if there is no justice, people would enforce it as in the time of Machado when mobs dragged corpses through the streets. . . . When one tries to do it legally, adverse reaction sets in. Unfortunately, this is people's hypocrisy, and we talked about it with Fidel in the Sierra. . . . They had been forewarned because we issued proclamations from the Sierra that justice would be applied to all those who robbed and murdered the peasants, and I thought we had to act accordingly.[5]

---

[1] In his biography of Fidel Castro, Tad Szulc quotes several people connected with these courts who have since left Cuba who felt the courts were justified since they prevented mobs from taking justice into their own hands. Tad Szulc, *Fidel: A Critical Portrait* (New York: William Morrow and Company, 1986), pp. 482-485.

[2] According to Szulc, Fidel Castro has acknowledged approximately 550 such executions. Ibid., p. 483.

[3] The Revolutionary Courts were disbanded in 1973. See, Chapter Four (The Judicial System).

[4] International Commission of Jurists, *Cuba and the Rule of Law* (Geneva: International Commission of Jurists, 1962).

[5] Quoted in Szulc, p. 484.

Even former United States Ambassador Philip Bonsal declared afterward that the Revolutionary Courts were an improvement over the bloodbath following the revolution that ousted dictator Machado.[6]

In the context of disorder and revolutionary fervor, it would have been remarkable if the leadership had replaced a biased, corrupt legal system with one that functioned smoothly with enhanced procedural protections. Passionate disdain for those responsible for the brutal repression under Batista played heavily in shaping the judicial attitudes of the newly appointed judges who were more concerned with "moral justice" than with process. Yet, neither during the most violent period of counter-revolutionary activity of the 1960s, nor since, has Cuba experienced the appalling, massive extra-judicial executions common in more recent years in other countries of the region, such as El Salvador, Guatemala, Chile and Argentina.

Criminal justice in Cuba has not only been scrutinized by outsiders but also by Cuban jurists themselves who have actively engaged in serious study and debate for more than four decades. Concern for improvement and modernization of the system is amply demonstrated by the substantial body of literature on criminal law authored by Cuban scholars.[7] While emphatically rejecting outside pressure to conform to foreign models, Cuban jurists interact with jurists from all over the world and study other experiences. A masters program in criminal law was instituted in 1999 at the University of Havana Law School, the first masters degree program to be offered. In addition, law faculty from Cuba have been contracted by Bolivia to organize a similar masters degree program there. Cuban criminal law experts enjoy international prestige and are invited to participate in many academic events.

Both substantive and procedural laws have been modified a number of times, with the active participation of all sectors of the criminal justice system, including defense attorneys, prosecutors, police, the judiciary and officials of the Ministry of Justice. The Code of Criminal Procedure was amended in significant ways in both 1991 and 1994. Until recently, improvement in procedure has been impeded by incompetence among members of the judiciary as well as the defense bar, police and prosecutors. Substantial efforts and advances in training and professionalism have begun to correct this problem.

Unfortunately, however, the stress of the current economic crisis has placed a heavy burden on a system struggling to be more efficient and fair. Cuba not only faces severe shortages of resources needed to maintain daily judicial and legal activities, but is also feeling the impact of increased crimi-

---

[6] Ibid., p. 483.

[7] In addition to numerous books, articles on the subject are published frequently in the *Revista Cubana de Derecho*, published by the National Union of Cuban Jurists, and the *Revista Jurídica*, published by the Ministry of Justice

nal activity, particularly robberies and economic crimes. Efforts to reform the system will most certainly be hindered by these objective conditions as well as a continuing deficit in numbers of well-trained personnel.

I. SUBSTANTIVE CRIMINAL LAW

The substantive provisions of Cuban criminal law have undergone three major revisions since 1959. The first Criminal Code enacted by the Cuban revolution was adopted in 1979. It was replaced by a far more liberal code in 1987, which in turn was substantially modified in 1997 and again in 1999 in response to increasing criminal activity that emerged as a result of the economic crisis.

The 1979 Code

Prior to 1979, Cuba continued to enforce, with some modifications, the Social Defense Code (CDS) adopted in 1936, which was heavily influenced by Spanish tradition and contemporary Italian law.[8] Efforts to develop a new criminal code that reflected socialist values began as early as 1969; a new code was not finally enacted until 1979. Despite desire to adapt the new code to the new "social, economic and political conditions of the country on the road to the construction of socialism,"[9] Cubans did not leap to copy codes of other socialist countries. Rather, the 1979 Code developed out of a long, laborious process.

In 1973, the Commission on Juridical Studies, established by the Party in 1969, presented its preliminary proposals to another commission composed of representatives of the Supreme Court, the University of Havana and the Ministry of Justice which studied the proposals and sent back a revised text in 1974.[10] The revised text was then reviewed by the Commission on Juridical Studies and by a third commission that was charged with revising the 1973 law on the organization of the judicial system as well as draft-

---

[8] In fact, the CDS incorporated the vast majority of provisions from the Penal Code of 1870 imposed during the Spanish colonial rule.

[9] Francisco Varona Duque de Estrada, "La Transformación de la Justicia Penal en Cuba," *Revista Jurídica*, No. 1, 1983, p. 157.

[10] Antonio Rodríguez Gavira, "El Sistema Jurídico Penal y el Sistema Judicial Cubano," *Revista Jurídica* No. 16, July-September 1987, pp. 53-54.

ing new codes of both criminal and civil procedure.[11] In 1977, a new draft was distributed for comment to deputies of the National Assembly, the heads of central organs of government, the provincial committees of the Party, the courts, the procurator general, the municipal organs of the Poder Popular, and the ONBC.[12] Consistent with the policy of incorporating public participation in the legislative process, a summary version was also submitted to the CDRs for public discussion. The final draft was elaborated by the Political Bureau of the Party incorporating 495 recommendations resulting from the various bodies that had reviewed the proposed text.[13] In December 1978, the Code was approved by the National Assembly and went into effect in February 1979.

A fundamental premise of the new jurisprudence was the destruction of class privilege. Corruption was rampant in the pre-1959 legal system, and prosecution almost always favored the middle and upper classes to the detriment of the poor and working class. One of Cuba's most prominent jurists, Francisco Varona Duque y Estrada, has written that the revolution "restored fundamental equality before the penal law."[14] Varona argued that the essential difference between the 1979 Criminal Code and its predecessor is that the former represented and protected the interests of the propertied class whereas the new Code reflected the interests of the workers and the socialist state.[15]

In the preamble, the Code explains that a new statute was necessary in order to replace "penal norms . . . which no longer correspond with the reality of our economic, social and political development" and to integrate socialist principles into the penal law. The purposes of the law were enumerated in Article 1: (1) to protect society, individuals and the social, economic and political order; (2) to protect socialist, collective and personal property; (3) to promote the observance of both the rights and duties of citizens; and (4) to contribute to the respect for socialist legality.[16] Although maintaining much of the structure of the previous law, the 1979 Code introduced many new substantive concepts and provisions.

The 1979 Code, like its predecessor, treated criminal conduct severely, but it also contained major jurisprudential advances. It provided for the first time a definition of a punishable crime: "every socially dangerous action or

---

[11] Ibid.
[12] Ibid.
[13] Ibid. See also the preamble to the 1979 Criminal Code which discusses the process by which it was developed.
[14] See, for example, Francisco Varona Duque de Estrada, "La Transformación de la Justicia Penal en Cuba," *Revista Jurídica*, No. 1, 1983, p. 157.
[15] Ibid., p. 134.
[16] Código Penal (Ley No.21), Art. 1, *Gaceta Oficial*, No.3, March 1, 1979.

omission, prohibited by law resulting in penal sanction."[17] The CDS contained no definition and simply provided that no act that was not found in the Code could be considered a crime. Cuban jurists considered the new provision important because it established as a legal principle that only conduct that was socially harmful could be punished.[18] Second, the new Code introduced a range of alternatives to incarceration for lesser offenses and first-time offenders. Thus, instead of being put in prison, a person convicted of a crime could remain in the community but with certain restrictions on personal liberties for a designated period of time. For example, a person could be required to stay within a described area or denied entrance to taverns or bars.

The new Code, which also recognized defenses of necessity[19] and impossibility of compliance,[20] strengthened provisions that exempted from criminal responsibility those who suffered from mental incapacity.[21] In addition, the age of criminal responsibility was raised from twelve to sixteen,[22] and the 1979 Code gave judges flexibility in applying sanctions to those who were under the age of twenty.[23] Thus, a judge could reduce a sentence by half for a defendant who was between sixteen and eighteen years of age and by one third for those between eighteen and twenty.

Socialist legality also required lawmakers to promote compliance with the new economic norms and to protect socialist and collective property. Among the crimes added in the new Code were those acts that harmed the national economy.[24] New provisions punished malfeasance by those in charge of economic activities,[25] as well as abuse and misuse of social property by officials and functionaries. The Code also included provisions related to the destruction and illegal exploitation of natural resources and the environment[26] and crimes against cultural patrimony of the nation.[27] Collective forms of property received special protection. Penalties for robbery

---

[17] Ibid., Art. 8.

[18] Juan Vega Vega, "Comentarios a la Parte General del Código Penal Cubano de 1979," *Revista Cubana del Derecho*, No. 17, 1981, p. 159.

[19] Código Penal (1979), Art. 22.

[20] Ibid., Art. 14.

[21] Ibid., Art. 20.

[22] Ibid., Art. 16. This change had already occurred in 1973 by an amendment to the Code of Social Defense. In 1983, legislation created a separate process for dealing with juveniles which does not involve the court system.

[23] Ibid., Art. 17.

[24] Ibid., Arts. 262-294.

[25] Ibid., Arts. 262-269.

[26] Ibid., Arts. 287-294.

[27] Ibid., Arts. 295-299

were substantially enhanced under aggravating circumstances, among which was listed the theft of socialist, state or cooperative property.[28]

In addition to protecting the socialist economy, the 1979 Code contained provisions dealing with crimes that threatened the security of the state. Included in this category were act of espionage, sabotage, treason and armed rebellion. Sanctions for such crimes could be imprisonment for periods of four to twenty years or death in cases where violence was used or the threat to security particularly serious.[29] Also included was the crime of "Enemy Propaganda" which penalized conduct that incited opposition to the social order, international solidarity and the socialist state. Sentences for violation of this section were lighter, ranging from one to eight years.[30] The Code continued the criminalization of unauthorized entry or departure from the country, which had become part of Cuban criminal law in the 1960s when such activity was linked to counter-revolutionary attacks.[31]

With the exception of "illegal departure," these provisions were not a dramatic departure from previous Cuban law, which traditionally prohibited both acts and expression in opposition to the state as well as those that threatened the existing order. What was different was the severity of the penalties imposed after 1959. For example, the 1936 Code provided penalties of up to ten years for those who promoted violence against the state or who impeded the functioning of organs of government, even for brief periods of time.[32] Further, it also penalized shouts, demonstrations, posters, writings or similar conduct that "provoked an alteration in the public order."[33] The sanction was up to six months in prison and/or a fine. Another

---

[28] In the case of robbery with the use of force or intimidation the penalty was increased from a maximum of six years to a maximum of twenty years with the possibility of the death penalty in egregious circumstances. Ibid., Arts. 386.3(g) and 387.2(d). These provisions were later eliminated in the 1987 Code.

[29] Ibid., Arts. 95-136. Included in this section also are crimes which violate international law such as the crime of genocide (Art. 124) and of racial violence and persecution (Art. 128).

[30] Ibid., Art. 108. The sentence for the distribution of false information or malicious information for the purpose of stirring public alarm or discontent under this section is one to four years unless the convicted has used mass media to distribute the information in which case the sentence is seven to fifteen years. Ibid.

[31] Ibid., Arts. 246 and 247. Failure to comply with legal formalities for entry into the country may be sentenced to one to four years; illegal departure could be punished by six months to three years unless aggravating circumstances such as the use of violence were present in which case the sanction was three to eight years.

[32] Código de Defensa Social (1936), Arts. 148 and 149. Curiously, the sentence for temporarily impeding the functions of the congress, the president or the supreme court, were harsher than those for interfering in the process of elections.

[33] Ibid., Art. 246.

provision of the 1936 Code made it a crime to incite "hatred among the social classes putting public tranquility in danger."[34]

The 1987 Criminal Code

Although providing significant improvements over the law inherited from the previous regime, the 1979 Criminal Code left much to be desired. It maintained a system of severe sentencing for major offenses and gave judges insufficient flexibility to treat individually first time offenders.[35] Although the 1979 Code was ten years in the making, its imperfections were recognized even as it was enacted. According to one jurist, it was enacted anyway because Cuba needed a new code that gave coherent definition to its criminal law, and the 1979 Code was perceived to be far better than the former code.[36] The new Code was not in effect long, however, before Cuban jurists embarked on an extensive analysis of its effectiveness and consistency with principles of justice.

Some insight into the evolution of thinking with respect to criminal justice in Cuba is found in a statement by then Vice Minister of Justice Carlos Amat in June 1987:

> In the first period, we operated under the idealistic criteria which governed law-making in the country. One of the basic principles governing our philosophy was that if delinquency and criminal behavior is a product of the social system of exploitation and oppression, then if we change that situation and do away with exploitation and oppression, then crime and criminals would be eliminated. That was the "bobo" [stupidity] at the beginning. So we began to deal with crime very severely, imposing very heavy penalties to suppress crime, because we thought that any manifestations of crime had to be carry-overs of the prior system. And this same approach was adopted in the Criminal Code of 1979, which was very severe.

---

[34] Ibid., Art. 218. The sentence was one to six months.

[35] See Rodríguez Gavira, p. 67. For example, theft without the use of force carried a sentence of three to eight years. Theft with the use of any kind of force, such as breaking a car window to steal something inside, carried mandatory sentencing of ten to twenty years. Theft of state property regardless of value also carried a sentence of ten to twenty years.

[36] Interview with Carlos Amat Fores, then Vice Minister of Justice, Havana, Cuba, June 12, 1987. In 1990, Amat was promoted to Minister of Justice to replace Juan Escalona Reguera who was elected president of the National Assembly.

> But experience has shown us that severe treatment has neither prevented crime nor eliminated criminals. New forms of crime developed, and harsh sanctions did not serve as the slightest deterrent to crime.[37]

Thus, the philosophical framework within which the 1987 Code was drafted was different. Whereas there had been a tendency in the early years to treat delinquents as enemies who were unable to conform to the values of the new society,[38] jurists later recognized a dialectical relationship between social development and criminal behavior and the impact of criminal law on both. Cubans acknowledged that severe sentences had not only failed to deter crime, but that they carried social costs as well—the human and material price of incarceration.

Efforts to revise the four-year-old code were facilitated by important changes among the top officials of the legal institutions. In 1983, Juan Escalona Reguera was appointed Minister of Justice, filling the vacancy left by the death of former minister Osvaldo Dórticos Torrado. Escalona's appointment was followed by changes at the top of the Ministry of Interior, which is responsible for running the prison system, and the appointment of Ramón de la Cruz as Attorney General. Both Escalona and de la Cruz energetically pursued continued modernization of Cuban criminal law and organized a commission to analyze the 1979 Code and to propose reforms.

In the course of its work, the commission studied the contemporary criminal codes of both socialist and capitalist countries, including some state codes from the United States. Moreover, several international conferences were held in Cuba to discuss approaches to criminal justice. Cuban legal literature suggests that the work of the United Nations in this area was also important in shaping the Cuban approach.[39] As a result of the commission's work, a proposal for a new criminal code was presented to the National Assembly and adopted in December 1987.

One of the objectives of the commission was to substantially reduce the prison population, which had grown to about 30-40,000. The size of the prison population was perceived as partly the result of unduly long sentences meted out by the courts. Moreover, even though the 1979 Code permitted alternatives to incarceration, many judges did not apply such alternatives when possible.[40] The 1987 law reduced the prison population by lowering sentences, by permitting alternative sentences for more offenses and

---

[37] Ibid.

[38] See Francisco Varona, p. 167.

[39] Antonio Cejas Sánchez, "El Régimen de Peligrosidad Social y las Medidas de Seguridad en la Legislación Vigente," *Revista Jurídica*, No. 14, January-March, 1987, p. 69.

[40] Interview with Juan Escalona Reguera, June 16, 1988, Havana, Cuba.

by allowing greater flexibility in sentencing for first-time offenders. Further, it decriminalized a number of minor offenses, such as traffic violations and some misdemeanors that had been included in the 1979 Code.[41]

Even before the National Assembly considered the proposed reforms, justice officials began reviewing the sentences in individual cases pursuant to a decree-law passed in 1985[42] giving the Supreme Court authority to review cases to determine whether the sentences imposed were too severe. Under this process of *revisión*, review could be requested by the person convicted, a relative or a state official. A commission comprising persons from the Ministry of Justice, the president of the Supreme Court and judges of the Provincial Courts studied more than 4,000 cases in 1986 and 1987. By June 1987, 1,000 cases had been submitted to the Supreme Court for *revisión*, and many of the prisoners were released or received reduction of their sentences.[43]

In addition, a broad effort was made to review all cases of prisoners eligible for conditional release, a process similar to parole. According to Escalona Reguera, this process was available under the 1979 Code but had not been implemented consistently.[44] As a result of the review process, approximately 15,000 prisoners were given conditional release between August 1985 and April 1988.[45]

Although following the basic structure of the 1979 Code, the 1987 Code eliminated some crimes and reduced sentences for many others as well as substantially revising numerous provisions. For example, the penalty for theft of property was reduced from six months to three years to a penalty of six months to two years and/or a fine.[46] In cases of robbery with the use of force, the difference is even more marked: The 1979 Code provided for a sentence range of ten to twenty years or death when certain aggravating

---

41 Among the crimes transferred from criminal prosecution to administrative proceedings were certain forms of misfeasance, violations of regulations and traffic violations. Acts of misfeasance that were decriminalized included conduct of managers of state enterprises, such as failure to fulfill legal obligations resulting in harm to the enterprise or in the production or sale of below-standard goods.

42 Decreto-Ley 87 (Del Procedimiento de revisión en material penal), *Gaceta Oficial Extr.* No.7, July 22, 1985 A decree-law is a law adopted by the Council of State or the Council of Ministers while the National Assembly is in recess. The statute is then presented to the Assembly at its next session for rejection or approval. It takes effect, however, upon adoption by the Council.

43 Interview with Juan Escalona Reguera. For example, under Art. 380.5 of the 1979 Code, theft of state property (such as goods from a factory) could be punished by a sentence of up to ten years. After review, the sentence could be reduced to three years in cases where no force or violence was used (unless the economic loss was substantial).

44 Interview with Juan Escalona Reguera.

45 Ibid.

46 Compare Art. 380 of the 1979 Code with Art. 322 of the 1987 Code.

circumstances were present; the 1987 Code eliminated the death penalty for this crime and reduced the prison term to four to ten years.[47] Whereas the theft of socialist property had been considered an aggravating circumstance under the 1979 Code, the 1987 Code draws no distinction between theft of state property and theft of private property.

The adoption of the 1987 Criminal Code was not without controversy. Some members of the Party leadership, including Fidel Castro, initially opposed the revisions, arguing that it was too soon after the enactment of the 1979 Code. In fact, in a statement made to the Third Congress of the Party at the end of 1986, Castro had called for stiffer penalties for those who committed robberies.[48] Moreover, a substantial segment of the population protested the new law as being too lenient on criminals and delinquents. Some jurists and Party members reported that their neighbors were alarmed by what they perceived to be the weakening of the criminal code and felt that the leadership was wrongly bowing to international pressure to moderate its penal law. They predicted that Havana would soon resemble crime-ridden New York.[49] The commitment of the new leadership, however, held firm. The Minister of Justice, the Attorney General and the President of the Supreme Court all participated in televised addresses and newspaper interviews in an attempt to convince the population that the new Code was not only just but would not result in an increase in crime.

A contemporaneous report indicated that recidivism rates were quite low.[50] Some lawyers questioned the significance of these figures since the report was based on statistics gathered only a short time after the release of many of the prisoners. The statistics of cases handled by the *bufetes colectivos* from 1987 to 1989 does show a substantial increase in the number of criminal cases handled. Contracts for criminal defense rose from 42,482 in 1987 to 49,480 in 1989. These statistics may not, however, indicate high rates of recidivism as more criminal cases were handled by the *bufetes colectivos* in 1982 and 1983 (55,710 and 59,446 respectively) than in 1989.[51]

---

[47] Compare Art. 386.3 of the 1979 Code with Art. 327.3 of the 1987 Code.

[48] Fidel Castro, "La Educación Jurídica y el Cumplimiento de la Legalidad Socialista," in *La Educación Jurídica de la Población* (Havana: Ministry of Justice, 1988), p. 15.

[49] I heard numerous such complaints from people I talk to in Havana, and a number of lawyers and officials related to me that they had also encountered such reactions among their neighbors and the members of their CDRs.

[50] "Menos de uno por ciento de los ex reclusos de la capital han reincidido," *Granma*, June 26, 1988, p. 3.

[51] "Principales Indicadores de la Prestación de Servicios Jurídicos," mimeograph report (ONBC, 1989).

1999 Modifications

As the economy plummeted in the early 1990s, criminal activity began to rise, bringing new challenges to the criminal justice system. An alarming increase in ordinary thefts and burglaries created insecurity among Cubans struggling to make ends meet. Increase in workplace thefts and embezzlement threatened economic recovery. The virtual elimination of prostitution, street crime and drug trafficking were among the proud achievements of the Cuban revolution. However, the combination of the severe economic crisis and the influx of foreign tourists dramatically changed that. Havana quickly became a haven for sex tourism already flourishing in the Caribbean as many young women and girls eagerly sought to provide tourists with a good time in exchange for goods and cash not accessible to them through ordinary work. Tourists also became prey to the husslers and muggers common to other capitals but hitherto unknown in Cuba. Further, for the first time in 40 years a fledgling narcotics traffic surfaced in Cuba,[52] spurred by a market provided by tourists.

Although measures to increase policing began earlier and some amendments to the Criminal Code were adopted in 1994 and 1997, it was not until February 1999 that Cuba modified its criminal code in direct response to these changed circumstances. The measures were decidedly harsh in contrast to the liberal approach of the 1987 Code which reflected the view that harsh sentences did not deter crime. Although many who backed the 1999 revisions acknowledged that increasing prison sentences would not solve the problem,[53] the consensus in the National Assembly was that harsher penalties along with increased police presence on the street and community involvement was needed. It is significant that the earlier amendments were adopted by Decree Laws of the Council of State when the National Assembly was not in session whereas the 1999 amendments were considered of such public importance that they were debated in a special session of the legislature.

In addition, the modifications added penalties for conduct not previously included in the Criminal Code. Prostitution, which had been absent from the 1987 Code, was reintroduced as a crime along with punishment of those who facilitated and participated in prostitution.[54] The provisions on drug

[52] Narcotics, primarily cocaine find their way into Cuba in two ways: 1) brought in small amounts by foreign visitors or 2) bundles destined for the US which are dropped in the ocean to be picked up by speed boats but are carried by the currents to Cuban shores despite efforts to intercept them. Small amounts of marijuana are grown on the island.

[53] See, for example, "Las Modificaciones velan especialmente por los Niños y los Jóvenes, " *Juventud Rebelde*, February 2, 1999, p. 2.

[54] Ibid., Art. 17, modifying Art. 302 of the Criminal Code.

trafficking were expanded.[55] Other new provisions include those punishing money laundering,[56] trafficking in minors[57] and crimes related to the promotion, organizing and facilitating of illegal immigration.[58] The latter was in specific response to the growing number of operations in which smugglers are paid to take Cubans illegally to the United States. U.S. immigration law, which offers parole to Cubans who reach the shores of the United States, whether legally or illegally,[59] encouraged smuggling and has cost the lives of many who caste their fate with profiteers and board unsafe boats.

Sentences for theft and violent crimes were increased substantially,[60] and the death penalty was introduced for some crimes for which it was not previously included among the range of sanctions: drug trafficking, sexual abuse of minors and armed robbery. Further, Cuba introduced for the first time the sanction of life imprisonment. Previously the maximum sentence was 20 years or thirty years in cases where the death penalty was commuted to time in prison.

Judicial Reaction to the 1999 Modifications

Differences of approach and philosophy have surfaced again between the judiciary and the legal institutions and the popular assembly. As in 1984, the judiciary has reacted to soften the harshness of sanctions embodied in the 1999 amendments to the Criminal Code. In 2000, the Governing Council of the Supreme Court issued a statement of policy that lower sentences should be applied when reasonable to do so.[61] Accordingly, judges should look for elements that allow the imposition of the lowest sentence provided by the statute. The statement was part of policy of seeking rationality and serving the social interest—not simply applying the law in a formal way.

---

[55] Ibid., Art. 10, modifying Art. 190 of the Criminal Code.
[56] Ibid., Art. 21, adding Chapter II, Art. 346 to the Criminal Code.
[57] Ibid., Art. 19, modifying Articles 315 and 316 of the Criminal Code.
[58] Ibid., Art. 22, adding Title XV, Articles 347 and 348 to the Criminal Code.
[59] Known as the Cuban Adjustment Act, this regulation offers special treatment to illegal immigrants coming from Cuba permitting anyone who arrives in the United States to apply for parole, leading to residency. The explosion in number of "rafters" trying to cross the Florida Straits from Cuba, gave rise to the controversial "wet feet/dry feet" policy. Those intercepted at sea by the US Coast Guard are generally repatriated to Cuba; those who make it to shore are permitted to apply for parole.
[60] Ley No. 87 (Modificación del Código Penal), Art. 20, modifying Arts 322-329 of the Criminal Code, *Gaceta Oficial Ext.*, No.1, March 15, 1999.
[61] Interview with Dr. Jorge Bodes, President of the Supreme Court of Cuba, May 10, 2002.

In addition, the lower courts were urged to apply alternative sentences wherever the Code permits.[62] Alternatives to 24 hour imprisonment include internment with work outside prison and furloughs to visit family;[63] work without internment,[64] limitations of liberty and supervision outside prison.[65] As a result, judges increasingly sentence first time offenders to work outside of prisons for a period of time equivalent to the number of years of incarceration provided for by law. Unions were resistant at first to having convicted offenders in the workplace. To assuage the unions and to discuss conditions for alternative sentences, judges from the Supreme Court as well as prosecutors and defense lawyers met with union leadership to convince them of the importance of providing this opportunity, particularly to first time offenders.[66] It has been reported that in 2002 that in some courts, such alternatives are applied in up to 60% of sentences.[67] The results appear to have been quite positive.[68]

As part of the implementation process of applying alternative sentences, the Supreme Court issued an instruction establishing a special unit of judges "charged with the oversight of the execution of sentences and other corrective measures alternative to imprisonment."[69] Pursuant to this program one or two professional judges are assigned in each municipality to supervise the enforcement of criminal sanctions such as correctional work outside of prison, limitations of liberty and conditional probation as well as those who have received parole. These judges make periodic visits to the workplace to assure the sentence is being fulfilled and to check on the adaptation of the person convicted. In cases of other alternative sentences, the judges work with neighborhood groups and the heads of the local police unit.[70]

The "enforcement judge" is empowered to recommend to the trial court that the sentence be revoked, suspended or modified; that is that the offender be re-sentenced to prison for failure to fulfill the requirements of the alternative sentence, that the sentence be lifted or shortened, or that parole be re-

---

[62] Article 33.1 of the Criminal Code as modified in 1997 permits work as an alternative sentence when the prison term allowed by the law does not exceed five years.
[63] Código Penal (as amended in 1999), Art. 32.
[64] Ibid., Art. 33.
[65] Ibid., Art. 34.
[66] Id. Interview with Dr. Ruben Remigio Ferro, President of the Supreme Court of Cuba, April 15, 2002.
[67] Interview with Dr. Jorge Bodes, President of the Supreme Court of Cuba, May 10, 2002.
[68] Ibid. See also, Lidia Mercedes Miquet Ortiz, Maria Teresa Cuesta Rodriguez and Humberto Cartaya Monaga, "El Trabajo en las sanciones alternatives de la privativa de libertad, medio de readaptacion social," Paper presented at the 4th Interamerican Conference on Labor Law and Social Security, Havana, Cuba March 24-25, 2002. This paper details experiences of three young defense lawyers in Mantanzas Province.
[69] Instrucción No. 163 (Consejo de Gobierno del Tribunal Supremo), 2001.
[70] Interview with Jorge Bodes.

voked.[71] However, the instruction does not state what recourse the defendant has in the event of a negative recommendation by the "enforcement judge."

Although the Criminal Code was modified as recently as 1999, there is consensus in the legal community that a new Code should be drafted that is more coherent and better integrated. A commission has been formed consisting of members of the judiciary, representatives of the Office of the Attorney General, the Ministry of Interior, the Armed Forces and the Ministry of Justice. The proposed code will incorporate military law as a chapter of the criminal code. It is not expected that a draft will be presented to the National Assembly until 2003. Defense lawyers have not been included in the drafting commission, but it is inconceivable that they will not be consulted before a draft is presented to the National Assembly.

Crimes Against State Security

Although the 1999 amendments to the Cuban Criminal Code will have far greater significance for the Cuban population, international attention focussed exclusively on another law adopted at the same time: The Law on the Protection of the National Economy and Independence[72] that was enacted to implement the 1996 Law Reaffirming Cuban Dignity and Sovereignty.[73] Both laws are a response to specific legislation and actions by the United States government expressly designed to inflict economic harm by extending the effect of the U.S. embargo and to undermine the Cuban government by giving direct support to dissident groups in Cuba.[74] It can hardly be disputed that the objective of the hostile policies of the United States is to overturn the current government of Cuba and to compel radical internal political and economic changes. Thus, from the Cuban perspective acts in support of this policy are tantamount to treason even if there is no armed aggression.

Contrary to the general foreign commentary at the time, Law 88 does not suppress all dissenting views in Cuba. The express purpose of Law 88 is to protect national sovereignty and it applies only to persons who intention-

---

[71] Instrucción No. 163 (2001), Art. Decimo Tercero.

[72] Ley No.88 (Ley de Protección de la Independencia Nacional y la Economía de Cuba), *Gaceta Oficial Ext.*, No.1, March 15, 1999. The law was adopted on February 16, 1999.

[73] Ley No. 80 (Ley de Reafirmación de la Dignidad y Soberanía Cubanas), *Gaceta Oficial Ext.*, No.2, December 24, 1996.

[74] Most notable are the Torricelli Law of 1992 and the Helms-Burton Law of 1996.

ally cooperate with implementation of defined aspects of U.S. policy towards Cuba. Article 1 states:

> The objective of this Law is to define and sanction those acts which are undertaken to support, facilitate or collaborate with the objectives of the "Helms Burton" Law, the blockade and the economic war against our people, the purposes of which are to undermine internal order, destabilize the country and eliminate the Socialist State and the independence of Cuba.

Thus, the law prohibits specific acts such as the intentional supply of information to agents in the United States for the purpose of facilitating the application of the Helms-Burton law[75] and actions undertaken for the purpose of interfering with Cuba's economic relations.[76] Despite fears raised in the international press, to date no one has been prosecuted under this law.

On the other hand, the Criminal Code, as amended, contains broader provisions regarding crimes against the security of the state. The article on "enemy propaganda," identical to the 1979 Code,[77] has been applied to scores of people prosecuted for activities such as giving false reports to the international press, distributing leaflets against the Party, and for making an illegal film. In 1992, there were also a number of armed raids and attempts at sabotage perpetrated by individuals and groups based in Miami. Even more dramatic were the bombs set off in tourist facilities in the summer of 1997 by persons reportedly paid by anti-Castro groups outside of Cuba.[78] No one has been prosecuted or sentenced simply for voicing criticism of the government, its leaders or its policies. However, Cuban officials perceive all attempts to organize activities designed to undermine the socialist economy and political stability as being tied to or supported by outside forces, most notably elements of the ex patriot communities in Miami and Spain. Much of it clearly is.[79] In addition, the U.S. government now provides funding for the activities of what it describes as "dissident groups." As the United States administration takes a more aggressive stance towards Cuba,

---

[75] Ley No. 88 (1991), Art. 4.

[76] Ibid., Art. 9.

[77] Código Penal (1987), Art. 103.

[78] A Salvadoran citizen and two Guatemalans confessed, after arrest, to having been paid to plant explosives in Cuban hotels.

[79] In 1992, Jorge Más Canosa, then president of the Cuban American National Foundation, even used U.S. funded broadcasts over Radio Martí, a project of Voice of America which broadcasts to Cuba, to call for a revolt. In July, when Fidel Castro was attending the Earth Summit in Rio, Más gave a speech in which he called on the Cuban military to block Castro's return to Cuba. He arranged to have the speech broadcast over Radio Martí.

even accusing Cuba of cooperating with "terrorist" nations,[80] and the Cuban economic situation remains critical, the government has made it clear that it will not tolerate either the organization or incitement of internal unrest.

Death Penalty

Current Cuban law does permit imposition of the death penalty, but only in exceptional cases and in the gravest circumstances in which it is permitted.[81] However, it cannot be applied to a defendant who was under twenty years of age at the time the crime was committed. Nor can a woman be executed who is pregnant or has a minor child under the age of one year.[82]

A mandatory review is designed to assure that the death penalty is not applied arbitrarily. Thus, in every instance in which the trial court imposes the death penalty, it is automatically reviewed by the Supreme Court.[83] The appeal involves complete review of the evidence tantamount to a new trial. If the Supreme Court ratifies the death sentence, it must be reviewed again and confirmed by the Council of State (the highest executive body of the state) before it can be carried out. Once the final decision has been made, the sentence is carried out within twenty-four hours. Execution is by firing squad.

The death penalty is applied only in egregious cases of violence,[84] and when it is, the Supreme Court generally commutes the sentence to the maximum prison term permitted by law which, prior to 1999, was thirty years.[85] Reportedly there were no executions in 1985 or 1986.[86] In 1999, the Criminal Code was amended to permit life imprisonment. Although the amendments expanded the number of crimes for which the death penalty may be applied, many believe that the alternative offered by the sanction of

---

[80] In April 2002, shortly before the scheduled visit to Cuba by former President Jimmy Carter, a State Department official accused Cuba of trafficking in bio-weapon technology. Carter refuted the charges after visiting Cuba's biotechnology installations. Still, Cuba remains on the State Department list of "terrorist" nations.

[81] Código Penal (1987), Art. 29.1.

[82] Ley No. 5 (De Procedimiento Penal) as modified (1994), Art. 498.

[83] Ley No.5 (Ley de Procedimiento Penal), Art. 60, *Gaceta Oficial*, No.37, August 26, 1977.

[84] Interview with Ruben Remigio Ferro, President of the Supreme Court, Havana, Cuba, September 16, 1999.

[85] The maximum prison sentence under Cuban law is twenty years with the exception of those who have been sentenced to death. If the death sentence is commuted, the prison term imposed is thirty years.

[86] Interview with José Raúl Amaro Salup, former President of the Cuban Supreme Court, Havana, Cuba, June 14, 1987.

life terms will actually reduce the number of cases in which the death penalty is applied or carried out. In fact, no executions have taken place since 2000, suggesting that the government has imposed an implicit moratorium.[87]

Because of the spotlight focused on Cuba, the application of the death penalty in Cuba has attracted disproportional international attention. Yet, since the 1960s, there has been no occasion where the death penalty has been imposed on any civilian for what might be considered a political offense that did not involve acts of violence.[88] In one case decided in early 1992, the defendant murdered a police officer in cold blood during an attempt to flee Cuba in a stolen boat, a crime punishable by death in virtually every state in the United States that has the death penalty.[89] The sentence received a great deal of attention in the international press. In an earlier case, the Cuban courts condemned an ex-patriot, Eduardo Díaz Betancourt, who had illegally entered Cuban territory with arms and explosives, which he admitted were to be used for sabotage. The death sentences of two co-conspirators were commuted by the Cuban Supreme Court to thirty years imprisonment. Betancourt acknowledged he was in charge of the operation and was part of a terrorist group based in Miami. Numerous heads of state as well as the Pope sought clemency for Betancourt, but they showed no concern for the fourteen people executed in the United States in the same year.[90]

Amnesty International sent a protest to the Cuban government concerning these executions and expressed alarm that Cuba would use the death penalty against those convicted of "political" crimes. Although Cuba continues to deal harshly with those who oppose the regime, it has not sentenced to death or executed anyone who did not engage in or conspire to commit serious acts of violence. The only exceptions were the 1989 executions of General Ochoa and three other military officials: they were sentenced for crimes related to drug trafficking while in military service, but not for political opposition.

The application of the death penalty in the case of military officers Arnaldo Ochoa, Jorge Martínez, Amado Padrón and Tony de la Guardia

---

[87] Interview with Jorge Bodes, President of the Criminal Law Chamber of the Supreme Court, Havana, Cuba, May 10, 2002.

[88] Interview with Amaro Salup, Havana, Cuba, October 10, 1992.

[89] Newspaper accounts of the trial reported that several Cubans had tried to steal a boat in order to leave the island. When they were discovered in the act by a police officer, they first tied up the officer on shore and then tried to start the boat. When they could not get the boat started, they shot the officer and fled.

[90] According to a report published by the Bureau of Justice Statistics, eight states executed 14 prisoners in 1991, increasing to 157 the total number of executions in the United States between 1977, when the Supreme Court reaffirmed the death penalty's constitutionality, and Dec. 31, 1991. U.S. Newswire, October 22, 1992.

sparked controversy inside Cuba as well as outside, although for different reasons. The court's rationale for the death penalty was derived from the Law of Military Crimes[91] and the civilian Criminal Code. Article 13 of the Law of Military Crimes provides for a penalty of two to ten years' imprisonment for abuse of office when such abuse results in serious consequences for the activities or interests of the military. If such abuse occurs during time of war, as in the case of these defendants, the penalty may be increased to ten to twenty years or death.[92] Article 110.2 of the Criminal Code provides for the death penalty in cases in which a person commits an act hostile to a foreign state which results in retaliatory measures against Cuba or its citizens, humiliation or the alteration of diplomatic relations with Cuba. The prosecutor sought the death penalty for seven of the fourteen defendants; the Court imposed the penalty on four.

In the case of General Ochoa and Captain Martínez, the defendants were shown to have made contact with the Medellín drug cartel in Colombia for the purpose of negotiating a deal on drug trafficking during the time that Cuba was in active military engagement in southern Africa. Thus, these acts and other acts of corruption admitted to and demonstrated at trial were arguably the kind of abuse covered by the Law on Military Crimes. Given the gravity of the offense, even though no drug deal was actually consummated, the court imposed the death sentence.

In the case of Amado Padrón and Tony de la Guardia, who were not involved in the war in Angola, the drug trafficking could not be considered an "abuse of office in time of war." Rather, the prosecutor looked to the article in the Criminal Code related to hostile acts against a foreign country. It is indeed ironic that Cuban officers would be sentenced to death for hostile acts against the United States which had pursued a course of extreme hostility toward Cuba for more than thirty years in its attempt to topple the Cuban government. At the time of trial, however, no acts of reprisal or alteration in diplomatic relations had occurred unless intensification of the U.S. anti-Cuban campaign was to be considered an act of "reprisal." Arguably, the relentless campaign against Cuba by the United States with respect to alleged drug trafficking placed the country in some danger of reprisal, demonstrated by the U.S. invasion of Panama a few months later. The statute also speaks, however, of resulting "humiliation" to the Cuban nation and people, and unquestionably the scandal seriously damaged the prestige of the nation. Since the drug dealing also threatened the security of the nation by compromising Cuba's territorial integrity as well as the loyalty of its

---

[91] Ley No.22 (Ley de los Delitos Militares), Art. 37(d), *Gaceta Oficial*, No.6, March 5, 1979.

[92] Ibid., Art. 37(d). Cuban troops were engaged in military combat in Angola at the time.

military officials, it was considered within the realm of treason, and the prosecutor called for the severest of penalties.

Had the defendants been involved in almost any other type of crime, theft for example, the penalty would most certainly have been imprisonment, not death. The gravity of having engaged in drug trafficking when the Cuban government had consistently denied long-standing U.S. allegations was profoundly shocking to Cubans. Even so, there were questions concerning the legal foundation for the application of the death penalty.[93] Rumors circulated at the time that several members of the Central Committee dissented from the majority vote approving the decision to impose the death penalty. A number of lawyers also engaged in debate over the legality of the sentence and the quality of defense counsel.[94] Nevertheless, even among those who did not like the decision, many believed that the country had no choice under the circumstances but to execute the officers. The collective needs won out.

In the United States, on the other hand, commentators in the media set aside discussion of legal questions and focused primarily on speculation that General Ochoa had been tried because he represented a political challenge to the leadership of Fidel Castro and/or that Castro himself had approved or been involved in the drug schemes. No credible evidence has yet been offered to support either speculation.[95] There was, however, ample evidence that the drug dealing did take place and that the persons charged were in fact key figures in the scandal. Much of this evidence is corroborated by testimony given at trials in the United States of drug traffickers who had dealt with the Cuban officials.[96]

Although the death penalty in Cuba has been politicized internationally, it has not become a political issue in Cuba. It is likely that the majority of the Cuban population, like those in the United States, support the death penalty in exceptional cases. Moreover, in Cuba, there is not a popular perception that it has been used arbitrarily. Further, the continued effort by the

---

[93] I was in Cuba during the trials, and this observation is based on notes of informal discussions I had with Cuban jurists at the time.

[94] None of the fourteen defendants exercised their right to appoint their own defense counsel, and all were appointed military lawyers to defend them. This decision was controversial among some in the legal community because some of the defense counsel had little experience in criminal trials, and their efforts at trial were not adept. For a discussion of the impact of the trial on Cuban lawyers, see Chapter three.

[95] Several U.S. journalists have attempted to educe such evidence, but their versions rely on conjecture and not evidence. See, for example, Julia Preston, "The Trial that Shook Cuba," *New York Review of Books,* December 7, 1989, p. 24; Andres Oppenheimer, *Castro's Final Hour* (New York: Simon and Schuster, 1992).

[96] For a description of the connections, see Debra Evenson, "Dealing With Drugs in Cuba," *Covert Action Information Bulletin*, No. 33, Winter 1990, p. 59.

United States to topple the Cuban government and the socialist revolution has heightened tensions and concern for national security. Given the sporadic, but continuing acts of violence and sabotage against the Cuban revolution[97] as well as the perception that violent crime is increasing, the climate is not conducive to abolition of the death penalty, or other security measures for that matter.

Yet, there are signs of changing attitudes towards the death penalty. The June 2000 execution of Shaka Sankofa in Texas was given wide publicity in Cuba. Numerous television and radio shows tracked the dramatic debate in the United States sparked by the revelations of abuses in the application of the death penalty. Some believe that these discussions encouraged debate in Cuba on the death penalty. In the 1999 legislative session of the National Assembly, delegate Raúl Suarez, a Baptist minister, publicly expressed his moral opposition to the maximum penalty. As noted previously, there has been an implicit moratorium on executions since 2000.

Social Dangerousness

Perhaps one of the more controversial substantive provisions in Cuban criminal law is that entitled "Social Dangerousness," which gives the state authority to take preventive measures with respect to persons who have certain indicia of anti-social behavior. This provision, which existed in the 1936 Social Defense Code, also appeared in the laws of other countries.[98] Although the 1936 provision was influenced by the contemporaneous Italian Criminal Code, post-1959 jurists who favored its retention, albeit with modification, found support in the codes of the former socialist countries of Europe. Its retention was viewed as consistent with the function of law as the instrument of social change. Nevertheless, the provision has been modified substantially since the revolution. Its character and validity remain the subject of internal debate.

The Social Defense Code of 1936 provided that an individual could be detained if found to have "a certain unhealthy, congenital or acquired predisposition . . . which favors the inclination to commit a crime,"[99] whether or not the individual had actually committed a crime.[100] The 1936 Code

97 See, e.g.,"Cuba says U.S. Turns blind eye on Terrorists in Florida," United Press International, October 14, 1992.

98 See, for example, the Italian Criminal Code (1977), Arts. 202 and 203.

99 Código de Defensa Social (1936), Art. 48(a).

100 Ibid., Art. 48(b).

listed twelve categories of behavior considered to be indicia of a dangerous state that predisposed one to criminal behavior. Among the categories were mental illness as well as mental retardation, drug addiction, habitual drunkenness, gambling and vagrancy, habitual use of physical threats, habitual lying, infection with contagious venereal diseases, practice of prostitution among minors, infraction of regulations legally imposed by authorities, and the practice or exploitation of morally repugnant vices.[101]

In 1942, a thirteenth category was added: suspicious behavior during a State of Emergency or at any time the Constitutional Guarantees were suspended because of disruption of the public order.[102] Persons subject to this provision included both nationals and foreigners who were suspected of cooperating in whatever form with the enemy or with those creating public disturbances.[103] Those found to be "suspicious" were tried by the *Tribunal de Urgencia*, a special court which conducted summary proceedings based on accusations made by the military or police authority.[104] After the triumph of the revolution, the section on "suspicious behavior" was repealed when the *Tribunales de Urgencia* were abolished, but in all other respects the provision remained identical to the pre-revolutionary law until 1979, with one notable exception. As an expression of the policy to eliminate prostitution altogether, the provision was broadened to specifically include all forms of prostitution, not just prostitution involving minors.

The 1979 Code narrowed the definition of "dangerous state" to signify habitual behavior that showed a "special proclivity . . . to commit criminal acts, as demonstrated by observed conduct which is manifestly against the norms of socialist morality."[105] The list of indicia of such pre-delinquent behavior was reduced from twelve to seven categories: habitual drunkenness, drug addiction, pandering, prostitution, vagrancy, the exploitation or exercise of socially repugnant vices, and a catch-all category designated as antisocial conduct that is defined in the statute as habitually engaging in acts of violence or use of provocative or menacing gestures or phrases that threaten the rights of others or frequently disturb the order of the community.[106] The phrase "morally repugnant vices" was replaced by the phrase "socially repugnant vices" perhaps indicating that social values have replaced the religious moral values of the past era. Under the 1979 law, mental illness or retardation was considered a dangerous state only when the

[101] Ibid.
[102] Acuerdo-Ley No.3 (Ley de Seguridad y Orden Público), Art. 8, *Gaceta Oficial*, January 5, 1942.
[103] Ibid.
[104] Ibid., Art. 9.
[105] Código Penal (1979), Art. 76.
[106] Ibid., Art. 77.

person was not able to comprehend or control his actions and posed a threat to the safety of others.[107] The measures to be applied to those adjudicated to be "socially dangerous" included therapeutic treatment, re-education programs and supervision, but not imprisonment.[108]

The 1987 reforms further reduced the categories of conduct to include only three: habitual drunkenness, drug addiction and antisocial behavior.[109] Today, a person may be considered to be in a "dangerous state" when his or her antisocial conduct

> habitually breaks the rules of social coexistence by acts of violence, or whose other provocative acts violate the rights of others or whose general comportment harms the rules of social coexistence or disturbs the community order, or who lives as a social parasite . . . or who exploits or practices socially repugnant vices.[110]

According to one lengthy analysis, the provision with respect to "socially repugnant vices" was rarely, if ever, applied since conduct that fell under the term was treated separately under the Code in sections entitled "public scandal," and "corruption of minors."[111]

Despite this effort to more narrowly restrict the reach of "social dangerousness," some lawyers in Cuba argue that security measures, whether punitive or therapeutic, should only be legally imposed in cases of criminal conduct and that drug addiction, alcoholism and dangerous conduct of the mentally ill should be treated outside of the criminal process altogether.[112] A commission of the ONBC, charged with making proposals for the modification of the Code of Criminal Procedure, concluded that detention of one presumed to be dangerous should be clearly prohibited, and that the process by which therapeutic measures could be imposed should be based on more precise legislation with the same guarantees of defense granted those accused of committing a crime. Some have taken note of criticism that the doctrine imposes sanctions on those who have not yet committed a crime

---

[107] Ibid., Art. 7
[108] Ibid., Art. 82.
[109] Código Penal (1987), Art. 72.
[110] Ibid., Art. 73.2.
[111] Cejas Sánchez, p. 60.
[112] For example, see Mario Alberto Taglo y Babé, "Contribución para el Perfeccionamiento del Vigente Código Penal Cubano," in *Enfoques Jurídicos de Abogados Cubanos* (Havana: Organización Nacional de Bufetes Colectivos, 1989), pp. 202-264; Carmen López González, et al., "Algunas Consideraciones Sobre el Estado Peligroso en Cuba," in *Ponencias Derecho Penal* a compilation of papers presented at the National Juridical Conference of the National Organization of Bufetes Colectivos, November 30 to December 2, 1989, pp. 153-178.

and thus risks violating fundamental rights of individuals to due process. Others, like Antonio Cejas Sánchez, chair of the department of criminal law at the University of Havana, defend the doctrine on the grounds that it is important to the prevention of crime and that the statute establishes a sufficiently narrow definition that is capable of proof.[113]

The subject remains the object of debate in Cuba.

Homosexuality

In the 1960s, homosexuality was considered not just deviant behavior but against socialist morality and linked with counter-revolutionary activities. As a consequence of repressive measures, many homosexuals were denounced as counter-revolutionaries and sent to the infamous UMAP work camps (Military Units to Aid Production) established in 1965 in which inmates were required to do mostly agricultural labor. Castro ordered their closure in 1967 after receiving protests about the brutal treatment of UMAP draftees.[114] A number of military officers responsible for mistreating inmates were court-martialed.[115] Despite the closure of these camps, discrimination and harassment of homosexuals persisted.

Antagonism toward homosexuals had social, religious and political origins. First, Cuban society is traditionally and pervasively homophobic, stemming from the influence of both the Roman Catholic church as well as the Afro-Cuban religions. Second, the revolutionary forces initially considered homosexuality a remnant of bourgeois, capitalist decadence that the "new society" would eliminate. Homosexuality was, thus, considered an affront to socialist morality. Over time, official attitudes and policy changed, eliminating the political basis of discrimination, and today an atmosphere of tolerance, if not total acceptance, prevails in Cuba supported and promoted by most state agencies.

Homosexual conduct was not expressly mentioned in the criminal code of Cuba before 1979. To the extent that it was penalized, it would have had to been considered "socially dangerous" conduct under an interpretation of morally repugnant or socially repugnant behavior or implicitly included in other provisions that sanctioned behavior that corrupts the morals of minors or that creates a public scandal. None of these sections, however, specifically referred to homosexual behavior.

---

[113] Cejas Sánchez, pp. 46-48.
[114] Domínguez, p. 357.
[115] Ibid.

In contrast, the 1979 Code explicitly listed homosexual conduct among misconduct defined in Article 359 as constituting a "public scandal" and in Article 367 on the corruption of minors. It was never, however, included in Article 76 on "social dangerousness." With respect to homosexual conduct, the article on "public scandal" provided for a sanction of three to nine months, a fine, or both in cases where (1) a person made a public display of his homosexuality or solicited another to engage in homosexual conduct; and (2) a person engaged in homosexual acts in a public place or in a private place exposed to the involuntary view of others. Article 367, dealing with the corruption of minors, stated in subsection 1: "He who induces a minor of less than 16 years, of either sex, to engage in homosexuality . . . incurs a sanction of one to eight years in prison."

Reflective of changing attitudes, the provisions penalizing public display of homosexuality or even engaging in homosexual acts in public view were eliminated from the Criminal Code in 1987. Bothering or pestering another with solicitations to engage in homosexual acts, however, is included as conduct creating a public scandal, and may be punished by three months to one year imprisonment, or a fine.[116] The provision regarding corruption of minors under the age of 16 remains unchanged.[117]

Thus, consensual homosexual relations in Cuba have been freed from the reach of criminal law. Although the criminal code still defines some conduct with specific reference to homosexuals, it is limited to conduct in which either unwelcome advances are made or which involves a minor under the age of 16. In addition, homosexuals are no longer subject to official harassment for simply being identified as homosexuals, and there are a growing number of public places where gay men and lesbian women openly meet and socialize.

Moreover, public agencies attempt to overcome social biases. Since the late 1980s sex education books describe homosexuality as a normal expression of human sexuality. Restrictions on employment have also been virtually eliminated. Although Party statutes never explicitly excluded homosexuals from membership, personal biases among Party members have limited access to those who profess their homosexuality. However, there are nationally known members of the Party who are widely known to be gay or lesbian.

Perhaps more importantly, the subject is no longer taboo for public discussion. In an interview with Tomás Borge, Fidel Castro expressed opposition to policies that discriminated against gays and lesbians.[118] The subject

---

[116] Código Penal (1987), Art. 303(a).

[117] Ibid., Art. 310. The provision which also includes soliciting a minor under 16 years to engage in acts of prostitution provides for a punishment of two to five years' imprisonment.

[118] Tomás Borge, *Un Grano de Maíz* (Mexico: Fondo de Cultura Económica, 1992), p. 235.

also arose at the April 1992 congress of the Union of Young Communists (UJC) at which Vilma Espín, president of the Federation of Cuban Women and member of the Council of State, called for an end to discrimination and said that gay and lesbian youth should be respected and accepted. The release of the film "Fresa y Chocolate" by Cuba's most famous filmmaker Tomás Gutierrez Alea in 1993, was a national box office hit.[119] The film dealt sensitively and directly with the injustice of discrimination and prejudices against Cuban homosexuals and argued for valuing each individual on his merits, not on sexual orientation.

Today, the situation for gays in Cuba is in many ways better than that of gays in the United States and other Latin American countries. In 1986, more than twenty states in the United States still had statutes penalizing private, adult, consensual homosexual relationships.[120] Although Cuban society remains largely homophobic, as does most of the rest of the hemisphere, Cuban homosexuals are not subject to the kind of violent attacks that have been prevalent in the United States, Colombia and Mexico. Nor has the advent of AIDS resulted in a backlash against gay men in Cuba where AIDS is not publicly viewed as a gay disease. Until recently, the majority of HIV cases in Cuba were found among heterosexuals, and educational programs were primarily targeted at heterosexual conduct. Although failure to direct educational efforts at gay men may itself be a form of discrimination, the initial Cuban policy of limited quarantine of those found to be HIV-positive, whatever criticism it may provoke, was not a measure to repress gay men.[121]

III. CRIMINAL PROCEDURE

Soon after the new Criminal Code was adopted in 1987, Cuban lawyers and officials also began a review of the Code of Criminal Procedure, long the object of criticism for being imprecise, inefficient and out of date. At a

---

[119] The film won the prize for best film at the Havana International Film Festival in 1993 and was nominated for an Oscar for best foreign film the following year.

[120] *Bowers* v. *Hardwick*, 478 U.S. 186 (1986). In *Bowers*, the Supreme Court ruled that the criminalization of private, consensual homosexual conduct does not violate the constitutional rights of gays and lesbians.

[121] When AIDS first began to appear in Cuba in the mid-1980s, Cuba adopted a policy of quarantine for all those who tested HIV positive. Over time, the policy relaxed so that those who are living in quarantine could go home for weekly visits and return to their normal work. In 1994, the general policy of quarantine was eliminated altogether. For a description of Cuba's AIDS program, see Chapter 2.

forum organized by the Cuban Society of Penal Sciences in 1990 to discuss reforms of the procedural law, then Procurator General Ramón de la Cruz remarked that the problems in the current procedural law were profound: "We cannot simply reform the law. We have to revolutionize it." For de la Cruz the fundamental issue was "how to construct the proper balance between individual guarantees and the guarantee of the security of society and between the need for swiftness and the need for quality." After more than four years of debate, modifications to the Code of Criminal Procedure were adopted in 1994 correcting some of the deficiencies of the previous law, but they failed to introduce the advances many had hoped for.

Cuban criminal procedure is derived from the investigatorial or inquisitorial system of Spain rooted in the civil law tradition of Europe. However, most modern inquisitorial systems also incorporate some elements of the accusatorial or adversarial system related to the rights of the accused. Cuba is no exception. The U.S. occupation from 1898 to 1902 left a significant imprint on Cuban criminal procedure. Thus, although Cuba maintains the formal procedural aspects characteristic of the inquisitorial system, it also guarantees rights of the defendant typical of the accusatorial system.

Many procedural guarantees are established in the Cuban Constitution such as the right to defense[122] and the right not to testify;[123] confessions must be voluntary and those that are not voluntary are considered void.[124] No one may be prosecuted or sentenced except by a competent court "by virtue of laws which existed prior to the crime,"[125] and criminal laws may be applied retroactively only when they "benefit the accused or person who has been sentenced."[126] The Constitution also provides protections against unauthorized searches and seizures.[127]

In addition, Cuban authorities have made many reforms designed to prevent undue delays in bringing an accused to trial. The expansion of the number of municipal and provincial courts since the mid-1970s has helped cut delays in trials. The Supreme Court also created sections of the Chamber of Criminal Law in the provinces most distant from Havana to avoid delays in appeals and other difficulties caused by the "special period". Moreover, under current criminal procedure, a case should normally be brought to trial within 60 days of indictment, a term which can be extended up to six months upon petition to the chief prosecutor or the court. A further extension requires that the petition be submitted to the Procurator General

---

[122] Constitución (1992), Art. 59.
[123] Ibid.
[124] Ibid.
[125] Ibid.
[126] Ibid., Art. 61.
[127] Ibid., Arts. 56-57.

by the highest police or prosecutorial authority of the province in which the case is being brought.[128]

As in other inquisitorial systems, there is no such thing as a plea of guilty or plea bargaining that would vitiate the need for a trial. Moreover, since Cuba expressly maintains the presumption of innocence until convicted by a court,[129] the burden of proving guilt remains on the prosecution. The accused may not be forced to make any declaration,[130] and even if the accused should voluntarily confess, he cannot be convicted based on a confession alone or solely on the statements of his spouse or relatives up to the fourth degree of affinity.[131] Thus, in all cases, the prosecution must prove guilt by submitting evidence independent of any statement made by the defendant in order to obtain a conviction.[132] The rule is taken seriously. In cases where the trial court fails to observe it, the Supreme Court will overturned the conviction.

Cuba, like most civil law countries, does not provide for a jury trial in either civil or criminal matters. However, Cuba has introduced the participation of the community in the form of lay judges who have equal status with professional judges in judicial determinations.[133] In contrast to the traditional inquisitorial process where the only the court conducts the examination at trial, Cuban procedure allows both the prosecutor and the defense to question witnesses as well as the court.

Pre-Trial Procedure

The pre-trial process has been the subject of much debate and reform. Prior to the revolution, Cuban law provided that the investigation and instruction of the charges be carried out by a judge called the *juez instructor*. The pre-trial process was divided into two phases: the *sumario* during which it was determined whether to bring charges, and the *fase preparatoria* during which the case was prepared for trial. The involvement of the court via

---

[128] Ley No. 5 (1977), Art. 107 (as amended in 1994).
[129] Ley No.5 (1977), Art. 1 (as amended in 1994).
[130] Ibid., Art. 161. Article 161 states: No accused is obligated to make a statement against his interest. The instructor, once fulfilling the formalities referred to in the preceding article, shall have the duty to inform him of what he is accused, by whom and the charges made against him, and instruct him of the right to make a statement, if he should want to do so, which can be made at any time and as many times as he requests.
[131] Ibid., Art. 1.
[132] Ibid.
[133] For an explanation of the selection and function of the law judges, see Chapter 3.

the judge instructor in both the pre-trial and trial process was viewed as prejudicial to the accused. Thus, since 1977, the tasks of instruction and investigation have been separated from the judicial function and delegated to instructors, special personnel in the police department, who work under the supervision of the public prosecutor.[134] The two phases were combined into one, the preparatory phase, which combined all procedures preliminary to trial.

Under current criminal procedure as modified in 1994, the police instructor commences an investigation from the time the police have knowledge that a crime has been committed, either because someone has filed a complaint or the police have knowledge of the crime from other sources. When the instructor determines there is sufficient evidence of a crime and the probable identity of the author, he makes a ruling to that effect which is to be communicated immediately to the prosecutor along with the files in the case.[135] The prosecutor may at this time decide whether to maintain the action against the accused or to drop the charges.

If the accused has been arrested, the police must turn him over to the instructor within twenty-four hours or release him.[136] The instructor then has three days to determine whether there is sufficient evidence to proceed against the accused and present the case to the prosecutor, and if the accused is still in custody, make a recommendation of preventive detention.[137] The prosecutor then has three days to review the file and determine whether or not to approve the continued detention of the accused or to impose some other security measure such as a bond. Prior to the 1994 modifications, an accused could not be detained beyond 10 days without court approval of the detention. Under current law, the decision to provisionally detain an accused must be confirmed within seven days of arrest, but the decision falls solely within the discretion of the prosecutor and is not submitted to the court for approval.[138] Security measures other than provisional detention, such as a bond, may be imposed by the instructor without requiring approval of the prosecutor.

After communicating the evidence to the prosecutor, the instructor continues to develop the case through investigation to gather the evidence to be presented at trial. By law, this phase should be completed in not more than sixty days at which time the case is to be submitted to a court for a determi-

---

[134] Ley No.5 (1977) Art.105 (as amended in 1994).
[135] Ibid., Art. 106.
[136] Ibid., Art. 245.
[137] Ibid., Art. 246. Estimates of the numbers of accused held in pre-trial detention in 1987 ranged from 25 to 35 percent. Interview with Dr. Ramón de la Cruz ormer Procurator General, Havana, Cuba, December 10, 1987.
[138] Ibid., Art. 247.

nation whether there is sufficient evidence to proceed to trial. This time period may be extended to six months by the Chief Instructor[139] and may be further extended by the Attorney General upon petition justifying the delay submitted by the Chief Attorney General of the province or by the Chief of the Ministry of Interior of the province where the trial is to be held. At any time the prosecutor believes that there is insufficient evidence to demonstrate guilt, he may also dismiss charges.

Right to Defense Counsel

One of the provisions most debated among Cuban jurists has been the point of time in the process when the accused has a right to defense counsel. The pre-revolutionary procedure provided for a right to defense from the time of formal indictment, but there was no time limit set for the issuance of the indictment. Thus, although a person detained had to be brought before a judge within 24 hours of arrest for a determination whether or not to ratify a decision to detain the accused provisionally, a decision that the court had up to three days to make, the person could be held for long periods without a right to defense until the indictment issued. If the defendant had not appointed counsel at the time of indictment, the court would appoint one.

The law criminal procedure adopted in 1977 was an improvement over the prior procedures. Since that time, the right to defense counsel arises at one of two points depending on the situation of the accused: (1) when the prosecutor or instructor issues an order for provisional detention or any other precautionary measure to assure the presence of the accused at trial; or (2) when the court ratifies the indictment and opens the case for trial at the end of the preparatory phase. Alternative provisional measures for those arrested included release on signature; release with special conditions; and release on money bail. As in other civil law systems, there was no requirement that a defendant be arrested in order to be charged with a crime. He or she could be simply cited to appear to answer the charges.

From the moment that the instructor communicates to the accused the decision to impose pre-trial detention or other pre-trial measure provided by law, the accused "becomes a part of the process and may, by himself or through his defense attorney, propose proofs or evidence in his favor."[140] Thus, pursuant to modifications adopted in 1994, the right to defense counsel may not attach for up to seven days after arrest in cases where the in-

[139] Ibid., Art. 107.

[140] Ley No. 5 (1977), Art. 249 (as amended in 1994).

structor or prosecutor decides to apply provisional measures against the accused since that is the maximum time for the measure to be imposed by the prosecutor although it could occur as early as the second day after arrest.

Once appointed, defense counsel have the right to communicate immediately with and interview their client in privacy, if detained.[141] In addition, the defense lawyer may examine all of the files and evidence obtained by the instructor during the preparatory phase with the exception of specific cases involving state security designated by the prosecutor. The defense may also propose evidence and present documents in favor of his or her client. If the instructor should refuse to obtain the evidence proposed, the defense may petition the prosecutor to insist that such evidence be sought.[142] Either the defense lawyer or the accused may petition for release from provisional detention and if denied by the prosecutor may appeal to the court.[143]

In cases where no provisional measures are taken, the right to counsel does not attach until the case is certified for trial at the end of the preparatory phase. In the latter case, the defense counsel has no opportunity to propose evidence in the preparatory phase that would counter the conclusions the prosecutor presents to the court prior to the case being opened for trial. Once the case is opened for trial, the accused must appoint a defense lawyer who must respond to the written charges and propose evidence for the court's consideration at trial.

If a lawyer has not been designated by the accused within 5 days of the court's having opened the case for trial, the court will assign a defense lawyer to the accused. Since there is no office of public defender, the court requests the local *bufete* to provide a defense lawyer for the accused, and the state pays the *bufete* for these services. In cases in the municipal courts where the potential sanction is less than one year imprisonment, there is no right to a state appointed defense counsel, and apparently the majority of defendants in such cases appear in court without lawyers. The prosecutor may decide to present the case at trial or let the police instructor do so.

The unfairness of the differentiation in the right to defense during the preparatory phase has been pointed out by Cuban lawyers who note that the accused to whom some security measure is applied—whether provisional detention or bond or other measure—has greater rights than one who is not subject to such measures. The role of the defense counsel during the preparatory phase is important, if not critical, to obtaining a dismissal before the trial since it is during the preparatory phase that the prosecution devel-

141 Ibid.
142 Ibid.
143 Ibid. Art. 249, 251.

ops its case.[144] In either case, the defense counsel does not formally participate until after the prosecutor has determined whether or not to charge the accused.

In practice, a family member frequently contracts for the services of a defense lawyer from the time the accused has been arrested. Although there is no formal right to defense at this point, the lawyer may begin on his or her own to gather evidence. The lawyer might also begin to prepare arguments to oppose provisional detention in the event the prosecutor should seek detention. However, the lawyer may not formally interview the defendant or have access to the case files or propose lines of inquiry or witness testimony until the accused becomes "part of the process," that is, subject to some provisional measure or the charge is communicated to the court and the case is accepted for trial.

Today, there is virtual consensus among Cuban officials and jurists that the right to defense should attach earlier in the process; the debate has been over just how early. The proposal of the Cuban defense bar, formulated by a national commission of the ONBC in 1989 to analyze the deficiencies in the criminal procedure,[145] would require the prosecutor or instructor to charge the accused within seventy-two hours of arrest at which time the instructor or prosecutor must interview and permit the accused to make a formal declaration. The ONBC argued that the accused should have the right to have counsel present at this interview.[146] Ten years later, José Candia Ferreira, the Director of the Division of Criminal Prosecutions of the Office of the Attorney General, also argued that the defense counsel should participate in the process from the time the accused is charged.[147] Candia underscored the necessity of strengthening the role of the defense "to protect the guarantees of the process and the correct application of the law" as a means of protecting the social interest, not only the interests of the accused.[148]

---

[144] Mariano Mieres Martí, "El Abogado en la Fase Preparatoria," *Ponencias Derecho Penal*, a collection of papers presented at the National Legal Conference of the ONBC (1989), p. 55. The defense counsel has the right to establsih communication with his-her client and interview him-her in private if detained. Counsel also has the right to review the relevant police and prosecutor files, propose proofs and present documents. The lawyer may also see modification or revocation of provisional detention or other measures.

[145] The ONBC commission was comprised of eighteen members, one from each province and four others.

[146] In some cases, the ONBC suggested that the accused be permitted to represent himself *pro se*.

[147] José Candia Ferreira, "Problemas Actuales del Proceso Penal en Cuba," *Revista Cubana de Derecho*, No. 13, 1999, pp. 11-16.

[148] Ibid., p. 13.

With respect to the definition of participants in the preparatory phase, the ONBC submitted that the accused and the defense attorney as well as the victim and his or her representative should be full participants in the process, including the possibility of questioning and being questioned during the oral trial. Accordingly, the defense attorney would have the ability to intervene at any point in the process and have the right to propose evidence in favor of the accused. In light of the unsatisfactory experience many defense attorneys reported with the police instructors, the ONBC proposed that the preparatory phase be entrusted to the prosecutor who should be authorized to determine the provisional measures to be taken. They also proposed that the accused have greater rights with respect to provisional detention.[149]

It took approximately two years to develop a consensus among the various sectors on the general content of the reforms. All sectors of the penal system took part in shaping a legislative proposal. In addition to the work of the ONBC, the Cuban Society of Penal Sciences held several forums where proposals were discussed, as did the Ministry of Interior, the Supreme Court, the Office of the Attorney General and the Ministry of Justice. The *Revista Cubana del Derecho* published articles by several experts on procedural reform. At an April 1992 meeting of the Society of Penal Sciences, some of Cuba's top experts and officials met to discuss a draft of the legislation prepared for submission to the National Assembly.

However, the draft was never presented to the legislature. The reasons why it was derailed are not clear, but undoubtedly it had to do with growing concerns over the increase in crime and the lack of resources necessary to implement proposed modifications that would have placed heavy burdens on defense lawyers as well as the courts. During the early 1990s public transportation was devastated by lack of fuel and spare parts for buses requiring lawyers and judges alike to move around on bicycles. Energy shortages left courtrooms and law offices without electricity during many working hours. Further, since defense lawyers had not taken full advantage of the right to participation in the preparatory phase already permitted by law by investigating and proposing exculpatory proofs,[150] such material obstacles made it

[149] The ONBC also argued for other changes including that special procedures should be eliminated because they violate the principle of equality of persons before the law. The 1977 law provided for special procedures to be implemented in three specific instances: (1) the prosecution of members of the Political Bureau of the Party, high officials of the government and judges of the Supreme Court (Arts. 385-393); (2) presidents of the lower courts, professional and lay judges, and prosecutors (Arts. 394-397); and (3) crimes against the security of the state in exceptional cases (Arts. 398-403). Additional arguments for their elimination were that, in practice, they have not been used in Cuba and they never appeared in the laws of other socialist countries.

[150] Mariano Mieres Martí, "El Abogado en la Fase Preparatoria," *Ponencias Derecho Penal*, a collection of papers presented at the National Legal Conference of the ONBC (1989), pp. 55.

unlikely they would do better under the proposed reforms. Moreover, the changed conditions had halted, at least temporarily, the liberal reform movement in Cuban criminal law that had emerged in the 1980s.

The 1994 Modifications

Although disappointing to many, the 1994 modifications to the Code of Criminal Procedure made some improvements even if they did not "revolutionize" Cuban criminal procedure. First, consistent with the view of many, the 1994 reforms enhanced the supervisory role of the prosecutor during the preparatory phase to improve the quality of work during this phase and to better assure the procedural guarantees of the accused.[151] The preparatory phase was explicitly divided into two independent stages: the investigative and the preparatory. The former consists of the investigation of the crime by the police beginning from the moment it receives a complaint or knowledge of the possible commission of a crime and ends with the discovery and apprehension of the presumed perpetrator. The latter consists of the process of determining whether charges are to be brought and preparing the case for presentation to the court for ratification of the charges and opening the case for trial.

One of the more significant modifications adopted in 1994 is the introduction of an abbreviated process in cases in which the sanction is less than 8 years in prison and the accused is caught in the act of committing the crime or where the accused has confessed and there is other evidence clearly indicating the participation of the accused in a criminal act.[152] In such cases, the prosecutor will determine within 72 hours of having received the file whether or not to initiate an abbreviated procedure and will direct the instructor to complete the necessary steps and procedures within 20 days.[153] The prosecutor may also order that no further proofs are necessary and present the case immediately to the court for ratification of the charges.[154] Once the prosecutor has determined that the case is one to be dealt with by this abbreviated procedure, he must immediately advise the accused of this fact.[155] From this point the accused becomes a part of the process and has

---

[151] Decreto Ley No. 151 (1994), Art. 105.

[152] Ibid., Arts. 481-482. For an extensive analysis of this procedure see José Candia Ferreira, "El Procedimiento Abreviado en el Derecho Procesal Cubano," in *Temas Sobre el Proceso Penal* (Havana, Cuba: Prensa Latina, 1998), pp. 14-96.

[153] Ibid., Art. 484.

[154] Ibid.

[155] Ibid.

the right to defense counsel who must propose lines of investigation within 48 hours.[156]

Once the case is presented by the prosecutor to the court, the court has three days in which to review the file and decide whether use of the abbreviated procedure is appropriate. If the case proceeds pursuant to this procedure, then the accused must appoint a defense lawyer within 48 hours if he or she hasn't already done so. In the event, the accused does not name a defense lawyer, the court will appoint one.[157] The Defense has 3 days from the time the court opens the case or from the time the defense counsel is appointed to present its arguments and conclusions based on the evidence shown by the files.

Although Cuba does not permit "plea bargaining," that is a negotiation between the defense and the prosecution over the charges, the defense can declare to the court its agreement with the charge formulated by the prosecutor, leaving only the issue of sentencing for argument before the court.[158] The court, which has already reviewed the file and evidence proposed to support the charge, will then dispense with the trial of the facts and hear arguments relevant to sentencing. Thus, only in cases where the maximum sentence is 8 years imprisonment may the accused accept the charges and vitiate the necessity of a trial of the facts before the court.

Cuban law permits two types of appeals: what is called an appeal and an appellate process known as *casación*. The former allows the defendant to seek a new trial at the next highest judicial level during which the court hears evidence and makes a determination of guilt and sentencing. The decision of the lower court is suspended during the appeal process. *Casación* is akin to appellate procedure in the United States where the argument is that the lower court made an error of law in the procedure. The 1994 modifications eliminated some of the unnecessary formalities and paperwork plaguing the appeal process which had caused long delays in obtaining a remedy.

Thus, Cuba has taken some important steps to improve its criminal procedure to make it more efficient and fair to the accused. Although these steps fell short of the objectives sought at the beginning of the decade, the process of reform has not ended. The commission appointed in 2002 to draft a new criminal code will analyze and present a proposal for a new code of criminal procedure as well. Further modifications await consensus among the sectors involved.

---

[156] Ibid., Art. 485.
[157] Ibid., Art. 487.
[158] Ibid.

IV. PRISONS

Consistent with the reforms in criminal justice, including the expansion of the opportunities to apply alternative sentences, considerable attention has been paid to the rehabilitative function of incarceration. Cuba has both maximum and minimum security facilities. At Combinado del Este, one of the newer maximum security prisons located outside Havana, prisoners are housed in units holding 600-800 inmates. Each unit contains dormitories with approximately fourteen to twenty inmates to a cell, sleeping in double bunk beds. Prisoners have space for personal belongings such as books, pictures, etc. Although the space is quite small allowing little room to move about in the dormitories, inmates spend little time in these quarters. They spend the entire day either at work, recreation, classes or meals. Each unit has a dining room, classrooms, a library, and a common lounge area where there is a television set.

Some prisons are known to be rougher than others because of the prison population, for example, Kilo 7 in Camagüey province. Others offer extremely supportive environments such as Melena del Sur in Havana Province, where a local chapter of the Union of Writers and Artists provides programs for prisoners interested in the arts. In Combinado del Este, prisoners have related that the relationship between inmates and guards is not tense, although there are occasional blows from guards, but not beatings.[159] Guards do not carry firearms. Inmates also report occasional fights between prisoners over personal differences.

The Cuban prison system also includes work farms (*granjas*) where those convicted of minor offenses or deemed eligible for early release live in open barracks with minimum security. These farms have no walls or gates. The prisoners engage in agricultural work, much of which provides food for the prison system. Some are engaged in experimental hydroponic cultivation. Prisoners in these facilities often have furlough privileges and go home on weekends to visit their families. In addition, there are two women's prisons in Cuba.

Innovative programs for counseling, education and training are employed in the prison system which takes an individualized approach to rehabilitation. After an initial orientation program, each new prisoner is assigned to a group—called a detachment—of approximately eighty inmates supervised by a rehabilitation counselor. Civilians and prison officials also work directly with the prisoners. The prisoner is provided educational programs in basic learning skills, if needed, and courses in history and the sci-

---

[159] National Lawyers Guild, *Criminal Justice in Cuba* (New York: National Lawyers Guild, 1987), p. 14.

ences. Prisoners who have the requisite education may work as teachers within the prison. There are also a variety of cultural and sports activities.

With the exception of prisoners considered violent or dangerous, each prisoner is expected to work, although it is not obligatory, and everyone is expected to learn a trade if he or she does not already have one. At Aguica, a maximum security prison for men in Matanzas Province, the major enterprise is the construction of prefabricated parts for housing. There is also work in carpentry and crafts. Combinado del Este also has several enterprises including one in leathercraft. About 10 percent of the prisoners work outside the prison in areas such as maintenance, carpentry or electrical work.

Cuban inmates who engage in productive work are paid the same wage as workers on the outside doing comparable work whether it be construction work, repair work or handcrafts. In this way, inmates can continue to assist their families or save money for themselves for use later on. The prisoners pay one-third of their salary to the prison administration to cover costs of their food and maintenance. This is a significant improvement over the pre-revolutionary system, which made work obligatory and gave none of the income to the prisoner.

Moreover, the system encourages family contact. When a prisoner first enters the prison, his or her family is interviewed by the head of the prison. The prisoner's counselor is also supposed to convene regular meetings with the family and inmate to discuss the inmate's progress. Visits are normally scheduled monthly. Families and friends can be seen visiting every day of the week. At Aguica, they meet inmates in a large open pavilion with long tables. Even in maximum security prisons, such as Combinado del Este, there are no glass or other barriers between them, allowing physical contact `between inmates and visitors. Guards are present, but do not hover over the inmates or visitors.

Another striking feature, which is unheard of in most U.S. prisons, is the general right to conjugal visits. Prisoners (both men and women) are normally permitted three-hour conjugal visits every three to four months and some more frequently. Special quarters--pavilions--are provided for these visits. The rooms are separate and private and look much like normal bedrooms—each brightly decorated with a double bed, private bathroom and a small kitchen. Combinado del Este has twenty-six such rooms. Denial of conjugal visits is frequently used as punishment when an inmate violates prison rules.

Prisons also provide comprehensive medical care to all inmates, including dental services. Every prison of significant size, such as Aguica and Combinado del Este, has a hospital that is clean and well equipped. The hospital at Combinado del Este has 200 beds and three operating rooms for general surgery. In addition, the prison also has its own pharmacy, an area for out-patient services and an area for physical therapy. The prison also has dental care facilities with a full complement of equipment. Smaller prisons have infirmary facilities, and prisoners are transferred to hospitals when necessary.

Until the late 1980s, physical conditions at some of Cuba's maximum security prisons were below international standards in some aspects. But as a result of improvements and the decrease in prison population, which permitted the closure of some of the older prisons, physical conditions improved markedly. In the late 1980s, Cuba's prisons were operated well below capacity and some were being phased out. For example, Aguica, built in the mid-1960s to accommodate 1000 inmates, housed approximately 700-800 male prisoners in 1987. Combinado del Este, which has three times the capacity of Aguica, was also operating below capacity in 1987 with a population of approximately 2500. Officials report that the prison population in Cuba in the first half of 1987 numbered approximately 40,000. After implementation of sentence reduction and conditional release policies, it was reduced to about 25,000 to 30,000.

In the mid-1980s, Cuba's prisons became a focal point of accusations of human rights abuses. Some anti-Castro groups made exaggerated allegations about the number of prisons and prisoners in Cuba. Some of these estimates ranged as high as 100,000 to 200,000 prisoners supposedly being kept in more than 200 identified installations. In 1988, a team of British journalists working on a film documentary attempted to find the alleged prisons and found that many did not exist, calling into question the exaggerated claims of these critics.

In 1987, Cuban authorities began to let outsiders visit the prisons. A number of delegations of U.S. lawyers and researchers did visit as did a delegation from Amnesty International. These delegations found no widespread complaints from common prisoners about their treatment in the prisons.[160] As a result of Amnesty's review of the Cuban prisons, the Cuban authorities took measures to bring all prisons up to international standards. For example, Combinado del Este has isolation or punishment cells located in a building separate from the other dormitories. These cells are used for non-political prisoners who have committed acts of violence in prison. The

---

[160] See, for example, Amnesty International, *Cuba: Recent Developments Affecting the Situation of Political Prisoners and the Use of the Death Penalty* (New York: Amnesty International, 1988); Institute for Policy Studies, Preliminary Report: Cuban Prisons (Washington, D.C.: Institute for Policy Studies, 1988); National Lawyers Guild, *Criminal Justice in Cuba.* A similar tour of U.S. prisons by Cuban authorities was barred by the State Department, which refused to grant visas to a delegation invited by the Institute for Policy Studies in Washington, D.C., as reciprocation for permission granted by Cuban authorities to visit the island's prisons.

attachment contained 140 single cells that were small, rectangular rooms. In May 1988, the cells were closed for renovation to bring them up to international norms. Additional ventilation was added as well as increased artificial light to augment the natural light that reaches each cell.

The prison system is administered by the Ministry of Interior. The Office of the Attorney General, however, has oversight authority to assure that the prisons follow the law and respect prisoner rights. A representative of the Attorney General's office, whose responsibility it is to inspect prison conditions and to hear and investigate prisoner complaints, is attached to each prison. In addition, inmates have their own governing bodies. Each detachment elects a council that expresses the concerns of the detachment to the prison management. Prisoners who commit crimes while in prison are charged and tried in the same manner and in the same courts as those who commit crimes outside of prison. They also have the same entitlement to a defense attorney.

Reports of mistreatment have come primarily from prisoners who were convicted for crimes against the security of the state, particularly those who fought against the regime in the 1960s and who refused to work or accept other prison programs. The major group of such prisoners was known as the *plantados*, the planted ones, because of their resistance. The *plantados* rejected the authority of the Cuban government, engaging in a number of hunger strikes and refusing to wear normal prison garments.

Until the mid-1980s, when the small number remaining were moved to the more modern facility at Combinado del Este, most *plantados* were kept at the century-old Boniato prison on the east coast of the country. There have been several written accounts of mistreatment of these prisoners, especially at Boniato. Even among these prisoners, however, the complaints date primarily to the 1960s and 1970s. When it visited Cuba in 1987, Amnesty International reported on information it received from *plantados*. Although Amnesty cited incidents of ill-treatment, it found no evidence to substantiate charges of torture.[161]

According to prison officials, all prisoners convicted of crimes against the security of the state are now housed at Combinado del Este. In the mid-1980s, partly as a result of the personal intervention of French author Regis Debray, Jesse Jackson and others, Cuba began releasing political prisoners, including the *plantados*. Officials reported that there were approximately

---

[161] Amnesty International, *Cuba: Political Imprisonment* (1988), pp. 150-154. In 1986, treatment of prisoners in Cuba had become a major focus of anti-Cuban political movements. In February 1987, the United States used the issue to attempt, but failed, to obtain censure of Cuba by the United Nations Human Rights Commission for what it characterized as outrageous violations.

1,000 political prisoners in June 1987, including about fifty to sixty *plantados*; by 1990 all long-term political prisoners had been released.

Estimates on the numbers of political prisoners have always varied. Generally, those convicted of acts of violence are not considered political prisoners under international conventions. In 1993, Cuba contended that there are about 200 prisoners who had committed crimes against state security, including acts of sabotage.

Prisoners who do not resist or habitually violate prison regulations are integrated with the regular prison population during daily activities. One former prisoner, who chose to stay in Cuba after being released from prison in 1987, agreed to a private interview that was arranged through a neighbor.[162] Having left Cuba during the 1980 Mariel boat lift, he settled in Miami for a short while before becoming a member of Alpha 66, a known anti-Castro group based in Miami that has engaged in armed attacks against Cuba. In 1980, the former prisoner had been the driver of the boat that carried four saboteurs in an operation organized by Alpha 66 to infiltrate Cuba. He was caught, convicted and sentenced to 20 years in prison but released after seven years for good behavior. He reported that he was well treated and was unaware of any mistreatment or abuse of any other political prisoner. Upon release he was given a job and now resides with his family in Cuba.

As with every other sphere of Cuban life, the prisons are affected by the current economic crisis. Shortages of materials and fuel affect prison conditions and services, as well as the quality of food. Moreover, if criminal activity continues to increase, the prisons may be once again filled to capacity putting further strain on the system. Given the other pressing priorities of the government, it is unlikely that scarce resources will be allocated to continue to improve prison conditions at this time.

In an effort to reduce incarceration, in 2001, the government increased its efforts to prevent delinquency and to cut recidivism. Unemployed youth are encouraged to enroll in special education programs to learn marketable skills, like computer technology. The educational programs in prisons have also been expanded and improved. Moreover, first offenders as well as those convicted of minor offenses are generally given alternatives to incarceration, thus avoiding incarceration.

[162] Interview with Luís González, Jaimanitas, Cuba, June 10, 1988.

V. CONCLUSION

With respect to criminal justice, the Cuban revolution vastly improved the system it inherited, and Cuba has come a long way since 1959 and the turbulent 1960s. Now in its fifth decade, the Cuban revolution has progressively reformed and modernized its criminal law and procedure. Reform of the written law, however, cannot correct deficiencies without substantial efforts to raise the level of competency and commitment of not only the criminal defense bar, but of the judiciary, the prosecutors and the police. Cuba has made substantial strides towards that goal. Although there is much room for improvement, there are few examples in Latin America where the criminal justice system is as fair and efficient as it is today in Cuba.

Chapter 8

PRIVATE PROPERTY

Fundamental change in property relations was a goal of the revolution well before it was openly declared to be socialist. In his 1953 courtroom defense of himself and others who took part in the attack on the Moncada Barracks, Castro described five revolutionary laws which would have been declared had the assault succeeded. The first would have reinstated the 1940 Constitution. The other four had profound implications for specific property rights: The second would have given land to "tenant and sub-tenant farmers, lessees, sharecroppers and squatters;" the third would have granted "workers the right to share in thirty percent of the profits" of all large commercial enterprises; the fourth would have granted "sugar planters the right to share fifty-five percent of the sugar production;" and the fifth would have confiscated "all the holdings and ill-gotten gains of those who had committed frauds during previous regimes."[1] This was not all. Castro declared that these measures would be followed by further agrarian reform as well as the nationalization of utilities, reductions in rent and massive construction of public housing.[2]

Once in power, the revolutionaries moved quickly to implement some of these objectives. Fulfilling promises of agrarian reform made in the 1940 Constitution,[3] the agrarian reform acts of 1959 and 1963 targeted large agri-

---

[1] Fidel Castro, *History Will Absolve Me* (New York: Center for Cuban Studies, undated), pp. 25-26.

[2] Ibid., pp. 127, 131.

[3] Constitución de la República (1940), Art. 90. The article reads:

> Latifundio are prohibited, and in order to dissolve them, the Law will establish the maximum size of property which each person or entity may possess for each kind of use to which land can be put.
>
> The Law will strictly limit the acquisition and possession of land by foreign persons or companies and will take measures which will tend to revert foreign land holding to Cubans.

cultural landholdings for expropriation and redistribution. Further, in the early months of 1959, landlords were prevented from evicting delinquent tenants,[4] and in 1960 all commercialization of housing was prohibited.[5] At the same time, whether the result of conflict or design, all major industries and oil refineries were nationalized. In early 1961, Castro declared the socialist character of the revolution, and by the end of the decade all the means of production, with the exception of small farms, were in state hands.

Yet not all private property was socialized by the Cuban revolution. Unlike the Soviet Union, which eventually eliminated all private farm holdings,[6] Cuba specifically recognized rights of small private farmers to own and work their land within the socialist system.[7] Moreover, individual ownership of primary and vacation homes has been promoted,[8] and individual rights to other forms of personal property protected.[9] Further, while most commercial enterprises were nationalized, some individual service businesses were tolerated as long as no one other than immediate family members was employed.[10] In 1993, the government expanded the possibilities for self-employment.[11] The socialist regime also created property rights in agricultural cooperatives formed after the revolution.

Imposition of a Cuban-styled socialist economy was highly experimental at first, and only in the mid-1970s did the Cubans adopt models and formulas from the Soviet Union. Even then, Cuba continued its own innovations in housing, agricultural and other private property rights. Thus, the development of property law has not always followed a smooth progression, undergoing continuous, sometimes abrupt, modification.

If there has been a unifying principle guiding the experimentation, it is that private property should always be used in ways which serve social goals and not private enrichment. For example, rights to agricultural property depend on its productive use, and housing law is based primarily on recognition of its important social function as opposed to its commercial or invest-

---

[4] Jill Hamburg, "Cuban Housing Policy," in Sandor Halebsky and John Kirk, eds., *Transformation and Struggle* (New York: Praeger, 1990), p. 235.

[5] Ley No.60 (Ley de Reforma Urbana), *Gaceta Oficial Ext.,* No.23, October 14, 1960.

[6] George M. Armstrong, Jr., *The Soviet Law of Property* (The Hague: Martinus Nijhoff, 1983), pp. 51-52.

[7] Both the 1976 and 1992 Constitutions contain provisions recognizing the right of small farmers to own their lands and other means and implements of production. See Articles 20 and 19 respectively.

[8] Ley No. 65 (Ley General de la Vivienda), Art. 2,*Gaceta Oficial Ext.*, No.3, February 8, 1989.

[9] Constitución (1992), Art. 21. This is virtually identical to Article 22 of the 1976 Constitution.

[10] Ibid.

[11] See Chapter nine, "Economic Law."

ment value. Further, inheritance and property transfer laws take into account the needs of those dependant on the testator or owner whether closely related or not, and the division of marital property is also influenced by social concerns.[12] Thus, rights to private property in Cuba continue to exist but within a sphere of use and enjoyment bounded by social, economic and political considerations. This is still true today, even though foreign investvestment is encouraged and there are new opportunities for individual economic activity. Regulations as well as new tax laws provide a source of funding for universal social benefits and prevent the accumulation of individual wealth or the exploitation of resources for private benefit by Cuban nationals.

Although personal property law has been the object of continual analysis and adjustment, the post-1989 economic crisis compelled dramatic changes in commercial property law in order for Cuba to integrate into the international market and obtain needed capital investment. The law governing commercial enterprises, including joint ventures with foreign companies, is discussed in Chapter Nine. The present chapter focuses on individual property relations and interests, specifically housing, personal property, and agricultural property. Inevitably, however, changes in the law affecting socialized property will have consequences for private property as well.

I. HOUSING

Housing law in Cuba has been guided by the social objective of providing shelter to all citizens. Individual rights to housing and to home ownership, although protected and promoted, are limited by this goal as well as a policy that eschews the enhancement of personal property interests through investment or speculation. The principle is expressed in the introduction to the second General Law on Housing adopted in 1988:

> Personal property in housing must be understood . . . essentially as a right to enjoyment of the house by the owner and his/her family, without having to pay anything after paying its price, but in no case can this right of personal property in the house become a mechanism of enrichment or exploitation.[13]

---

[12] See Chapter six, "Family Law."

[13] Ley No. 65 (1989), Preamble.

Cuban citizens may own both a primary resident and a vacation home, but no more. In sum, "housing is to live in, not to make a living from."[14]

Housing disparities in pre-revolutionary Cuba dramatically illustrated the contrast between the haves and the have-nots. The worst conditions were in the rural areas where more than four-fifths lived in thatched-roof shacks with dirt floors, and less than 10 percent had electricity or plumbing.[15] Although better than rural housing, more than half of urban dwellings were considered substandard and lacked complete sanitary facilities.[16] Despite pre-revolutionary laws providing for rent control, landlords found ways to circumvent restrictions, and new housing development in the 1950s centered on condominiums for which mortgage holders charged usurious rates.[17]

The eradication of profiteering and speculation in housing was one of the first items on the revolutionary government's agenda in 1959. Within the first months, the government prohibited evictions and ordered the reduction of rents by 30 to 50 percent, depending on the income of the lessee.[18] Other measures encouraged individual home construction such as tax exemptions for newly constructed owner-occupied homes.[19] Finally, the Urban Reform Law of October 14, 1960, prohibited all private rental housing, converting housing into a public service and making the state the primary landlord. Tenants continued to pay reduced rents to the state for a period of time ranging from five to twenty years depending on the age of the building, after which time they became the owners of their dwellings. Most landlords were permitted to retain their own homes and received monthly payments from the state in compensation for the loss of their investment property.[20]

The government, however, did not nationalize private housing, nor did it embark on any program of housing redistribution. Rather, those who remained in Cuba were entitled to maintain ownership of their homes regardless of size. The homes of those who left Cuba, however, were considered abandoned and were confiscated and either given to legal occupants, sold or rented to other families or converted to social or government uses.[21] The

---

[14] Rodolfo Dávalos Fernández, *La Nueva Ley General de la Vivienda* (Havana: Editorial de Ciencias Sociales, 1989), p. 2.

[15] Jill Hamburg, *Under Construction* (New York: Center for Cuban Studies, undated), p. 2.

[16] Ibid.

[17] Ibid.

[18] Hamburg, "Cuban Housing Policy," p. 235.

[19] Hamburg, *Under Construction*, p. 3.

[20] Ibid.

[21] Ley No. 989 (Sobre la Nacionalización mediante Confiscación a favor del Estado Cubano de los Bienes y Derechos de los que se ausenten con carácter definitivo del país), *Gaceta Oficial*, No. 237, December 6, 1961. Dávalos Fernández, pp. 216-223.

housing policy set forth in the Urban Reform Law projected a second stage of implementation during which the government would begin to build housing and lease it to citizens who would pay no more than 10 percent of family income.[22] The idealism of the time was reflected in the expressed goal of a third projected stage whereby the state would provide free housing to all.[23]

Despite efforts that have been made, the government has not been able to keep up with the demand for housing, particularly in urban areas, a point of considerable frustration for the population. Virtually all of the substandard rural housing has been replaced, but shortages and deteriorating housing stock in the cities has remained a serious problem that has been exacerbated since the economic crisis of the 1990s. Thus, although the constitutional guarantees of economic and social rights such as employment, health and education have been substantially realized,[24] the state has not yet been able to guarantee the right to housing. Recognizing the inability of the government to fulfill such a pledge, the Constitution states that the "socialist state . . . strives to provide each family a comfortable place to live."[25]

In the 1980s, the government embarked on a new housing policy, one that was intended to stimulate individual initiative in both rehabilitation and new housing construction. The General Housing Law adopted in 1984 paved the way for a private housing market in which individual owners could freely sell primary and vacation homes. In addition, the law permitted individuals to borrow funds and obtain materials for new construction and remodeling.[26] Further, the law simplified procedures to encourage those who continued to rent their homes or apartments from the government to convert their tenancy into ownership.

The 1984 law reflected the contemporary liberalization of other market mechanisms in Cuba, including the introduction of farmers' markets where small farmers could sell surplus produce at unregulated prices.[27] In operation, the measures designed to stimulate home improvement and construction almost immediately led to speculation and black marketeering in housing.[28] Unregulated, housing prices soared. Within two years, officials in the National Housing Institute began to propose revisions to the 1984 law to deal with the distortions taking place in the housing market. A commission

---

[22] Ley No. 60 (1960), Art. 1.

[23] Ibid.

[24] Constitución (1992), Art. 8(b). The same provision appeared in the 1976 Constitution.

[25] Ibid., Art. 8(c).

[26] Ley No. 48 (Ley General de la Vivienda), Arts. 38, 60-63, *Gaceta Oficial Ext.*, No.22, December 31, 1984.

[27] Medea Benjamin, Joseph Collins and Michael Scott, *No Free Lunch* (San Francisco: Institute for Food and Development Policy, 1984), pp. 66-80.

[28] Dávalos Fernández, p. 27.

was formed composed of representatives of the National Housing Institute, the Ministry of Justice, the Courts, the Office of the Attorney General, the National Assembly and the Council of Ministers.[29] As a result, in 1988, the National Assembly adopted a new law that eliminated private speculation without reducing private ownership. Similarly, the farmers' market was also eliminated around the same time because it had produced distortions in food production and a cadre of middlemen who were profiting at the expense of consumers.[30]

The new housing law reorganized the entire structure of the previous statute. In contrast to the 1984 law, which emphasized sale and transfer of ownership, the new statute gave primary consideration to legal issues surrounding construction. After setting forth general principles, the law begins with sections devoted to regulation of the microbrigades that had become the chief force in housing construction.[31] The microbrigades are made up of workers assigned from different work centers. Employees of the centers that contribute workers to the microbrigades have a say in decisions regarding the distribution of the housing built.

Second, the law deals with the rights and regulations governing individual construction and rehabilitation.[32] Cubans who construct their own homes gain title to and retain them as long as they do not have another primary residence. The significance of individual initiative is seen in the fact that more than two-thirds of housing built between 1959 and 1990 was built by individual efforts as opposed to public projects.[33] Such private building, however, is regulated. The builder must obtain a building permit for all construction projects, and materials and equipment can be legally obtained only from authorized state agencies.[34] The builder may contract for labor with state agencies or hire workers who are self-employed.[35] Construction

---

[29] Interview with Rodolfo Dávalos Fernández, then Legal Director of the National Housing Institute of Cuba, Havana, March 24, 1989.

[30] The reasons given for elimination of the farmers markets vary. The government claimed it was closed down because of price gouging as well as development of a corrupt merchant class of brokers. Castro also contended that some small farmers were using state resources, particularly fertilizer, to produce crops for the private market instead of for the crops contracted to the state. See debate at the Fourth Congress of the Cuban Communist Party, October 10-14, 1991, published in *Este es el Congreso Más Democrático* (Havana: Editora Política, 1991), pp. 111-117. Still another reason put forth was its negative impact on the cooperatives whose members argued for its elimination at the May 1986 meeting of ANAP. Jean Stubbs, "Gender Issues in Contemporary Cuban Tobacco Farming," *World Development*, Vol. 15, No. 1, 1987, p. 52.

[31] Ley No.65 (1989), Art. 8, *et seq.*

[32] Ibid., Art. 13, *et seq.*

[33] Hamburg, "Cuban Housing Policy," p. 238.

[34] Ley No.65 (1989), Art. 13.

[35] Ibid.

is financed by the Popular Savings Bank, and the loan is considered a personal debt, unsecured by the home.[36] The bank may require, however, that other adult inhabitants co-sign the loan or that the debtor have someone else guarantee the loan.[37]

State constructed housing is transferred through sale to individuals by the Popular Savings Bank.[38] Prices of newly constructed homes are based on square footage, location and amenities such as gardens.[39] The price is amortized over a period ranging from fifteen to twenty years, and buyers make monthly payments to the bank. Other adults who live with the buyer at the time of purchase are considered to be co-debtors.[40] Title passes upon full payment, which can be accelerated if the buyer so chooses.[41]

Because the main purpose of the policy is to assure that individuals and families have adequate housing, the state is not interested in dispossessing a home owner who has defaulted on payments either for construction or purchase loans. Since the loan is considered unsecured personal debt, failure to repay does not result in foreclosure but rather attachment of the salary of the purchaser-debtor or of the co-debtors.[42] Alternatively, the bank can renegotiate the loan to reduce the monthly payments and stretch out the amortization period.[43] Even in the event that no suitable arrangement can be made for payment, the bank will not foreclose, but will seek attachment of other property of the debtor. Only in the rare case that there is no other recourse and the debtor fails to make payments for three months, will he or she lose the right to purchase the house and be converted into a lessee of the state.[44] Failure to pay rent, however, can result in the occupancy being declared illegal,[45] but even in that case, the remedy would generally be removal to other, perhaps less desirable, housing.[46] Policy considerations reject a result that would leave a debtor or any illegal occupant living on the street except in cases of flagrant violation of the law.[47]

An interesting question unanswered both by the statute and commentators is whether the co-debtors living in the home who are called upon to pay the debt thereby acquire any ownership interest in the property. Since these

---

[36] Ibid., Art. 33.
[37] Ibid., Art. 35.
[38] Ibid., Art. 41.
[39] Ibid., Art. 42.
[40] Ibid., Art. 41.
[41] Ibid., Art. 45.
[42] Ibid., Art. 35.
[43] Ibid., Art. 43.
[44] Ibid., Art. 44.
[45] Ibid.
[46] Ibid., Art. 112.
[47] Ibid., Art. 115.

persons are generally related to the owner and have lived in the dwelling, they may have already acquired some tangible interest in occupancy as discussed below, but it is not clear whether they gain any equity interest in the home. Thus, if the co-debtor is not an occupant or heir, he or she may have no legal property interest in the dwelling and may be left with an uncollectible debt against the purchaser in default.

Another initiative that looked to private arrangements as a way of alleviating the housing shortage was found in Article 74 which permitted those who have title or the lease to their homes to rent rooms.[48] In 1997, four years after the legalization of the use of hard currency, Article 74 was amended to permit Cubans to rent rooms and entire apartments in hard currency.[49] This legislation regulated an existing situation: many Cubans had begun renting rooms to foreign tourists and to Cubans visiting from the provinces or looking to install themselves in Havana. The lessors pay a fairly steep tax to be paid in US dollars or pesos depending on the currency charged to the lessee.[50]

Renters under such private agreements have no rights arising from their tenancy other than what is part of their contract with the lessor. However, once giving someone permission to occupy a room in the house, the owner may have difficulty removing the tenant because the law does not make it easy to evict tenants. If the tenant does not leave within thirty days of notice to do so, the owner may apply to the courts for an attachment of salary of up to 30 percent.[51] If the tenant has not left after three months the attachment may be increased to 50 percent of income.[52] Only in the case of clear anti-social conduct will the authorities intervene to forcibly remove the unwanted tenant,[53] who will be relocated to another dwelling.[54] However, it is not at all clear what recourse the lessor might have against a tourist who skips without paying.

Although most tenants generally occupy the property at the will of the owner and have little protection, certain kinds of occupants receive special legal protection. Thus, the owner cannot evict close relatives, a mother with one or more children fathered by the owner or who has lived in the house for

---

[48] Ibid., Art. 64.

[49] Decreto Ley No. 171(Sobre el arrendamiento de viviendas, habitaciones o espacios), Art. 1, *Gaceta Oficial Ext.*, No.3, May 15, 1997. Rooms and apartments may only be rented for residential purposes.

[50] Resolución No. 20 (Ministry of Finance and Prices), May 22, 1997. For example, the tax per room in tourist areas is $200 per month. In 2002, most rooms in these areas rented for $25 to $35 (US) a night yielding a comparatively substantial income after taxes.

[51] Ley No.65 (1989), Art. 64.

[52] Ibid.

[53] Ibid.

[54] Ibid., Art. 112.

three or more years, elderly persons who have lived in the house for three or more years or anyone else whose eviction might be considered inhumane.[55]

A Nation of Homeowners

Cuba is a nation of homeowners. By 1984, more than half of the 2.5 million Cuban homes and apartments were owner occupied. Between 1984 and the passage of the new law in 1988, more than 750,000 additional homes were converted from rental to individual ownership.[56] Thus, the vast majority of Cubans now have equity in their homes and may exchange, sell and bequeath them. In order to eliminate the speculation that resulted from the 1984 law, the new statute provides that all sales must be authorized by the Provincial Housing Office, which has the right to purchase the house at the legally established price.[57] Parties to an illegal transfer of housing are punishable under the criminal law by three months to one year in prison and/or a fine.[58]

Because the transfer of ownership through sale may be cumbersome and restricted by regulations, most owners transfer homes through a popular process known as permutas (exchanges), which may be bilateral or multilateral. People wanting to move try to find someone else who wants to swap their apartment or home. For example, a single, elderly person may wish to exchange a large third-floor apartment for a smaller ground floor apartment in a certain neighborhood. Sometimes, the transaction may require multiple, simultaneous transactions in which owner A moves to B's apartment who moves to C's apartment who moves to A's. A popular Cuban movie made in the mid-1980s, entitled "Se Permuta," treats the subject with biting wit and satire. With the closure of the classified advertising section of the popular monthly publication Opina, advertisement is done through word of mouth and by posting a sign outside the front door. In 1988 there were approximately 20,000 such exchanges.[59]

Exchanges must be formalized in writing by a notary. Those who exchange their homes do not automatically exchange their debt liability and generally remain responsible for continuing to make any outstanding pay-

---

55 Ibid., Art. 65.
56 Interview with Dávalos Fernández.
57 Ley No.65 (1989), Art. 70.
58 Código Penal (1987), Art. 231.
59 A. Shelton, "Acerca del Proyecto de Ley General de la Vivienda (I)," *Granma*, December 17, 1988, p. 2.

ments to the bank.[60] They may, however, apply to the bank to have the obligation transferred partially or in full to the new owner where the swap was unequal in value. Further, an exchange may be prohibited if it is done for financial gain or if it might cause injury to the same classes of inhabitants protected from eviction—mothers, children, the elderly, etc.[61] In exceptional cases, depending on the size and structure, houses also may be divided or joined.[62]

Despite these regulations on exchanges, since 1993 many who had access to considerable sums of money from relatives living abroad[63] began to acquire new homes by making payments under the table. Indeed, such payments were common, especially for housing in better neighborhoods. Such purchases are illegal and, if detected, can result in fines as well as loss of the housing acquired. There have been reports that some foreigners have "purchased" homes putting title in the name of a Cuban citizen since foreigners cannot obtain title to housing except for specially built condominiums. Not only are such deals illegal, but even if undetected the "purchaser" takes great risk since he or she is not the title holder and has no recourse against the person in whose name title was placed.

Although dwellings may be bequeathed by will, the law sets out complicated inheritance rules of inheritance designed primarily to protect the rights of heirs or others who have occupied the house for a substantial period of time prior to the testator's death and continue living there.[64] Thus, an heir who has not lived in the house at the time of the testator's death may not claim a right to occupy the house unless it is unoccupied. Such heirs, however, have a right to compensation from the occupants for the value of their inheritance. If someone who inherits a house already owns another house, he or she must sell one of them since no one can have more than one primary dwelling. If the owner dies intestate, title to the house will go first to those heirs who occupy the house or, if unoccupied, to heirs according to succession provided by law.[65] In addition to the duty to compensate the other heirs, those who receive title acquire any debt outstanding to the bank related to the purchase or construction of the house.[66]

The complexity of the law and the unsatisfied demand for housing produces tens of thousands of claims and disputes annually that are resolved by

---

[60] Ley No.65 (1989), Art. 68.
[61] Ibid., Art. 69.
[62] Ibid., Art. 73.
[63] Soon after the Cuban government legalized the use of the US dollar as currency parallel to the Cuban peso in 1993, many Cubans began to receive substantial sums of money from relatives.
[64] Ibid., Art. 78.
[65] Ibid., Art. 77
[66] Ibid., Art. 79.

administrative procedures. The process of bringing a complaint is fairly informal and may take the form of a simple letter setting forth the facts.[67] Complaints are processed by Municipal Housing Institutes, of which there are 168 in the country. One of the approximately 400 lawyers working in these institutes will review the complaint and seek clarification or further information as deemed necessary. The lawyer then submits the file to the director of the institute who makes the final decision. If any of the parties is not satisfied with the decision, he or she can appeal to the provincial court. The court does not simply review the decision of the institute, it also reviews the entire case de novo and makes an independent decision.

According to Rodolfo Dávalos Fernández, former legal director of the National Housing Institute (INV), there were more than 100,000 claims filed in the first year.[68] Only about 10 percent of the cases are appealed, but that represents a significant number of cases appealed to the courts.[69] There is no fee for filing a complaint with the housing institute, but anyone seeking an appeal must contract a lawyer from one of the bufetes and pay the required fees.

In the case of someone who has been declared an illegal occupant, however, there is no right of appeal to the courts.[70] The determination is made in the first instance by the municipal housing office, and the defendant in the proceeding may seek review of that decision by the president of the National Housing Institute whose decision is final. The review process represents an improvement. Prior to 1986, there was no review of the municipal decision at all.[71] As noted previously, however, anyone declared an illegal occupant for any of the reasons set forth in the statute will not be put out on the street. Rather, he or she will be relocated, and, further, will be entitled to acquire title to the new dwelling if he or she so chooses. Even given the generosity of the law, a lawyer at the *bufete colectivo* in Sagua la Grande argues forcefully that administrative review is insufficient in many cases involving housing matters.[72]

Because the law has created some confusion and uncertainty with regard to rights, the newspaper *Trabajadores* publishes a regular column explaining various provisions of the law in response to letters from readers. In addition, after the law went into effect in 1988, the National Union of Jurists

---

[67] Interview with Rodolfo Dávalos Fernández.
[68] Ibid.
[69] Ibid.
[70] Ley No.65 (1989), Art. 111.
[71] Orestes Rodríguez Reves, "La Ocupación Ilícita de Viviendas. Medios de Impugnación," *Ponencias Derecho Económico, Agrario y Administrativo* (Havana: Organización Nacional de Bufetes Colectivos, 1989), p. 149.
[72] Ibid.

of Cuba sponsored a program of free consultations for citizens, two nights a month. Dozens of people showed up to have questions answered.

Neither changes in the law, nor construction efforts have solved the housing shortage in Cuba. Indeed, the housing situation has substantially worsened since 1990. The economic crisis virtually halted new construction in urban areas as well as impeded needed repairs from 1990-1993,[73] leading to further deterioration of existing housing stock. Since then, there have been substantial efforts to resume construction and repair existing housing, but recovery and advancement are an uphill battle.

Fortunately for Cuba, its rural and urban policies saved the country for many years from the problems related to large-scale migration to the cities that afflict almost every other Latin American country. Between 1970 and 1981, Cuba experienced only 12 percent internal migration to the capital, Havana.[74] Until the 1990s, authorities did not regulate internal movement; rural development programs and the dispersal of industrial development to areas outside Havana kept the population fairly evenly distributed. However, the economic crisis of the 1990s provoked increased migration to Havana particularly from the eastern provinces suffering high rates of unemployment and severe food shortages.

As a result, in 1997, the government adopted measures to control overpopulation in certain areas of Havana that overtaxed an already weak urban infrastructure.[75] The regulations did not prohibit migration; rather they required that a person wishing to migrate permanently to Havana show that he or she had the permission of the person who owned the proposed dwelling and that the conditions in the house or apartment were adequate. Included in the requisites for approval is that the domicile have at least ten square meters habitable space for each person living there.[76]

Cuba´s housing policy has converted the majority of Cuban adults into homeowners. In contrast to the often repeated axiom about property rights in the United States, occupancy, rather than possession, is "nine tenths of the law" in Cuba. Ownership, while providing some real benefits, does not give the owner complete control over the property. Social considerations override many decisions regarding use and disposition. Thus, occupants have substantial legal protection, are difficult to dislodge, and are rarely, if ever, left out on the street. Further, inheritance rights depend on whether an heir

---

[73] Viviana Togores Gonzaléz, "Cuba: Efectos Sociales de la Crisis y el Ajuste Económico de los 90's," in *Balance de la Economía Cubana a Finales de los 90's* (Havana: Centro de Estudios de la Economía Cubana, 1999), p. 103.
[74] Hamburg, "Cuban Housing Policy," pp. 243-44.
[75] Decreto No. 217 (Regulaciones migratorias internas para la Ciudad de La Habana y sus contravenciones), *Gaceta Oficial Ext,*. No. 2, April 22, 1997. 1997.
[76] Ibid., Art. 2(b).

already resides in the testator's house or not. As a result of these policies as well as shortages, one apartment may house two and sometimes three generations.

Although people complain bitterly about crowded conditions and the inability to find new housing, they still take a certain pride in the fact that, despite the difficulties, there are virtually no homeless people in Cuba. In addition, Cuban housing policies preventing speculation and pay-offs maintain a certain equality and economic integration of neighborhoods that would be lost if Cuba reverted to a free market in real property.

II. "ABANDONED" PROPERTY

One issue that has received considerable attention in the Cuban American community in the US since the fall of the socialist governments in eastern Europe is the status of property formerly owned by ex-patriots. Hundreds of thousands who left Cuba since 1959 left homes and other personal property behind, title to most of which is in held by the Cuban citizens who now live in them. In anticipation of political change, some lawyers in Miami have begun enticing ex-patriots into paying $150 in order to have their property claim listed in a book they planned to publish.[77] In 1996, the US Congress adopted and the president signed what is commonly known as the Helms-Burton law which conditions the end of the United States embargo against Cuba on the implementation of a policy of compensation or return of property in Cuba.[78]

Many factors make it highly unlikely, if not inconceivable, that any such return of property or compensation for personal property will ever occur. Under contemporary Cuban law, no such claims to personal property or personal realty would be valid. As a practical and legal matter, it is difficult to imagine any Cuban court dispossessing Cuban citizens of their homes or requiring them to make payments to those who abandoned them to take up residence in another country. If there is to be any restitution at all, it will likely come as the result of a political accommodation, not judicial decision. However, such measures would seriously affect the political stability of any government overseeing such restitution. In addition to practical and political concerns, pre-revolutionary law regarding acquisition of property by *pre-*

---

[77] Howard Kleinberg, "Don't Look for Castro's Fall Soon," *St. Petersburg Times*, August 15, 1990, p. 18A.
[78] 22 U.S.C. Sec. 6021ff (1996).

scripción weighs against claims to the personal property that was left behind by ex-patriots.

Since 1889, the Cuban Civil Code has recognized the legal doctrine of *prescripción* or *usucapión*, the term now used for adverse possession, by which a person who is in uninterrupted possession of property for a specified period of time may acquire legal title to the property in his or her possession. The Civil Code that was in force from before the revolution and which was not repealed until 1987 provided for two forms of acquisition by prescription: ordinary and extraordinary.[79] For ordinary acquisition the possessor was required to demonstrate a legitimate basis for the claim of ownership as well as possession in good faith.[80] In the case of personal property other than real estate, the term of required possession was three years.[81] In the case of real property the term of continual possession was ten years if the actual owner was present in the country and twenty years if absent.[82] However, with respect to extraordinary prescription, the law provided that even if there was no legitimate basis for the claim or good faith on the part of the possessor, title was perfected after six years for goods and after thirty years for real property.[83]

It seems apparent that even under long-standing pre-revolutionary law, few valid claims could be made with respect to title to personal property such as automobiles, furniture, jewelry, etc. The same law would clearly defeat claims to real property left more than thirty years ago, at least to the extent that the possessor could show uninterrupted possession. The Civil Code of 1987 recognizes acquisition by prescription (although it uses the more modern term *usucapión*), but has abolished the concept of extraordinary prescription.[84] Thus, there can be no such acquisition of title in the absence of just claim and good faith.[85] However, the 1987 Civil Code considerably shortens the period of required possession to perfect title: three years for goods and five years for real property.[86]

According to the General Law on Housing, title to the home of someone who "abandons the country definitively" passes to the state except in cases

---

[79] Código Civil (Annotated Edition) (Havana: Ministry of Justice, 1975), Arts. 1940, *et seq.* These articles were in force in 1959 and were not modified significantly prior to 1989.
[80] Ibid., Art. 1940.
[81] Ibid., Art. 1955
[82] Ibid., Art. 1957.
[83] Ibid., Arts. 1955, 1959.
[84] Ley No. 59 (Código Civil), July 16, 1987, Arts. 184-190, *Gaceta Oficial Ext.*, October 15, 1987.
[85] Ibid., Arts. 186.1 and 187.
[86] Ibid.

where there is co-ownership and one party remains.[87] Thus, title to housing that has been abandoned can only be acquired from the state, and anyone so acquiring the property would likely be deemed to have done so in good faith, thereby having a just claim to it. As with other aspects of housing law, preference is given to certain persons who have lived in the house for a period of five years or more (three years under the 1984 housing law).[88] Included in this class is the spouse or ex-spouse, ascendants and descendants, siblings, nieces and nephews, and first cousins. The 1988 housing law gives the local legislative assembly authority to make exceptions to the period of required occupancy in cases where it would be just to do so.[89] If there is no person entitled to acquire the property, the state may sell the property to any purchaser. Occupancy by anyone not within the recognized classes is considered illegal, making it impossible for anyone not granted title by the state to satisfy the just claim or good faith requirement for *usucapión*. Thus, title to abandoned homes can only be acquired pursuant to the housing law and, generally, only by purchase from the state.

Consequently, in order to challenge the title of anyone who has acquired title under Cuban law and who has occupied a home for five years, one would have to declare both the housing law and the Civil Code void and unenforceable and, in addition, demonstrate that the possessor did not acquire just claim to the property in good faith. Yet even under the pre-revolutionary law, persons in possession as a result of grant by legal authority would likely have been considered entitled to retain ownership of the property because they had obtained colorable title in good faith. Further, those in possession for thirty or more years would have rights recognized by both pre- and post-revolutionary law.

Experience in the former socialist countries of Europe shows that restitution of property is a particularly complex and thorny problem. The approaches have been varied, and none satisfactory to prior owners. Czechoslovakia, for example did not recognize claims by those who did not reside in Czechoslovakia or who took up citizenship in another country.[90] East Germany did not return property that had been acquired by others in good faith, but did provide some form of compensation.[91] Hungary decided

---

[87] Ley No.65 (1989), Art. 81. A person is considered to have abandoned the country when he or she has left the country without authorization or has violated the terms of the authorization to leave the country or one who has requested to leave the country permanently after 1959 giving up his or her property and who may only return upon receiving special authorization of the Cuban government. Ley No. 989 (1961).

[88] Ibid., Art. 81.

[89] Ibid.

[90] "Eastern Europe's Policy of Restitution of Property in the 1990s," *Dickinson Journal of International Law*, Vol. 10, No. 2, 1992, p. 368.

[91] Ibid., p. 367.

against outright return of property, favoring the issuing of bonds as compensation.[92] In every instance compensation was not for the full value since none of the fragile economies could absorb such enormous costs.

Restitution of or compensation for commercial property that was confiscated by prior governments in eastern Europe has raised other issues related to the needs of the national economy. Typically, the time for bringing a claim was exceptionally short because of the importance of resolving title in order to attract investment in commercial property. Further, to pay off fully such claims would bankrupt the country and prevent it from reorganization.

Given the severe economic crisis and the magnitude of Cuba's outstanding debt, it is very doubtful that any future Cuban government would offer full compensation if any. Nor is it likely that Cuba would restore property to former owners. Any attempt to do so would meet such public opposition as to make it politically and economically unfeasible. Moreover, in the case of Cuba the four decade economic embargo imposed by the United states has caused economic harm far in excess of the conceivable amounts of purported property claims by U.S. citizens or residents.[93]

III. INHERITANCE OF PERSONAL PROPERTY

The Constitution specifically protects the rights of citizens to personal property, which consists of one's income and savings, one's principle house and vacation house, means or instruments of personal or family work and other forms of goods that satisfy the material and spiritual necessities of the individual.[94] Further, the right of inheritance of personal property, either by a written will or by intestacy, is recognized in Article 24 of the Constitution and is regulated by Articles 466 to 547 of the Cuban Civil Code.

The particularity of Cuban law governing inheritance is found in various restrictions imposed on testamentary disposition. As noted previously, al-

---

[92] Ibid., pp. 373-374.

[93] Cuba has settled all outstanding property claims based on the nationalization or expropriation of property of nationals of all other countries. With respect to claims of US owners of property nationalized in Cuba, 8,816 claims were filed with the US Office of Foreign Claims Settlement. Of these, the Commission certified 5,911 as valid, and certified awards in the total aggregate amount of $1,799,548,568, together with simple interest from the time of the loss at the annual rate of 6%. In 1998, a law suit was filed in Cuban courts, based on declassified US government documents, claiming damages caused by the US sponsored Bay of Pigs invasion and other CIA activity in Cuba. In addition, Cuba claims economic damage from the 40 year embargo amounts to more than 120 billion dollars.

[94] Constitución (1992), Art. 21. The article is virtually identical to that contained in Article 22 of the 1976 Constitution.

though the intent of the testator will generally be respected, the disposition of a house or farmland is subject to legal limitations intended to protect social and economic interests. In addition, specific categories of persons are prohibited from receiving inheritance: those who have attempted to kill the testator or a beneficiary under the will;[95] those who have used fraud, deceit or violence to obtain a disposition or a change in a will;[96] and those who having an obligation to provide care of the testator have denied food or necessary attention to the testator.[97] Such incapacities can be overcome if the testator has expressly or tacitly forgiven the actions of the heir or beneficiary.[98]

Moreover, Cubans who "abandon" the country to establish residence or citizenship abroad lose their right to inherit property from Cuban nationals.[99] They will also not be able to make testamentary disposition of any property left in Cuba since it will have been acquired by remaining family members or confiscated by the state. On the other hand, United States law does not prohibit Cuban nationals from inheriting from United States residents although such Cuban nationals are prevented by U.S. law from receiving the proceeds of any inheritance situated in the United States.[100]

Unlike prior law derived from the Spanish Civil Code, contemporary Cuban law no longer gives special deference to either the spouse or children of the testator in opposition to a valid written will unless they qualify as "specially protected heirs."[101] Such protected heirs are persons who are incapable of working and who have been dependent on the testator and include the following: children or their descendants in the case the children predecease the testator; a surviving spouse; and parents.[102] If there is more than one protected heir, each will share equally in the estate.

The legal requirements for a valid will and the process of distribution in Cuba are governed by the Civil Code[103] and the law of civil procedure.[104] The procedures for validation of a will and distribution of the estate are very similar to those followed in other civil law systems, particularly those derived from Spanish law. Thus, there is no process analogous to probate. A will is generally validated and filed with a notary who is also empowered to

---

[95] Código Civil (1987), Art. 469.1(a).
[96] Ibid., Art. 469.1(b).
[97] Ibid., Art. 469.1(c).
[98] Ibid., Art. 469.2.
[99] Ibid., Art. 470.
[100] Cuban Assets Control Regulations, 31 C.F.R. Part 515.
[101] Código Civil (1989), Art. 492.1.
[102] Ibid., Art. 493.1(a), (b) and (c).
[103] Ibid., Art. 476.
[104] Ley No. 7 (Ley de Procedimiento Civil, Administrativo y Laboral), Arts. 567-577, *Gaceta Oficial,* No.34, August 26, 1977..

distribute the property upon the death of the testator.[105] Only where there is a dispute as to the validity of the will or its contents will the matter be taken before a court.[106]

IV. AGRICULTURAL PROPERTY

Farm workers in the 1950s earned little and lived in deplorable conditions. Most of the peasant population either labored as tenant farmers, sharecroppers or squatters or eked out a living as seasonal workers on large private sugar and tobacco farms. The average farm worker earned one-quarter the average national income. It was among this population that the guerrilla forces gained its greatest support. On the eve of the revolution, about three-quarters of the revolutionary soldiers were peasants.[107] It is not surprising, therefore, that government policies in the early years focused on improving conditions for the peasantry. Government efforts included not only measures that gave more than one hundred thousand peasants title to the land they worked[108] but also organized a massive literacy campaign, replaced shacks with new housing equipped with electricity and running water and provided farming equipment and supplies.

No one in Cuba in 1959 could have seriously doubted that the new government was going to make good on its promise of agrarian reform. Yet implementation ignited virulent hostility among landowners. The first measure, the Agrarian Reform Act of 1959,[109] confiscated large landholdings of more than thirty *caballerías* (approximately one thousand acres), but still left more than a quarter of the land in the hands of a small group of landowners, many of whom began to support resistance directly or by sabotaging or reducing production. The Agrarian Reform Act of 1963 [110] eliminated this group of farmers and left all agricultural land either in the hands of small farmers or under the control of state-run farms in a proportion of roughly 30 to 60 percent respectively.

---

[105] Ley No. 50 (Ley de las Notarias Estatales), Art. 10(c), *Gaceta Oficial*, No.3, March 1, 1985.
[106] Ley No.7 (1977), Art. 567.
[107] See, Benjamin, et al., p. 150; Leo Huberman and Paul M. Sweezy, *Socialism in Cuba* (New York: Monthly Review Press, 1969), p. 78.
[108] Benjamin, et al., p. 154.
[109] Ley No.59 (Ley de Reforma Agraria), *Gaceta Oficial Ext. Esp*. No.7, June 3, 1959.
[110] Ley No.63 (Segunda Ley de Reforma Agraria), *Gaceta Oficial Ext*., No. 1, October 2, 1963.

From the start, the plan was to maintain most of the land under state control, either as state farms or state-supported cooperatives, as the best way to increase food production and equitable distribution. The remaining land was to be farmed by small landowners who were assured by Castro that they would be able "to cultivate their land as they see fit."[111] Although there was a plan to also develop agricultural cooperatives, the cooperative movement did not take hold until the mid-1970s.[112]

Agricultural production and the maintenance of sufficient food for the population have been major concerns of the government since 1959. However, government policies have not been successful stimulating sufficient production. Moreover, since 1989, the loss of assured shipments from the former Socialist countries of wheat, grains, feed and other produce caused critical shortages in Cuba's food supply. Further, the halving of oil imports and breakdowns in machinery for lack of spare parts jeopardized the country's ability to sustain its own agricultural production.

Faced with this threat to national survival, the government intensified national coordination of production and use of limited resources. It expanded the agricultural labor force by recruiting idled factory workers and organizing volunteer brigades from the cities. Oxen replaced tractors idled by lack of spare parts and fuel. Several new agricultural projects, founded on a community based and ecological approach, such as the "Turquino Project" in the Escambray Mountains (started in the late 1980s), served to stabilize rural communities and increase productivity as Cubans continued to look to self-sufficiency in agriculture as a way out of the crisis. By stringent rationing, the government has been able to supply each citizen with basic staples at highly subsidized prices, although the rations are not sufficient for an adequate diet.

Throughout the past four decades, laws governing the property rights of private farmers have undergone analysis and revision in an attempt to assure that all agricultural land is used productively and primarily for social, rather than private, benefit. In the beginning, state policy favored the concentration of food production on state farms and agricultural cooperatives. While protecting certain rights of land ownership, the law did not encourage expansion of private ownership other than by incorporation into agricultural cooperatives. The cooperative movement got its first big boost at the Party Congress in 1975, and legislation since has favored the integration of small farms into the cooperatives. In addition, life at the cooperatives was made increasingly attractive by new housing construction, day-care centers and

[111] Huberman and Sweezy, p. 116.
[112] Ley No. 36 (Ley de Cooperativas Agropecuarias), *Gaceta Oficial*, No. 63, August 24, 1982.

other amenities. Between 1976 and 1983 there was a surge in the formation of cooperatives, and the number grew from forty-four in 1977 to 1,480 by 1983 when it peaked.[113] Agricultural production also rose significantly, tripling output in some sectors.[114]

After 1984, membership in the cooperatives declined partly due to the aging of members who for the first time had rights to pension at retirement.[115] The opening of farmers' markets in 1980 also had a negative impact on cooperative movement. In addition to other problems facing cooperatives, such as difficulties in organization, the farmers' markets created pressures for "illicit" extra-agricultural activities, which lowered morale as well as production at the cooperatives.[116] These markets were closed in 1986. Thus, until the early 1990s, although membership in cooperatives had increased slightly as did their land holdings, the number of cooperatives did not.[117]

In 1991, about 75 percent of agricultural land was owned by the state; the 25 percent that was privately owned was divided roughly equally between individual farmers and the agricultural cooperatives.[118] The proportion of state-owned to privately owned land varied both by crop and region. For example, state ownership of tobacco land was only about 25 percent of the total.[119] At that time, the state owned only about half of the agricultural land in Havana Province; the remainder was split almost evenly between cooperatives and individual farmers.[120]

Since 1994, this equation has changed substantially. Cuban law does not permit state-owned land to be sold to private persons, but in 1991 the Council of State approved a new law governing agricultural property that permits the state to both exchange property with individual farmers or cooperatives as well as grant them use of state land.[121] The creation of the Basic Unites of Cooperative Productions (UBPC)[122] was part of an effort to in-

---

[113] Benjamin, et al., p. 167; see also, Stubbs, p. 52.
[114] Stubbs, p. 52.
[115] Ley No. 36 (1982), Art. 20.
[116] Stubbs, p. 52.
[117] René G. Montes de Oca Ruíz, "Las Formas de Propiedad en Cuba," *Revista Cubana de Derecho*, Vol. 2, 1991, p. 26.
[118] "Aspects of the Food Program and the Status of Its Execution," speech by Adolfo Díaz, Vice President of the Council of Ministers at the opening sessions of the National Assembly, December 26, 1991 (Source: British Broadcasting Corporation transcript, January 8, 1991).
[119] Ibid.
[120] "Fidel Castro Addresses Party's Fourth Congress on Agricultural Policy," transcript in English by British Broadcasting Corporation, October 28, 1991 (Source: Cuba Vision Television).
[121] Decreto-Ley No. 125 (Régimen de Posesión, Propiedad y Herencia de la Tierra y Bienes Agropecuarios), Art. 3, *Gaceta Oficial Ext.*, No.1, January 30, 1991.
[122] Decreto Ley No. 142 (Sobre Unidades Básicas de Producción Cooperativas), *Gaceta*

crease production of sugar by breaking up the large state farms that dominated this sector into medium-sized farms of 1,700 to 2,000 hectares organized into cooperatives.[123] Similar cooperatives were formed in other sectors. While land ownership was not transferred to individuals or to cooperatives, the work force has been given both material incentives to produce cane for sale to the state and individual plots to grow produce for their own consumption.[124] The UBPCs are highly regulated.[125] The inflexibility of some of the regulations that has prevented them from meeting expectations has come under review for revision.

At the same time, land which was not being used for cultivation was given to individual farmers to cultivate specific products such as coffee and tobacco although the owners could also use a portion of the land to grow other crops for their own use. This policy of granting the right to usufruct free of charge to individuals committed to cultivation of certain products was first applied to tobacco.[126]

Thus, between 1992 and 1998, the percentage of land controlled by state owned farms shrank considerably. According to a 1998-99 report, state ownership of land declined from 78% in 1989 to 26% in 1995.[127] The highest gain went to the cooperatives: from 10% to 59%.[128] Foreign investment in the agricultural sector, permitted after the adoption of the new law on Foreign Investment in 1995, has helped the financing and marketing of certain products.[129]

The reopening of the farmers markets, known as "mercados agropecuarios," in late 1994 under new regulations[130] has stimulated food produc-

---

Oficial Ext., No.6, September 21, 1993.

[123] *Latin America Weekly Report*, February 18, 1993, p. 75. According to the report, 156 state-owned sugar estates were broken into medium-sized farms of 1,700 to 2,000 hectares with a work force of about two hundred workers each.

[124] Ibid.

[125] Resolución No. 354-93 (Reglamento General de las Unidades Básicas de Producción Cooperativas atendidas por el Ministerio de la Agricultur), and Resolución No. 160-93 (Reglamento General de las Unidades Básicas de Producción Cooperativa atendidas por el Ministerio del Azúcar), *Gaceta Oficial*, No.1, January 3, 1994. p.1, 10.

[126] Resolución No. 357-93 (Aprueba el Reglamento para la entrega de tierras en usufructo y el mayor aprovechamiento de las áreas de las Cooperativas de Producción Agropecuaria y Agricultores Pequeños destinadas al Cultivo del Tabaco), *Gaceta Oficial*, No.1, January 3, 1994.

[127] "Country Profile: Cuba, 1998-99," The Economist Intelligence Unit (1998), p. 22. See also, Santiago Rodriguez Castellón, "La Evolución y Transformación del Sector Agropecuario en los Noventa," in *Balance de la Economía Cubana a Finales del los 90's*, (Havana: Centro de Estudios de la Economía Cubana, 1999).

[128] Ibid.

[129] Ibid.

[130] The new farmers markets differ from their predecessors in that they are much more competitive and even government run farms and cooperatives may sell their produce in these

tion as have the growing number of "organopónicos" which are large urban gardens managed by the local municipality. The latter have increased vegetable production considerably and supply fresh produce directly to the population at prices substantially below those of the other markets. As of 1999, there were over 2,500 such gardens in 169 municipalities, selling mostly organically grown vegetables and herbs.[131]

Independent Farmers

Article 19 of the Constitution as amended in 1992 that recognize the rights of independent farmers to own their lands as well as structures and other property necessary to agricultural production.[132] Despite the recognition given to the rights of small farmers, however, government policy has generally favored incorporation of small farmers into agricultural cooperatives. Until recently, the number of independent, small farmers steadily declined from 1963 until 1994 when the government began to redistribute uncultivated lands to individual farmers to be used for specific crops such as tobacco and coffee. Since these measures were adopted, the percentage of land cultivated by individual farms increased from 12.5 to 16 percent by 1998.[133]

Ownership rights of farmers, like those of homeowners, are circumscribed by social policies. Because agricultural land is such an important resource, the government exercises considerable control over its use and transfer, even when privately owned.

In the case of independent farmers, continued enjoyment of property rights depends on continued productive use of agricultural land that contributes to social consumption and the national economy.[134] Thus, a farmer cannot simply live on his or her land and leave the fields unplanted. Nor can he or she engage in subsistence agriculture. Moreover, a farmer who becomes permanently incapable of farming due to age or illness may lose the right to retain the land unless a close relative continues to keep it productive.[135] Further, a farmer must produce crops in accordance with state production plans and may only employ others to work the land in accordance with Ministry of Agriculture rules.[136] Violation of these restrictions or ille-

---

markets. As a way of keeping some lid on prices, the government also created local produce markets where vegetables are sold at lower prices than at the "mercados agropecuarios."

[131] "Cuba Goes Green," *Washington Post*, November 26, 1999, p. A29.

[132] Constitución (1992), Art. 19.

[133] "Country Profile: Cuba, 1998-99," The Economist Intelligence Unit (1998), p. 22.

[134] Decreto Ley No. 125 (1991), Arts. 8-10.

[135] Ibid., Arts. 22-24.

[136] Ibid., Arts. 8 and 9. In the case of the lands redistributed since 1994, the grant of usufruct requires the farmer to plant and produce a certain estimated amount each year. The grant does not specify the price at which the product is to be sold. Resolución No. 357-93 (Ministry of Agriculture, 1993).

gal commercialization of products may result in the confiscation of the farm.[137] If confiscated, the farmer will receive payment for its appraised value.[138]

The transfer of land of a small farmer is also highly restricted. All sales must be authorized by the Ministry of Agriculture,[139] and transfer may only be made to the state, to a cooperative or to another farmer. However, the state cannot expropriate the land of an independent farmer except for violations mentioned above. With the exception of the lands redistributed for specific crops since 1994, sales to the state are strictly voluntary, but at prices established by appraisal in accordance with Ministry of Agriculture schedules.[140] Nor can farmland be rented, except to or from the state.[141]

Further, a farmer cannot dispose of his farm by a testamentary instrument.[142] Rights to inherit land by intestacy are also limited and have been further restricted by the 1991 statute pursuant to which land can only be inherited from the deceased by children, parents, siblings or spouses who have been actively working the land for five years, and in some cases grandchildren or nieces and nephews.[143] Exceptions are made for those heirs who have been away in military service or attending educational institutions or who were minors at the time of the testator's death if they demonstrate that they can personally work the land.[144] Decisions over the claims of heirs to the land are made in the first instance by the Ministry of Agriculture, which reportedly had been fairly flexible in applying the time requirements in the mid-1980s.[145] The right to cultivate lands subject to the recent redistribution policies cannot be inherited as the grant to their use is by contract.

Because rights to land are derived only from their use, only farmers and their dependents have legal right to compensation for their value. Certain heirs who have not worked the land for the requisite period have the right to receive the value of the land only if they do not have another source of in-

---

137 Ibid., Art. 10. If the owner has left the farm for other work, he or she may return within sixty days and reclaim rights to the land by reincorporating him or herself into the working of the farm. The farmer at risk of losing the land may also seek incorporation into a cooperative.

138 Ibid.

139 Ibid., Art. 12.

140 Resolución No. 171-84 (Ministry of Agriculture), September 20, 1984.

141 Decreto-Ley No. 125 (1991), Art. 26.

142 Ibid., Art. 28.

143 Ibid., Art. 18. Grandchildren and nieces or nephews can only inherit land if they have worked the land and their parent is either deceased or otherwise ineligible to inherit the land because he or she has not worked the land for the requisite period of time.

144 Ibid., Arts. 21-23.

145 Benjamin, et al., p. 160.

come and have been dependent on the testator for five years.[146] Otherwise, the land escheats to the state with no compensation. Goods or property not connected with farm production can be sold or transferred by inheritance according to the Civil Code.[147]

The previous statute governing inheritance of farms, enacted in 1982, established one year as the requirement for having worked the land or demonstrated economic dependency. The increase in the required period to five years is not explained and has been criticized as excessive by at least one Cuban lawyer employed by the Legal Department of the Ministry of Agriculture.[148] Moreover, the 1982 law did not limit inheritance to close relatives but permitted the testator to grant the land to anyone who had worked it for the requisite year.[149] The new restrictions may reflect impatience with the slowness of the integration of individual farms into the agricultural cooperatives and/or the intent to keep agricultural land only in the hands of experienced and dedicated farmers.

Special provisions are made with respect to persons who occupy the farmer's house at the time of his or her death if they do not have the right to inherit the property. According to the statute, they may continue to live in the house until they either find another place to live on their own or are relocated by the National Housing Institute or the Ministry of Agriculture.[150]

Small farms cannot be divided. Even in the case of divorce or inheritance,[151] one party will get the land if he or she has been working it, the other(s) will get the value of the portion due in cash. By law, heirs who are eligible to inherit the land itself receive equal shares but cannot divide the land except to cede their portion to the state or to join a cooperative.[152] They can, however, decide to own the land in common as a condominium as long as they continue to work the land.

In a 1981 opinion, the Cuban Supreme Court ruled that administrative decisions that affect legal rights may be appealed to the provincial courts.[153] The 1991 statute abrogated that decision. As a result, decisions regarding

---

146 Decreto-Ley No. 125 (1991), Art. 20. There is an exception to the five-year requirement for minors under five years of age.
147 Ibid., Art. 24.
148 Orlando Rey Santos, "Régimen de Sucesión de Tierras," *Revista Cubana de Derecho*, Vol. 4, 1991, pp. 54, 60.
149 Decreto-Ley No. 63 (Herencia de la Tierra Propiedad de Agricultores Pequeños),Art. 1, *Gaceta Oficial Ext. Esp.*, No.9, December 30, 1982.
150 Decreto-Ley No. 125 (1991), Disposiciones Especiales, Sexta.
151 Rigoberto Hernández León, "El Servicio Jurídico al Pequeño Agricultor en la Jurisdicción del Derecho Agrario," *Ponencias: Derecho Económico, Agrario y Admin-istrativo* (Havana: Organización Nacional de Bufetes Colectivos, 1989), p. 9.
152 Decreto-Ley No. 125 (1991), Art. 6.
153 Hernández León, p. 7.

transfer and expropriation are made by the territorial entities of the Ministry of Agriculture and are appealable only to the Ministry and not to the courts.[154] Exception is allowed for appeals to the provincial courts concerning the amount of compensation in cases of confiscation. Lawyers at the *bufetes colectivos* provide legal assistance to farmers. The subject of agrarian law and the role of lawyers in protecting the rights of farmers now features prominently in conferences and seminars of the *bufetes colectivos.*[155]

According to one author, Cuban officials had hoped to integrate 90 percent of all privately held farms into cooperatives by 1990.[156] However, despite policy and restrictions, the share of independent ownership remains fairly stable at about one half of private holdings. While encouraging integration into agricultural cooperatives, the state has nevertheless provided support to independent farmers. Most independent farmers are members of credit and service cooperatives that offer credit, technical assistance and shared use of farm equipment and other resources. Farmers may earn high profits by selling their produce in the public agricultural markets, but even sales to the government at government prices allowed farmers to enjoy a high standard of living compared to other Cubans.[157] Some blame the growth in the black market of food products before 1994 on illicit marketing by the independent farmers, but other officials deny this is the source of the problem, pointing the finger at thefts from state farms and warehouses.

Agricultural Cooperatives

It was not until 1982 that the government integrated regulations pertaining to the agricultural cooperatives into a single statute, the Law on Agricultural Cooperatives.[158] The statute establishes two main forms of cooperatives: (1) agricultural production cooperatives and (2) service and credit

---

[154] Ibid., Art. 41.

[155] See, e.g., collection of papers presented at a 1989 regional conference entitled *Ponencias: Derecho Económico, Agrario y Administrativo* (Havana: Organización Nacional de Bufetes Colectivos, 1989).

[156] Benjamin, et al., p. 167.

[157] Benjamin, et al., p. 160.

[158] Ley No. 36 (1982).

cooperatives.[159] The integration of individual farmers into cooperatives is voluntary,[160] and cooperatives enjoy a fair degree of autonomy over internal governance,[161] although production must be in line with national social and economic needs.[162] Cooperatives are governed democratically by a General Assembly of Members to which all members belong and which elects a board of directors.[163] One way in which the state encourages the growth of cooperatives is by providing special economic and technical assistance.

Any land or other property that an individual brings to the cooperative when becoming a member becomes the property of the cooperative. The individual is entitled to compensation for the contribution, which is paid out over time from the cooperative's earnings.[164] If a member should separate from the cooperative, he or she will receive both any unpaid portion of this contribution plus any accumulated share of profits.[165] Participation in the earnings of the cooperative, however, is not at all related to the value of property invested by the individual member, but rather on the basis of the member's work.[166]

Production and commercialization of produce are governed by the plan established by the national government in consultation with ANAP, but the cooperative may also set aside a portion of land for its own consumption. While the 1982 statute generally permitted the sale of cooperative land for reasons of public utility or the exchange of property to benefit the cooperative, the 1991 statute restricts such transfer to sales or exchanges between cooperatives or to the state.[167]

Consistent with the policy promoting the growth of cooperatives, the law protects the integrity of cooperative property. Thus, cooperative property cannot be subject to lien.[168] Nor can a member separate his or her land from the cooperative once joined. Further, cooperative property cannot be inherited as the land, most dwellings and structures belong to the cooperative, not the individual.[169] In the case of a house that was owned by the farmer before joining the cooperative, it can be inherited according to the housing laws, but it cannot be either sold or exchanged without approval by

---

[159] Ibid., Art. 2.
[160] Ibid., Art. 4.
[161] Ibid., Art. 5.
[162] Ibid., Art. 7.
[163] Ibid., Arts. 53-54.
[164] Ibid., Art. 25.
[165] Ibid.
[166] Ibid., Art. 36.
[167] Decreto-Ley No. 125 (1991), Art. 5.
[168] Ibid., Art. 33.
[169] Ley No.36 (1982), Arts. 45-48.

the cooperative.[170] In addition, the earnings as well as any unpaid portion of the value of the member's contribution will be transferred first to those heirs who are linked to the cooperative or to the deceased's dependents.

Credit and service cooperatives are formed by voluntary association of individual farmers who maintain ownership of their farms.[171] Membership in such cooperatives gives the farmers access to state resources, credit and technical assistance. To join, a farmer makes a contribution to a common fund, which is used to provide both credit and payment of services, including use of heavy equipment and materials. Membership in these cooperatives in no way encumbers the farmer's land.

The law governing agricultural cooperatives is now more than 20 years old and has not been modified to reflect changes which have taken place in Cuba and in the life of the cooperatives, themselves. At the same time, the number of cooperatives has grown substantially: Proposals arising from the 2000 Congress of ANAP formed the basis of a draft of a new law presented to the National Assembly in December of that year, but it was eventually rejected and sent back for further consultations. During the ensuing year, meetings were held with over 200,000 members of cooperatives nationwide to discuss the draft law and to obtain the criteria of those whom it would most affect.[172] The new law, expected to be enacted in October 2002, will give greater agility to the internal government of the cooperatives by creating an administrative council responsible for operational decisions. This council is to be named by and accountable to the Managing Board of the cooperatives and the assembly of the cooperative members.

In addition, the law will encourage the incorporation of agricultural workers into cooperatives, making them full members entitled to participate in profits and decision-making. Since many of the original members of the cooperatives have retired or are unable to carry out the physical work, many productive cooperatives have begun to hire laborers. This process created an anomaly in Cuban socialism: landowners benefiting from the labor of others. Under the proposed law, a cooperative may hire workers but must decide after a six month trial period whether or not the worker is qualified to continue at which point the worker must be dismissed or allowed to become a member of the cooperative with a right to participate in the cooperative's profits.

Moreover, the new law will augment to a degree the ability of the cooperative to manage its resources and profits. Reflecting the fact that most

---

[170] Ibid., Arts. 45, 48, and 52.

[171] Ibid., Art. 69.

[172] Interview with Leonardo Martinez, president of the Commission on Productive Activities of the National Assembly of Peoples Power, and Jose Garea, lawyer for ANAP, September 12, 2002.

cooperatives have repaid the value of the property contributed at the time the cooperative was formed, the amount of profits that a cooperative may distribute to its members will be increased from 50% to 70% with the remainder being set aside for contingencies (10%),[173] reinvestment and social programs benefiting the cooperative itself. The proposed law will also enhance the Credit and Service Cooperatives by permitting them to hire administrative staff to handle secretarial, technical and other paper work. The activities of these cooperatives will be expanded to permit pooling of resources for marketing and transportation of goods to market.

Yet, the overall scheme of supervision by the Ministry of Agriculture will remain unchanged. Policies governing agricultural production and development continue to be centralized in the Ministry. Thus, small farmers, production cooperatives and the UPBCs must still meet production quotas for certain crops and products designated by the Ministry and sell a substantial portion of their produce to the state at regulated prices. The state, in turn, facilitates purchase of fertilizers, equipment and technology and other supplies at preferential prices. Outside of this regulated relationship with the Ministry as major buyer, the cooperatives are responsible for contracting with state enterprises on a commercial basis for the other supplies and services they may need. Conflicts are decided by the Chamber of Economic Law of the Provincial Court.

V. PROPERTY OF MASS, SOCIAL AND RELIGIOUS ORGANIZATIONS

Property may also be owned by a wide variety of social, political and religious organizations. In addition to the mass and social organizations given special recognition in the Constitution, many professional and cultural organizations also function, such as the National Union of Cuban Writers and Artists, the National Union of Cuban Jurists, the Union of Cuban Journalists and so forth. Communities establish social clubs, and religious institutions may own property as well. The property belonging to these organizations is that which is used in the furtherance of their work or activities. It includes buildings, installations, vehicles and other goods as well as funds that come from the contributions of its members or affiliates.

[173] Under the proposed legislation, it will be obligatory for the cooperatives to create a contingency fund to cover losses caused by climatic changes such as drought or flooding, as well as other unforeseen damage as the state will no longer cover these costs as it had in the past.

Depending on their charters, these organizations can create enterprises that serve the work of the organization, and this property cannot be seized or burdened by liens. For example, the National Union of Cuban Jurists runs a small book shop and cafe for the benefit of its members and other visitors. Profits from sales are also used to support the activities of the Union.

Similarly, religious organizations own buildings where members worship as well as congregate for other institutional purposes. The Baptist church of pastor Raúl Suárez[174] formed the Center Martin Luther King to carry out social projects including independent economic development initiatives such as a bicycle repair shop, an agricultural cooperative and arts and crafts workshops.[175] The alienation of the property is controlled both by legislation as well as by the by-laws that govern the organization.

Because of shortages of goods and capital, institutions that formerly were able to pay in Cuban pesos for imported goods obtained from the state now must purchase such goods in "hard currency," meaning U.S. dollars. En- couraged to find ways of becoming economically self-sufficient and to earn this currency, many social and professional organizations have begun to organize seminars for foreigners or to sell products and services to foreign visitors as well as activities for Cubans who pay in pesos. In some cases, they may even offer cultural activities like musical or dance performances for tourists and Cubans. These activities are increasingly necessary for the survival of the sponsoring institution, but they also introduce experience with entrepreneurship and autonomous management of property and finances.

---

[174] Raúl Suarez was elected as a delegate to the National Assembly in February 1993.

[175] Mimi Whitefield, "Protestant Pastor Carves His Place in Cuba," *Chicago Tribune*, March 7, 1993, p. 21.

Chapter 9

ECONOMIC REGULATION

Today, as in the 1960s, the transformation of the economy is perhaps the most important task of the socialist government of Cuba. At the beginning of the revolution, the government radically altered existing economic policy and control of wealth by centralizing the ownership and management of productive property in the national government. Collectivization of the means of production was expected to provide the material basis and essential conditions for the evolution of the socialist state and society. The development of efficient institutions and measures to administer successfully a centralized, planned economy proved to be extremely difficult, exacting a constant process of experimentation and evaluation. The general inexperience in socialist economic practice was compounded by the adoption of the ineffective and inefficient models of Eastern Europe. Just as Cuba embarked on a process of reform to correct deficiencies in that model, the entire international socialist market system fell apart.

Survival after the economic free fall precipitated by the collapse of the Eastern Socialist bloc in 1990 required swift, pragmatic decisions, with little time to reflect on consequences. The urgency of action was analogous to that of the 1960s; reform and experimentation had to be accelerated in order to reorganize the economy. However, the circumstances were fundamentally different: In 1990, Cuba had to dismantle a highly centralized system designed to function in a socialist market in order to reintegrate into a world market dominated by capitalist transnationals.

At the outset of the crisis there was no comprehensive, coherent plan for restructuring a socialist economic system. None of the former European socialist countries had attempted to do so. Moreover, the changed circumstances all but nullified legal measures previously adopted to regulate state enterprises. The immediate objectives guiding decisions in the early 1990s were survival and preservation of basic social services and the egalitarian principles of distribution which were considered the bedrock of the Cuban revolution. A combination of reforms and foreign investment halted the downward slide in late 1994, but recovery has been slow impeded by many factors, not the least of which has been the intensification of the economic war waged against Cuba by the United States.[1] Nevertheless, at the beginning of the millenium the outlook appeared less than grim, buoyed by the 6.2% and 5.6% growth registered in 1999 and 2000, respectively.

It was not until 1993-1994 that the outlines of a new economic policy began to take shape, the principle measures of which included courting foreign investment, decentralization of the export industries, introduction of financial and management autonomy in the state enterprises and the creation of new, albeit limited, areas of private economic activity. After providing a brief overview of the progression of economic regulation during the first three decades of the Cuban revolution, this chapter describes the legal reforms implemented since the early 1990s that provide the basis for what the Cubans hope will be a sustainable socialist economic system.

I. OVERVIEW

Although Fidel Castro announced the socialist character of the Cuban Revolution in the early 1960s, legal regulation of the commercial relationships among state-owned enterprises did not begin until the mid 1970s. During the first fifteen years of the revolution, Cuba instituted a system of central budgetary accounting under which market mechanisms were rejected,[2] economic planning and management were centralized and all production and service units were financed out of a central budget.[3] The system was dedicated to radical egalitarianism, relying on moral incentives to promote discipline and productivity.[4] Thus, the directors of individual enter-

---

[1] In 1992, the United States adopted the "Cuban Democracy Act," known as the Torricelli Bill which prohibits trade by US subsidiaries incorporated in third countries from trading with Cuba. These subsidiaries had been an important source of goods, particularly food and medicines. In addition, US government officials and hostile leaders of the Cuban American community pressured foreign businesses not to invest in or engage in trade with Cuba. These efforts were codified in the bill signed into law on March 12, 1996, entitled the "Cuban Liberty and Democratic Solidarity Act, commonly known as "Helms-Burton," which punishes companies which "traffic" in property nationalized in Cuba. It is beyond the scope of this book to explore the legality of these measures, but numerous scholars argue they are in violation of basic principles of international law as well as treaties to which the United States is a party. See, e.g., Andreas F. Lowenfeld, "Congress and Cuba: The Helms-Burton Act," 90 Am. J. Int'l L. 419, 430-31 (1996).

[2] Economists have noted that Cuba in the mid-1960s relied less on market mechanisms than any other socialist country. Leo Huberman and Paul Sweezy, *Socialism in Cuba* (New York: Monthly Review Press, 1969), p. 164.

[3] Ibid., pp. 163-68.

[4] Ibid.

prises were not accountable for balancing costs and revenues or for profitability,[5] and material incentives were eschewed.[6]

The failure of the system of central budgetary accounting to achieve economic progress was painfully apparent in the early 1970s.[7] The errors specifically cited as problems in the Main Report of the First Congress of the Communist Party of Cuba in 1975 included the over-centralization of management and the lack of adequate market mechanisms, norms of commercial transactions and material incentives.[8]

The sweeping reorganization of economic planning and management in Cuba, announced at the 1975 Party Congress, signaled a new direction in Cuba's approach to the transformation from capitalism to socialism. As part of the institutionalization process, the Party Congress introduced the new "System of Economic Management and Planning" (SDPE) and adopted Cuba's first five-year economic plan. SDPE was modeled in large part, at least in form, after the systems adopted in the Soviet Union and numerous eastern European socialist countries.[9] The fundamental features of the SDPE included both the strengthening of centralized planning and the decentralization of production management through semi-autonomous state enterprises that were supposed to be self-managing, self-financing and profit maximizing. International trade was centralized in the Ministry of Foreign Trade. Cuba adopted a system of state arbitration in 1977 to assure compliance with the national economic plan and to resolve contract and commercial conflicts between enterprises.[10]

---

[5] Ibid., p. 164.

[6] Ibid., pp. 164-66.

[7] See, Joel C. Edelstein, "Economic Policy and Development Models," in *Cuba: Twenty-Five Years of Revolution*, Sandor Halebsky and John Kirk eds., (New York: Praeger, 1985), pp. 187-189; and Elaine Fuller, "Production Quotas and Profits," *CubaTimes*, No. 3, 1982, pp. 5-7. For a general discussion of the changes in economic policy in Cuba, see Edelstein, pp. 180-92; Edward Boorstein, *The Economic Transformation of Cuba* (New York: Monthly Review Press, 1968); Huberman and Sweezy; Carmelo Mesa-Lago, *The Economy of Socialist Cuba* (Albuquerque, N.M.: University of New Mexico Press, 1981); Arthur MacEwan, *Revolution and Economic Development in Cuba* (New York: St. Martin's Press, 1981); Andrew Zimbalist, *Cuba's Socialist Economy: Toward the 1990s* (Boulder, Colo.: Westview Press, 1987).

[8] "Informe Central," *Primer Congreso del Partido Comunista de Cuba* (Havana, 1976), pp. 102-05.

[9] Zimbalist suggests that while the form of SDPE may have been adopted from the Soviets, the new system was in practice distinctly Cuban, particularly with respect to broad popular participation in the planning process. Andrew Zimbalist, "Cuban Economic Planning: Organization and Performance," in *Cuba: Twenty-Five Years of Revolution*, Sandor Halebsky and John Kirk, eds., (New York: Praeger, 1985), pp. 214-217.

[10] Decreto-Ley No. 10 (Competencias de los Organos), Disposición autorizante, *Gaceta Oficial*, No. 44, December 21, 1977.

Implementation of reforms of the magnitude embodied in SDPE would challenge even developed economies. In the case of Cuba, the task was particularly difficult because many basic economic structures and systems essential to implementation of SDPE either did not exist or were insufficiently developed for rational economic planning.[11] For example, Cuba had not developed an adequate system for collecting, organizing and analyzing statistics and data essential to central economic decision-making.[12] Thus, from 1976 to 1980 the government created numerous institutions to manage information essential to the new system, including the State Committee for Statistics, a national accounting system and state committees to regulate prices and standards. It also restructured the banking system.[13] The difficulty of adaptation to the system was compounded by the fact that most officials and management personnel had little experience in economic affairs.

It was not until the early 1980s that the new economic regulatory agencies actually started to function. However, errors and deficiencies of the system soon began to surface. The Main Report to the Third Party Congress in 1985 pointed to the "absence of comprehensive national planning for economic development" as one of the most serious problems along with mismanagement and the lack of a coherent and disciplined approach to investment.[14] Moreover, distribution of goods was inefficient and, at times, irrational due to lack of flexibility in marketing mechanisms.[15] In response, the government embarked on a measured path of reform known as "rectification." The debate over the direction of reform centered on whether SDPE and the economic institutions it spawned were themselves conceptually inadequate or whether they simply had not been implemented effectively.[16] Resolution of this debate, however, would be of little help in the face of the disappearance of the socialist trading bloc which necessitated more radical alterations in Cuba's faltering socialist system.

---

[11] Zimbalist, "Cuban Economic Planning," p. 223.

[12] Ibid.

[13] In 1984, the Cuban government conferred new authority and responsibilities on the National Bank of Cuba. The Bank assumed financial control of the national production and became the exclusive organ which guaranteed and adjusted payments between enterprises and economic organs. For a report on changes in banking policy in the mid-1980s and the development of a consumer savings bank in Cuba, see Elaine Fuller, "New Developments in Cuban Banking," *CubaTimes*, No. 5, 1985, p. 3.

[14] Informe Central, *Tercer Congreso del Partido Comunista de Cuba* (Havana: Editora Política, 1985).

[15] Ibid.

[16] Julio Carranza Valdés, "Cuba: los retos de la economía", *Cuadernos de Nuestra América*, No.1, 1993, pp. 156.

The disintegration of the socialist bloc sent shock waves through the Cuban economy, which was already stagnating because of internal inefficiencies and the general depression in the international markets. Cuba's tie to the Council for Mutual Economic Assistance (CMEA) had previously facilitated its long-range planning by providing stable economic exchanges. In 1989, more than 85 percent of Cuba's foreign trade was with the socialist bloc of Europe. With the disappearance of the CMEA, the functions of centralized economic planning and management institutions had to be completely reoriented to interact with a diverse, competitive international market. Further, new sources of capital had to be found to replace the credits and trade benefits of the former Soviet block.

Moreover, domestic production was all but paralyzed as many factories built to supply the socialist bloc nations lay idled by lack of spare parts and fuel as well as orders. Where trade continued, the terms were no longer based on socialist prices, but on world market prices. Continuing United States hostility prevented Cuba from having access to credits from international financial institutions with which to finance its recovery. Because of a severe shortage of currency reserves, imports plummeted. Import of petroleum required for energy production was slashed from thirteen million tons of oil in 1989 to a little over six million tons in 1992 causing frequent and prolonged blackouts. An emerging informal economy, which operated in the black market of stolen state goods, grew rapidly, sapping needed resources and creating imbalances in distribution.[17]

Adjustment to this new situation posed a herculean challenge made all the more difficult by persistent United States attempts to cripple the Cuban economy and to prevent Cuba from entering international markets.[18] In the early 1990s, Cuba began to dismantle the former economic planning and management apparatus and to substantially decentralize international trade. By 1994, many Cuban enterprises dedicated to important exports were reorganized into free-standing corporations formally registered as *sociedades anónimas* with individual shareholders.[19] A new law adopted in 1995, broadened the sectors of the economy open to foreign investment and cre-

---

[17] Cuban economist Julio Carranza Valdés reported that the informal market as measured in pesos in circulation, grew from two billion pesos to ten billion pesos between 1990 and 1992. Ibid., pp. 131, 153.

[18] Andrew Zimbalist, "U.S. Blockade Policy: Mission Impossible?" *Cuba Update* , February-March, 1993, pp. 3, 6. The 1992 Cuban Democracy Act prohibited trade with U.S. subsidiaries incorporated in third countries, cutting off a large portion of Cuba's new trading partners.

[19] For example, Habanos, S.A. was incorporated in 1994 as an independent company to be the primary exporter of Cuban cigars. A similar reorganization of the rum industry took place at the same time with the creation of Cuba Ron, S.A. as the producer of rums for export. Since 1994, the number of such Cuban corporations has grown considerably.

ated new vehicles for investment. These measures introduced the use of market mechanisms in various sectors of the economy: those connected with foreign investment and tourism and those providing services or products to these enterprises as well as the sector of the Cuban economy dealing with exports and imports. On the other hand, at the beginning of the decade, domestic production and distribution of essential goods was more tightly controlled in order to be able to shift resources from one sector to another quickly to satisfy basic societal needs, particularly food.

A dual economy emerged as tourism, import and export enterprises began to operate in hard currency while most state enterprises continued to operate in Cuban pesos. Since the country could no longer offer most imported consumer goods to the public in Cuban pesos, new "dollar" stores opened that sold many consumer goods and food items in U.S. dollars. The use of the U.S. dollar was legalized in 1993, creating differentials between Cubans who had access to foreign currency and those who did not.[20] Although essential goods and food continued to be sold in Cuban pesos and education and health services remained free of charge, many of these measures created undesirable consequences which went against the grain of the egalitarian nature of the Cuban revolution. Yet, they were considered essential to the country's survival.[21]

Some Cuban economists suggested early on that greater decentralization was needed in the domestic economy as well as in the export and joint venture sectors, and even some amount of privatization in order to stimulate production and increase efficiency.[22] To study reforms undertaken in socialist systems, Cuba looked farther east than the Soviet Union. A number of Cuban economists visited China and Vietnam, including Carlos Lage, Secretary of the Council of Ministers, who has been in charge of coordinating Cuba's economic management during this difficult period. They also studied the experiences of other developing countries, particularly that of Latin American nations such as Chile. It is doubtful that Cuba will go very far in the direction of privatization, but already a measure of flexibility has been

---

[20] Although highly criticized by some for the inequalities it created, the introduction of the use of the U.S. dollar in the Cuban domestic economy was essential. Imports had to be paid for in hard currency and the only way to sustain them was to sell them in hard currency as well. The peso not only had no value on the international market, but was highly inflated in Cuba at the time. The purchase power of Cubans with access to hard currency through receipt of remittances from family abroad or earnings in the way of tips or from self-employment was an essential ingredient in the assuaging the crisis of currency reserves.

[21] See, for example, "Informe. Buró Político, PCC", published in *Granma*, March 27, 1996, pp. 2-3. The report details the negative consequences of many of the measures adopted, including the influence of tourism on the culture of consumerism.

[22] Carranza Valdés, p. 158.

introduced in specific areas of the domestic economy where goods and products are produced for local consumption.[23]

Modifications to the Cuban Constitution approved in July 1992 signaled a more flexible attitude toward new forms of property and economic organization. As amended, Article 14 introduced a potentially profound change in the definition of socialist property:

> The Republic of Cuba is governed by an economic system based on socialist property of the people over the *fundamental* means of production and the suppression of the exploitation of man by man. (emphasis added)

The 1976 text did not include the highlighted qualifier. Thus, the Constitution now permits forms of private ownership of property in sectors and activities that are not considered a fundamental part of the state economy.

Further, Article 15 specifically permits state property to be "transformed into private property" in exceptional cases if its "economic objective is destined for ends of development of the country and which do not affect the fundamental political, social or economic policy of the State." Such transfer must have the prior approval of the Council of Ministers or its Executive Committee. The willingness to relinquish complete state control over productive property reflected the need to instill greater flexibility in the economy and to uncover new ways of sustaining the society. Yet, it is clear that the state remains and will remain a central actor in the organization of the Cuban economy.

By the early 1990s, Cuba had already eliminated some of the economic planning and regulatory institutions developed in the late 1970s and early 1980s. For example, the State Arbitration System that resolved disputes between state enterprises was abolished in 1991. It was replaced by a new Chamber of Economic Law established in the Provincial Courts and in the Supreme Court to handle all commercial economic disputes. The Central State Planning Board was replaced by two ministries charged with directing the economic and fiscal policies of the country: the Ministry of the Economy and Planning and the Ministry of Finance and Prices. By 1997, when the Cuban Communist Party celebrated its Fifth Congress, the outlines of an economic plan to revitalize and sustain the Cuban socialist system had become evident.

---

[23] Some of these measures include the creation of new agricultural cooperatives and the breaking up of large state farms; the expansion of areas of self-employment and the development of independent artisans, the reorganization of state enterprises and the elimination of state subsidies.

As noted, the economy has shown a modest, but steady, recovery posting an impressive 5.6% growth in 2000 against the backdrop of extremely negative international conditions, specifically unusually high oil prices and low sugar prices both of which directly affect Cuba. In addition, Cuba alone among nations suffers the dual punishment of being denied access to the U.S. market, its natural trading partner, as well to credits from international financial institutions influenced or controlled by the United States. However, as a result of foreign investment, tourism and the ability to reactivate some of its domestic industries, Cuba has begun to increase its exports and its ability to substitute imports.[24] The implementation of fiscal reforms and reorganization of the state sector also contributed to recovery. That Cuba not only survived the extraordinary crisis against all odds, but shows potential for sustained recovery has infused the government with optimism for the future of Cuban socialism.

Cuba has embarked on a *sui generis* mixed economy composed of various elements, each with varying autonomy: joint ventures formed with foreign partners; autonomous Cuban corporations in the field of exports; reformed agricultural cooperatives and expansion of private farming; restructured state owned enterprises and an expanded, albeit limited, private service sector. The balance among these sectors is orchestrated by the government in an effort to achieve sustained growth without suffering massive dislocations. The reforms, however, have not altered the core beliefs underlying Cuban policy: that economic growth and efficiency can be achieved without surrendering the economy to privatization; and that a system based on collective "benefit" motive is viable.[25]

Yet, modifications to economic and commercial law, even small ones, will have consequences for the future direction of Cuban socialism. The introduction of forms of private ownership[26] as well as the use of market mechanisms have substantial implications for economic legal theory and practice. With the adoption of socialist legality, Cuba altered the civil law system's division of public and private law at least in practice if not in form. Under capitalist systems, economic law, which primarily comprises the law of business organization, contracts and commercial transactions, falls under

---

[24] See, *La Economía Cubana en el 2000: Desempeño Macroeconómico y Transformación Empresarial,* Centro de Estudios de la Economía Cubana, April 2001.

[25] The commitment to socialism was further underscored by the amendment to the Constitution adopted in June, 2002, declaring Cuba's socialist economic system unalterable.

[26] Examples of the creation and expansion of private ownership include: the introduction of joint ventures with foreign companies, the creation of agricultural cooperatives known as Basic Units of Production Cooperatives (UBPC), the distribution of new lands to individual farmers particularly in that areas of coffee and tobacco cultivation, and legalization of small private family businesses in limited commercial activities.

the area of private law. As in other socialist countries, economic law had until recently been a purely public, autonomous branch of law because virtually all economic organization and activity was managed by the state.[27] With its new approach to a mixed economy, Cuba must not only reform its socialist economic law and institutions but also begin to redevelop and modernize areas of private economic law.

Thus, as the elements of economic policy emerge, new laws are being adopted to support reforms taking place in many areas of the economy including the restructuring of banking system,[28] reorganization of the management of state enterprises,[29] implementation of new fiscal policies including the introduction of a tax law for the first time since 1959.[30] Cuba has also revised its trademark and copyright laws and strengthened measures to protect the environment.[31]

Although, the foregoing have been important developments, much remains to be done particularly in areas concerning commercial organization and relations. The Commercial Code of 1956, which has been amended but never repealed, is woefully out of date and must be revised substantially if it is to serve a modern economy. The Civil Code adopted in 1987 must also be updated, since its provisions on the law of contractual obligations were written to govern basically the contracts between state owned enterprises or non-commercial transactions between individuals such as the sale of personal property. Other areas of law must also be modernized, such as the laws governing business organization, personal injury and consumer protection. In addition, the concept of bankruptcy and its legal implications as

---

[27] *Derecho Económico* (Havana: Editorial de Ciencias Sociales, 1988), V. Laptev, ed., p. 26 (quoting Lenin).

[28] Decreto Ley No. 172 (Del Banco Central de Cuba), *Gaceta Oficial Ext.*, No.4, May 28, 1997; Decreto Ley No. 173 (Sobre los Bancos y las Instituciones Financieras No Bancarias), *Gaceta Oficial Ext.*, No.4, May 28, 1997. Until 1997, central, commercial and development bank functions were centralized in the National Bank of Cuba. As part of the overall restructuring of the economic institutions and the effort to increase efficiency and growth in the state sector, the government separated these functions by the creation of the Central Bank of Cuba, which will be responsible for implementing monetary policy and regulating and supervising the banks and non-banking financial institutions. As a result of the reorganization, Banco Nacional de Cuba retained its commercial banking functions and oversees a network of commercial and savings banks which serve the population and certain economic sectors. Today, there are numerous commercial and credit banks functioning in Cuba. See, "Respuestas del Sistema Bancario Cubano", Statement by Francisco Soberón Valdés, Minister President of Banco Central de Cuba at the plenary session of the National Assembly of Peoples Power, December 1997.

[29] Anexo al Decreto Ley No. 187 (Bases Generales del Perfeccionamiento Empresarial), *Gaceta Oficial*, September 14, 1998.

[30] Ley No. 73 (Del Sistema Tributario), *Gaceta Oficial Ext.*, No.8, August 5, 1994.

[31] Ley No. 81 (Del Medio Ambiente), *Gaceta Oficial Ext.*, No.7, July 11, 1997.

well as the concepts of unfair competition must be reintroduced into the Cuban legal system. The task is daunting, particularly since there is relatively little expertise in any of these fields in Cuba at the moment either to guide the drafting of new legislation or the implementation of that already adopted.

II. CONTRACT LAW AND STATE ARBITRATION PRIOR TO 1990

To understand the nature of the changes taking place and the subjective as well as objective impediments to their implementation, it is necessary to understand the system that had evolved in Cuba prior to 1990. Although radical transformations took place in the first years of the Revolution, it was only in the mid- to late 1970s that Cuba began to look to legal process as a tool to help build and direct a socialist economic system. As previously noted, the 1970s marked the institutionalization of the revolution when Cuba not only articulated its governmental, judicial, party and economic structure but also adopted several other important laws that governed social relations.[32] Central to the process was the institution of a national economic plan to be implemented by self-managing, state owned enterprises.

At the time the SDPE was introduced in 1975, however, a system regulating inter-enterprise transactions and accountability did not yet exist. Cuba had developed neither a system of contracts applicable to the enterprises charged with implementation of the central plan[33] nor a legal system to govern the execution, validation and enforcement of such contracts. In fact, Cuba did not adopt a new civil code reflective of the changes brought about by the revolution until 1987. Although the prior Civil Code had undergone piecemeal change from 1959 to 1975, the law of contract had not been revised to correspond to the new economic system until 1978 when the first law establishing basic principles for economic contracts between state enterprises was passed,[34] not as part of the Civil Code but as a separate piece of legislation. Simultaneously, the Council of State empowered the Coun-

---

[32] See, Chapter 1.

[33] Under the system of budgetary accounting, state enterprises did not contract with each other for supplies and services but fulfilled directives from central agencies. Thus, no system of inter-enterprise commercial contracts existed until 1978. Emilio Marill, "Sobre los Contratos Económicos y el Arbitraje Estatal," *Boletín Informativo*, No. 2, 1983.

[34] Decreto Ley No. 15 (Normas Básicas para los Contratos Económicos), *Gaceta Oficial*, No. 21, July 7, 1978.

cil of Ministers to organize an arbitration system to investigate and resolve conflicts of an economic character, both pre-contractual and contractual, flowing from monetary-mercantile relationships among state enterprises and other various national economic entities.[35]

The *Organo de Arbitraje Estatal* (OAE), as the state arbitration system of Cuba was called, was formally established by the Council of Ministers in 1978.[36] In general concept, the OAE was based on models found in the Soviet Union and other eastern European socialist countries.[37] Like many Cuban economic institutions that took their form from European socialist models, however, the OAE was shaped by decrees and regulations that reflected the specific circumstances and experiences of Cuba.[38]

State arbitration in socialist economies was as fundamentally different from arbitration in capitalist systems in its purpose and function as the economic system it supported. Private contract law is the fundamental regulatory device that enables competitive markets to function.[39] The sanctity of the private contractual relationship is so elevated in the United States that it enjoys constitutional protection against state interference. In contrast, in the Cuban socialist economy of the 1980s, a contract was not the expression of an independent bargain reflecting private interests, but an instrument in the implementation of a national economic plan that attempted to allocate resources to provide the greatest and most equitable societal benefit.

In theory, the creation of SDPE and the granting of management autonomy to enterprises made the contract the primary mechanism for the internal ordering of economic activities in accordance with the national plan. The plan outlined the annual production and service goals to be achieved by state

---

[35] Decreto Ley No. 10 (1977), Art. 1. In 1962, the government had created Arbitration Commissions to resolve disputes between state enterprises, government entities and the private sector. The law, however, had substantial deficiencies which made it ineffectual; arbitration was not compulsory and had no mechanism to assure compliance with decisions. Also there was no legislation dealing with contractual relations between enterprises. The commissions were disbanded in 1967. Miguel Reyes Salia, "El Sistema de Arbitraje Estatal en Cuba," *Revista Cubana de Derecho*, No. 20, 1982, pp. 73, 78.

[36] Decreto No. 23 (Del Sistema de Arbitraje Estatal), *Gaceta Oficial*, August 17, 1978.

[37] For a discussion of the Soviet state arbitration system see John Hazard, "Production Discipline: The Role of State Arbitration in the USSR," *Review of Socialist Law*, No. 4, 1982, p. 297.

[38] For a discussion of the differences between the functioning of economic institutions in Cuba and the Soviet Union see Zimbalist, *Cuba's Socialist Economy*.

[39] Although market exchanges could take place in the absence of contract law, Richard Posner suggests that private contract law serves three primary functions in the marketplace: It provides an efficient system for holding parties to their bargain; it reduces the complexity of market transactions; and it provides information which assists rational decision-making with respect to the bargain. Richard Posner, *Economic Analysis of Law* (Boston: Little Brown, 1972), pp. 67-69.

enterprises. In broad terms, the quantities and prices of goods to be produced were determined by the plan. The plan was then elaborated and made more specific and implemented through the negotiation of "planned" contracts between state enterprises.[40]

While the enterprises were supposed to be self-financing and self-managing, they were nevertheless obligated to negotiate "planned" contracts with other enterprises in order to fulfill the plan. The concept of state enterprises that were accountable for their profitability provided, at least theoretically, the incentive to negotiate terms that served efficiency and profit-maximizing objectives. Such terms would include specifications as to quality, quantities, date of delivery, terms of payment, responsibility for transport, storage, etc.

The state enterprises not only had a legal duty to enter into "planned" contracts but were also legally obligated to demand their execution and performance.[41] In the event a planned contract was not executed and neither party sought intervention by the OAE, the OAE could initiate a proceeding on its own, *de oficio*, to require execution of the contract.[42] Damages alone, however, were not a sufficient remedy since the contracted performance was not generally available from another source, causing harm to society as well as to the enterprise. Thus, to enable the injured enterprise to fulfill its obligations under the plan, the breaching enterprise was obligated whenever possible to perform the contract in addition to paying damages. Moreover, in addition to profit incentives, administrative personnel could be disci-

---

[40] "Planned" contracts were those which implemented the national economic plan. There were also unplanned contracts which an enterprise could enter into on its own initiative with surplus supplies or services not necessary to fulfill the national plan. Decreto-Ley No. 15 (1978), Arts. 4-5.

[41] Ibid., Arts. 4 and 33. Thus, state arbitration proceedings were brought not only to resolve disputes over performance of contracts, but also to resolve disputes that arose in the formation and execution of the contract. Where such expertise was lacking, the parties were unable to agree or one party refused to sign a proposed contract, one or both could request OAE intervention to resolve the dispute and to assure that a contract was executed and that it contained the necessary legal clauses. Decreto-Ley 15 (1978), Art. 33. Interview with Dr. Benito Besada, Vice President of the OAEN, Havana, Cuba, May 23, 1984.

[42] The OAE learned of failures of enterprises to execute required contracts by means of a third party who was affected by the situation, through other state reporting mechanisms, or by means of the OAE's own inspection procedures. In the initial years of its existence, the OAE frequently sent arbitrators to visit enterprises to discuss the system and to review contracts. The function of the OAE was not to impose terms on the parties, but to get the enterprises to agree on fundamental provisions necessary to fulfill their obligations under the national plan. Decreto No. 89 (Reglas de Procedimiento del Artibtraje Estatal), Art. 8(c), *Gaceta Oficial*,No.5, June 8, 1981.

plined for intentional or negligent failure to carry out contractual obligations, including execution of a contract.[43]

The system was designed to reinforce the fusion of the self-interest of the enterprises to maximize profitability[44] with the societal interest in fulfillment of the plan with maximum efficiency. As the juridical body charged with defending the social interest in the completion of the national economic plan, the OAE was to have played an essential role in balancing these interests. Further, the State Arbitration System was given jurisdiction to resolve disputes over economic impact of environmental harms.[45]

Some specialists contend that by the late 1980s the system was beginning to take root, instilling an understanding of the importance of contractual obligations.[46] The number of *de oficio* proceedings had dropped dramatically suggesting that enterprises were complying with the system.[47] However, it was precisely at this point that the government eliminated the OAE and transferred its jurisdiction to the newly established Chambers of Economic Law.

Whatever advancement had been accomplished in implementing this system of planned contracts, it has become obsolete since 1990 as have the underlying conceptions that guided the training and behavior of manage-

---

[43] Decreto-Ley No. 36 ((Sobre la Disciplina de los Dirigentes y Funcionarios Administrativos Estatales), Art. 4., *Gaceta Oficial* No.18, April 2, 1980. Because inexperienced management posed a significant impediment to implementation of the new system, the OAE, when it began functioning in 1980, provided technical assistance to management of the state enterprises, especially in the drafting of contracts. Regional seminars were organized by the OAE staff to teach management personnel and their legal advisors the importance of contracts in the new economic system, as well as how to draft and negotiate contracts. Seminars were also conducted to explain new regulations and to discuss problems which had been identified by arbitrators and management.

[44] This "self-interest" was largely theoretical as state enterprises were generally subsidized because of inefficiency. Only since 1997 have such subsidies been withdrawn, thus making the management accountable for losses.

[45] Moreover, the OAE's mandate went well beyond dispute resolution and included functions related to development and planning. For example, the OAE was charged with organizing a system of research and analysis concerning economic contracts and with investigating the causes of litigation for the purpose of proposing measures to prevent such disputes. Decreto No. 60 (Reglamento Orgánico de los Organos del Sistema de Arbitraje Estatal), Arts. 10(j) and (k), *Gaceta Oficial*, December 29, 1979. Thus, based on its experience with various industries, particular disputes, and its own research, the OAE made recommendations to the economic planning agencies such as the National Bank, the State Committee for Finance and others directly involved in state economic planning as well as to the management of particular enterprises. Interview with Dr. Benito Besada. Thus, the OAE served an important function in the process of developing the socialist economic system.

[46] Interview with Narciso Cobo, Havana, Cuba, October 7, 1992. Interview with Miguel Reyes Salia, Principal Arbitrator OAEN, Havana, Cuba, June 10, 1989.

[47] Ibid.

ment personnel as well as the lawyers and judges. Reforms undertaken since 1990, particularly the introduction of market mechanisms replacing centralized planning, have significantly altered contractual relations between state enterprises as well as their dealings with foreign businesses and joint ventures in Cuba. Overhauling the legal framework to support a more decentralized, market oriented socialist model is a daunting task in itself; preparing the very persons accustomed to centralized, hierarchical and inflexible regulatory schemes who must now manage decentralized and financially autonomous enterprises poses an even greater challenge.

III. THE NEW CHAMBER OF ECONOMIC LAW

In August 1991, the Council of State established new economic law chambers in the Supreme Court and the Provincial Courts with exclusive jurisdiction over contract disputes previously handled by the OAE.[48] The reason for the apparently abrupt decision to eliminate the OAE and transfer all such disputes to the courts is not entirely clear. It may have been a consequence of the general disruption in the economy. Since economic plans based on the former socialist market were useless and the availability of resources and imports extremely uncertain, factories and enterprises could not predict what was going to be produced and when. Consequently, the objectives of the OAE as originally designed were no longer applicable although the work of the OAE could have been adjusted to the new circumstances. In addition, although some experts contend that the arbitration system was just beginning to operate as planned, the state enterprises were notoriously inefficient, surviving not on self-financing but on state subsidies. Whatever the reasons for the elimination of the OAE, it is clear that Cuban managers still have a lot to learn about business economics, marketing and production management as well as contractual relations.

Another reason for the replacement of the OAE stems from the increasing number of "mixed" enterprises formed with foreign investors after 1991. Although a 1982 law permitted the creation of such joint ventures, none were established until the Cuban government began to promote foreign capital investment in Cuba after 1989. Although the OAE had been given jurisdiction over contractual disputes arising between "mixed" enterprises and state enterprises, it was tied to state economic institutions. As the number of joint ventures grew, it was clear that a forum for dispute resolution

[48] Decreto-Ley No.129 (De Extinción del Sistema de Arbitraje Estatal), *Gaceta Oficial Ext.*, No.9, August 19, 1991.

independent of the state economic planning system had to be established because the legal principles to be applied to such disputes would necessarily be different than those applied to cases arising from "planned" contracts between state enterprises. Thus, it was determined that disputes arising from their operations in Cuba should be resolved within the ordinary court system.[49]

However, the courts did not adopt new procedural rules for the new economic law chambers. To fill the void, the Supreme Court determined that the procedures which had governed the OAE would continue to apply to cases brought to the economic law chambers with some modifications and adjustments.[50] As of courts gained experience with such cases, judges began to draft a new law of procedure applicable to economic disputes in 2002.

Notably, the authority to initiate procedures *de oficio* was eliminated; thus, only complaints initiated by a party or the Attorney General in the case of violations of the environmental law may be decided by the court. According to the legislation abolishing the OAE, conflicts arising between state enterprises in the pre-contractual phase were to be handled administratively by the relevant ministries.[51] Further, the OAE procedures permitting the parties to negotiate an officially supervised settlement were revoked eliminating a judicially supervised settlement process. The parties, however, may reach a settlement out of court in which case the plaintiff withdraws the complaint. A complaint may be withdrawn as well in cases where the defendant pays the sum demanded or fulfills other contractual obligations which have been breached.

Economic law chambers were established in each of the Provincial Courts and the Supreme Court. Until 2001, the Supreme Court was the court of first instance in most cases, the Provincial Courts being given jurisdiction only over cases in which the value of the claim was less than the equivalent of $100,000US. Because of the heavy load of cases, this division was altered in August, 2001, giving the Provincial Courts jurisdiction over all cases in the first instance and the Supreme Court assuming the exclusive role as appellate court.[52] Between 1991-1998, the economic law chambers have primarily dealt with cases of non-payment of obligations (approximately 60% of cases) and shortfalls in delivery of goods (approxi-

---

[49] Ibid.

[50] Instrucción No. 141 (Tribunal Supremo), *Gaceta Oficial*, September 30, 1991.

[51] Decreto-Ley No. 129 (1991), Art. 6.

[52] Decreto-Ley No. 223 (De la Jurisdicción y Competencia de las Salas de lo Económico de los Tribunales Populares), *Gaceta Oifical*, August 16, 2001.

mately 20% of cases).[53] Other cases involve a variety of forms of breach of contracts. Although it has jurisdiction to decide cases brought under the 1997 Environmental Protection Law, very few such cases have been brought to the court.[54] In general, the courts hear claims between legal entities. Disputes involving individuals are decided by the civil law chambers.

In significant ways the economic law chambers must chart new territory in the Cuban legal system. The OAE was charged with not only safeguarding the rights of the litigants but also with taking into account the social interest in the dispute. It was after all an appendage of the Central Administration of the State and the Central Economic Planning Board. Today, the economic law chambers must apply the law to non-state entities, such as joint ventures and foreign subsidiaries, whose interests may diverge from those of the general society. The court can no longer take into account the specific impact on the national economy when deciding a dispute; it must simply apply the law. It is essential if Cuba is to continue to attract foreign investment in the form of joint ventures or the formation under Cuban law of wholly owned foreign companies that these parties have confidence in the impartiality of Cuba's judicial system.

In order to handle the growing case load, the Supreme Court has had to recruit and train more than 60 new judges for the Economic Law Chambers in the Provincial Courts. The Court has organized courses and seminars to train these judges in contract law and economic legislation, laws that had laid dormant for decades or that have been recently adopted. With new legislative developments on the horizon, the task of tooling and retooling both the judiciary and the bar is a constant challenge.

IV. FOREIGN INVESTMENT LAW

Like a number of other socialist countries, Cuba adopted legislation permitting joint ventures with foreign partners. Cuba did this in February of

---

53 Interview with Dr. Elpidio Pérez Suárez, President of the Chamber of Economic Law of the Supreme Court, Havana, Cuba, September 17, 1999.

54 The Environmental Protection Law was adopted in 1997. One of its primary enforcement mechanisms is the requirement of "environmental licenses" for all new investment and development which obligates the investor to undertake and submit an environmental impact statement which is reviewed by the Licensing Department of the Ministry of Science, Technology and Environment. See, Fredric Evenson, "A Deeper Shade of Green: The Evolution of Cuban Environmental Law and Policy", *Golden Gate University Law Review*, Vol. 28, No. 3, Spring 1998, pp. 489-525.

1982,[55] several years before the Soviets took similar steps. However, it was not until 1990, when the shortage of capital for investment became acute, that Cuba actively began to court foreign investment.[56] At the beginning, Cuba sought investments to expand facilities for international tourism, but it has since sought and obtained investment in other diverse areas including mining, energy production, light manufacturing, agriculture and marketing. In order to provide a measure of security to investors Cuban gave foreign investments constitutional recognition in 1992.[57]

Until 1994, the State Committee for Economic Cooperation (CECE) was given the task of developing and negotiating potential joint ventures. Since then, it has been the responsibility of the new Ministry of Foreign Investment and Economic Cooperation (MINVEC). A new law on foreign investment, adopted in 1995, governs the kinds of investments permitted, the rules regulating economic associations formed under the law and the process of approval.[58]

Major Provisions

The 1982 law permitted only one form of foreign investment: a joint venture between a foreign company and a Cuban entity in which the Cuban party was to retain at least 51% control.[59] The 1995 law encompasses not only such joint ventures, but also majority and wholly owned foreign companies and contracts of economic association between Cuban enterprises and foreign companies. Moreover, it expands the definition of investment to include both direct and indirect investment through stocks and other securities.[60]

The distinction between joint ventures, or "mixed enterprises" as they are called in Cuba, and other economic associations which include both Cuban and foreign participation lies in the fact that the former establishes a

---

[55] Decreto-Ley No. 50 (Sobre Asociación Económica entre Entidades Cubanas y Extranjeras), *Gaceta Oficial Ext.*, No.3, February 15, 1982.

[56] Carranza Valdés, pp. 155-156. For a complete description of the 1982 law and its provisions, see Jean G. Zorn and Harold A. Mayerson, "Cuba's Joint Venture Law: New Rules for Foreign Investment," *Columbia Journal of Transnational Law*, Vol. 21, 1983, p. 273.

[57] Constitución de la República de Cuba(1992), Art. 23.

[58] Ley No. 77 (Ley de Inversión Extranjera), *Gaceta Oficial Ext.*, No.3, September 6, 1995.

[59] In practice, on occasion, the percentage of foreign ownership was approved at levels above 50%.

[60] Ley No. 77(1995), Art. 11.

juridical personality distinct from the investor partners whereas the formation of an economic association is a contractual relationship in which the contracting parties remain independent juridical persons.[61] Contracts of economic association are used primarily in areas of promotion, packaging, distribution and marketing.

One of the major changes forged by the 1995 law that received the most attention in the foreign press is that a foreign investor may in some circumstances establish and operate a wholly owned enterprise in Cuba. Such investors may be individuals or companies that create a Cuban affiliate of a subsidiary of the foreign parent.[62] They have the right to manage the business, but are subject to all the regulations concerning commercial enterprises and foreign investment in Cuba. Although theoretically a highly significant development, the magnitude of this change should not be exaggerated; there is no indication that such wholly owned enterprises will be permitted in the key sectors of the national economy. Further, all such investments require the highest level of scrutiny and approval.[63]

Perhaps more important, the new law opens all sectors of the Cuban economy to foreign investment and association with three exceptions: health services, public education and the armed forces. With respect to the latter, however, foreign investment is permitted in the commercial enterprises operated by the military.[64] Thus, as had been announced at the 1995 Havana Trade Fair, even the highly important sugar sector is now open to foreign participation. Moreover, for the first time, investments may be made in real estate that may be developed for residential or office purposes for foreigners, and investments may also be made in real property to be used in tourism operations.[65] The law, however, maintains the rule that property ownership is confined to structures and goods but not to land. Foreign investors as well as Cuban nationals obtain only rights to usufruct with respect to land.

---

[61] Ibid., Arts. 13-14.
[62] Ibid. Art. 15.2.
[63] Ibid., Art. 21.2.
[64] Ibid., Art. 10. The army as well as the Ministry of Interior have developed a number of commercial enterprises in various economic sectors, including tourism, agriculture, manufacturing and services.
[65] Ibid., Art. 16. In the case of residences constructed by joint ventures or foreign enterprises, such apartments or houses may be sold to foreign residents.

Authorization

Although the new law introduces greater flexibility, the role of the government in overseeing the investment process remains substantial. In each instance of investment, government authorization is necessary before the venture can go forward. Authorization involves distinct layers of review, depending on the type of investment. In the case of joint ventures, the initial contract is negotiated between the Cuban and foreign partners. It is then submitted for approval to the Executive Committee of the Council of Ministers or to a Commission that it designates.[66] The statute sets out the formalities of applications for approval of foreign investments.[67]

In some circumstances, the Executive Committee of the Council of Ministers has exclusive authority to approve the investment. These circumstances include: investments in excess of ten million dollars; wholly owned foreign companies; investments in the areas of pubic services such as transport, communications, aqueducts, electricity, etc.; investments by foreign states; exploitation of natural resources; when the investment involves the transfer of state property or real estate; and investments in enterprises of the armed forces.[68]

In the case of wholly owned foreign enterprises, a foreign investor must first communicate with MINVEC which will indicate the appropriate Cuban entity in the relevant commercial sector responsible for evaluating the proposal. When the investor and the Cuban entity come to agreement on the proposal, it is presented jointly by the foreign investor and the Cuban entity to MINVEC which then makes an initial determination if the proposal should be submitted to the Council of Ministers for approval.

Joint ventures and contracts of economic association must also be approved initially by MINVEC and then approved by the Executive Committee of the Council of Ministers or the designated Commission.[69] Approval or denial of all proposed investments is supposed to be determined within 60 days from the date the proposal is presented.[70] This latter provision responds to complaints concerning the slowness of the approval process. However, it is unstated what would occur if the authorization or denial is not issued within 60 days, and there are accounts that delays continue to extend well beyond 60 days—up to a year in some cases.[71]

---

[66] The Council of Ministers is the administrative branch of the government.

[67] Ley No. 77(1995), Arts. 20-25.

[68] Ibid., Art. 21.

[69] Ibid., Arts. 20-21.

[70] Ibid., Art. 23.6.

[71] See, "Cuba Responds to Complaints from Investors," AP July 7, 2002.

Autonomy and Guarantees

The law specifically addresses the issue of security of investments and prohibits expropriation of foreign investments except when such action is for a public use or in the public interest that must be declared by the government in accordance with the provisions of the constitution, legislation and international agreements on the promotion and protection of investments.[72] In addition, before expropriation can take place, the investor must be compensated for the commercial value of the property that is to be established by mutual accord. If no agreement is reached as to the value of the investment to be expropriated, the appraisal is to be submitted to an international expert body authorized by the Ministry of Finance and agreed upon by the parties.[73]

Investment agreements are authorized for a fixed term of years giving either party the possibility of pulling out of the deal at the end of the term. However, the term may be renewed by the parties or the relevant authority. If there is no agreement to renew the term, the entity will be liquidated at the termination of the authorization pursuant to the terms of the contract between the parties.[74]

Foreign investors in joint ventures or economic associations have the right to sell or transfer their share or a portion of their share in the enterprise to the state or to a third party at any time with the prior agreement of the other investor.[75] In the case of a wholly foreign owned enterprise the investor may also transfer or sell its entire interest or a portion thereof to the state or a third party with prior authorization of the Cuban government. The price established for such sales or transfers is to be fixed by mutual agreement or a recognized international body as in the case of expropriations.[76]

Moreover, a joint venture is governed by the Articles of Incorporation to which the parties agree to subscribe which set forth the rules of governance, permitting the company to appoint its own board of directors to manage the enterprise.[77] The enterprise is also free of government regulation pertaining to production plans, prices, staffing patterns and other aspects of management. It may also contract with foreign personnel for executive, high level administrative and skilled technical positions, and these employees may be

---

[72] Ibid., Art. 3.
[73] Ibid.
[74] Ibid., Art. 4.
[75] Ibid., Art. 6.
[76] Ibid., Art. 7.
[77] Ibid., Art. 13.

paid in convertible foreign currency.[78] In the case of technical personnel, it must be shown that the post cannot be filled with a Cuban worker.

Foreign investors are expressly authorized to freely transfer out of the country in convertible currency, free of taxes or other encumbrance, the net earnings or dividends obtained from the investment as well as payments received as the result of expropriation or sale or transfer of its share in the enterprise. The individual foreign investors are not taxed on personal income obtained from profits of the business.[79] However, subject to certain exemptions, the joint ventures themselves, as well as other economic enterprises are required to pay taxes including taxes on earnings, employment and social security taxes, fees on ground transport and vehicles, and fees for documents.[80] All taxes and fees are to be paid in convertible currency. In general, taxes on profits are set at 30% of net earnings.[81] Taxes on profits earned from the exploitation of natural resources, however, may be set as high as 50%.[82]

The law provides tax incentives for reinvestment, allowing a total or partial waiver of taxes if the profits are to be reinvested in the country and the Executive Committee of the Council of Ministers determines that it is in the national interest to do so. Employment taxes are 11% of payroll, and the contribution to social security is 14%.

As of the end of 2002, there were 412 joint ventures and economic associations functioning in Cuba.[83] However, as Cuba becomes more selective, pursuing larger, targeted investments as opposed to small investments, the number of new agreements with foreign companies has diminished: 58 investments approved in 1999 as compared to 34 in 2000. A new modality of economic association introduced at the end of 2000, the cooperative agreement, provides for 3 to 5 year contracts by which a foreign company may guaranty assets such as raw materials, technology or equipment in the production process in return for exclusive foreign distribution rights during the term of the agreement. The foreign party to such a contract, however, does not share in the profits of the enterprise, which remains entirely stated owned and managed.

---

78 Ibid., Art. 31.2.

79 Ibid., Art. 39(d).

80 Ibid., Art. 39.

81 Ibid., Art. 39(a).

82 Ibid., Art. 39(b).

83 "Cuba Responds to Complaints of Investors," AP, July 17, 2002. Spain lead with the majority of investments, followed by Canada, Italy, France, Mexico and Great Britain.

Labor Relations

Aware of the impact investment might have, the Cuban trade unions became involved in the early stages of the drafting of the 1995 law and continue to monitor and participate in policy developments. Early drafts of the 1995 law prompted the CTC to make a number of proposals and counter-proposals concerning issues related to worker rights and labor relations. Specifically, the CTC rejected a provision that would have permitted direct hiring by the foreign investment enterprises and insisted that all hiring of Cuban workers be done through a Cuban employment agency. While direct hiring was attractive to management, the proposal augured serious consequences for the role of the trade unions and the intensification of inequality of income among Cuban workers. The proposal was rejected in the final text of the law.[84] Moreover, the CTC insisted that no concessions be made to the foreign investors with respect to compliance with labor laws and that the new law explicitly obligate the foreign investment enterprises to fully comply with them.[85]

Thus, with the exception of high-level administrative posts, foreign investment enterprises may not contract with workers directly but must hire Cuban citizens or permanent residents through a special employment entity. An aspect of the indirect hiring procedure that has been the focus of attacks by some outside critics is that the enterprise pays the special employment entity the salaries of the workers in convertible currency (US dollars), and the entity in turn pays the workers in Cuban pesos. Detractors call this practice "slave labor," but in fact it is designed to maintain parity among Cuban workers doing similar jobs while at the same time providing the government hard currency needed to subsidize social programs. Moreover, workers at joint ventures are generally more privileged than workers in state enterprises. Although paid their salaries in Cuban pesos, they receive benefits not often available to other Cuban workers in the form of bonuses,[86] tips and other perks such as meals, transportation and goods.

---

[84] However, in special circumstances the enterprise may seek authorization to contract all workers directly. What constitutes such special circumstances or the process for its authorization are not yet spelled out by implementing regulations. ETECSA, the telephone company jointly owned by an Italian and Cuban company, hires employees directly.

[85] For an analysis of labor rights and labor relations in Cuba, see Debra Evenson, *Workers in Cuba: Unions and Labor Relations* (Detroit: Guild Law Center, 2001). Cuban workers enjoy substantial universal rights, including: a month's paid vacation; an 8-hour work day; sick leave and free health care; a year's maternity leave with guaranty of return to the same job; free education and training; and the right to join a union.

[86] The amount of bonuses is to be agreed upon with MINVEC, but all enterprises formed under the 1995 Investment Law must create a fund for such bonuses.

Salaries of workers in Cuba are established by law based on categories of work and skills. Much has been written about how the average Cuban worker today receives the equivalent of $8-15 US at the going conversion rate of $1 for 26 Cuban pesos in 2002. However, the conclusion to be drawn from this simple equation must take into account other factors in order to calculate the real income of Cuban workers. Although low and in many cases insufficient, the income of Cuban workers has a much greater purchasing power than a simple conversion rate of currency suggests.[87] To begin with, most Cubans own their own homes, and if they are renting or paying off a mortgage, that payment is approximately equivalent to $1 or less a month. Utilities cost around 25 cents of the dollar. Basic food rations are likewise extremely inexpensive although insufficient for an adequate diet and must be supplemented. Health care and education are free. Public transportation is virtually free.

Moreover, the vast majority of Cuban workers who are employed by profitable enterprises, whether joint ventures or wholly state-owned, receive bonuses which in some instances may amount to the equivalent of double their monthly salary. Still, the CTC argues that salaries remain insufficient and lobbies for increased salaries and benefits.

There are no separate unions for workers in the foreign investment enterprises; rather workers may join the national union representing workers in that sector. For example, the National Union of Chemical, Mining and Energy Workers, represents the workers in the joint venture nickel mines as well as those at the wholly state-owned mines. As a consequence, workers in an industry or sector are fully aware of conditions and circumstances from one enterprise to another regardless of its ownership. A union representative is entitled to attend the monthly meetings of the management councils of the enterprise. In accordance with Cuban labor law, each enterprise must sign a collective bargaining agreement with the corresponding union. The collective bargaining agreement is similar in basic content to that negotiated and signed with state enterprises in the new system of decentralized management.

Free Trade Zones and Industrial Parks

The Foreign Investment law of 1995 also authorizes the creation of free trade zones and industrial parks in specific areas of the country. Established

---

87 See, Ana Julia Jatar-Hausmann, *The Cuban Way*(West Hartford: Kumarian Press, 1999), pp.113-15.

with the objective of stimulating production activities and increasing employment opportunities, the free trade zones and industrial parks are meant to cover primarily financial, import, export, warehousing, production and re-export activities. Special customs, immigration and other regulations have been established for these zones, but the same labor regulations that govern Cuban enterprises are applied. Decisions concerning both the free trade zones and the industrial parks are controlled by the Executive Committee of the Council of Ministers. Norms and regulations were announced in October 1996 which detail how such zones will be established and regulated.[88]

Environmental Protection Provisions of the Foreign Investment Law

Preservation of the environment and rational use of resources are two criteria that are supposed to guide approval of investments.[89] MINVEC is charged with submitting all proposals to the Ministry of Science, Technology and Environment (MSTE) to evaluate the proposal from an environmental perspective and to decide whether an environmental impact evaluation is necessary before approval. MSTE is also to determine whether certain licenses, or controls and inspections are required pursuant to current legislation. The procedures for environmental impact licenses and implementing environmental controls were given strength in the new Law on the Environment adopted in July 1997.[90]

In addition, under the 1997 Environmental Law, all new economic development projects and expansions of existing businesses must submit studies of the potential environmental impact and obtain an environmental license before the project is approved. This applies universally and not only to foreign investments. MSTE is authorized to dictate measures required to resolve situations in which the enterprise causes damage or risks to the environment or natural resources. According to the statute, the individual or company responsible for damage to the environment will be obligated to restore the environment to its previous condition, repair the material dam-

---

[88] Instrucción Z.F. No. 1/96 (Ministerio de Inversión Extranjera y la Colaboración Económica), *Gaceta Oficial*. December 4, 1996; Instrucción Z.F. No. 2/6 (Ministerio de Inversión Extranjera y la Colaboración Económica), *Gaceta Oficial*. December 4, 1996.

[89] Ley 77(1995), Arts. 54-55.

[90] Ley No. 81 (1997). For a description of the development of this law and its application, see Fredric Evenson, "A Deeper Shade of Green: The Evolution of Cuban Environmental Law and Policy," *Golden Gate University Law Review*, Vol. 28, No. 3, Spring 1998, pp. 489-525.

age or pay damages. The project may also be rejected if the impact is significantly harmful.

Impact of the Foreign Investment Law

The 1995 law did not lead to an avalanche of new investment proposals. Nor did the Cuban government predict that it would. In fact, Carlos Lage, Secretary of the Council of Ministers, has made it clear that Cuba views foreign investment as complementary to other reforms and not the cornerstone of Cuba's economic recovery.[91] As of the end of 1998, there were 350 deals concluded with foreign investors, either as joint ventures or contracts of economic association. Numerous interviews with foreign investors which have appeared in the Cuban press and elsewhere reveal that they find investments in Cuba attractive for a variety of reasons: the signs of stable economic recovery; the very good potential for tourism—unspoiled beaches and other tourist locations; Cuba's highly educated work force; competitive labor costs; a stable political situation; and the low level of corruption. Some of the drawbacks include: weak, but improving infrastructure (actually telephone service has begun to improve in the last few years as the result of foreign investment); and bureaucratic red tape creating delays in issuing required approvals and permits.[92]

Cuba does not allow foreign lawyers to practice law in Cuba except in the Duty Free Zones; rather, it has set up special law offices staffed by Cuban lawyers to do the necessary legal work, including contract negotiation, for the formation of these ventures.[93] Thus, the joint venture and foreign investors must rely on Cuban lawyers—whether from a special law office or hired as in house counsel—to represent them before the courts and administrative authorities. In the early 1990s, most Cuban lawyers had no training or experience in the field of commercial law whatsoever. Those that did were primarily lawyers who practiced law before the revolution. Thus, there has been a lot of catch up required and the law school as well as other institutions have offered numerous opportunities for post-graduate study.[94]

---

[91] "Amplio análisis para Mejorar y Controlar el Proceso de la Inversión Extranjera," *Granma*, March 16, 1999, p. 3.

[92] According to press reports, foreign investors continue to complain about delays and red tape. In 2002, the delay in obtaining approvals was approximately a year. See, "Cuba Responds to Complaints from Investors," AP July 17, 2002.

[93] See, Chapter 3.

[94] Ibid.

In addition to the economic benefits the joint ventures provide, their presence has introduced a new dynamic. Not only do they generally operate differently and more efficiently than state enterprises, thereby providing new experience for the Cuban personnel, they also generate an entrepreneurial spirit fueled by the quest for profits. They also offer opportunities and economic advantages that many talented Cubans find more attractive than those offered by state enterprises. Thus, the foreign investment enterprises compete with Cuban enterprises for the best and brightest.

In addition, the growth in tourism brought about by foreign investment has been the engine for economic recovery in other areas of the Cuban economy. At the end of 2001, Cuban enterprises supplied over 65% of the goods and services purchased by the tourism industry compared to 35% in 1999.[95] Other investments have been equally important for substantially increasing nickel and domestic oil production as well as introducing energy innovations developed with foreign investment. Undoubtedly, the opening to foreign investment has benefited Cuban workers as well as the economy as a whole.

IV. REFORM OF STATE ENTERPRISES

State enterprises were established in the early years of the Cuban revolution under the various ministries and central state administrative bodies. These enterprises had both independent legal personality and their own assets, but their structures and management systems were dictated by statute. Moreover, their production plans formed part of the larger national economic plan, and the contracts they entered into to fulfill those plans were mandated by the central planning agency. The state enterprises were notoriously inefficient as the workforce was usually bloated, there was little incentive for workers to be efficient and little accountability on the part of management given the assurance of state subsidies and the absence of rigorous accounting and auditing systems. Although the workers and unions participated in the development of work plans to meet production quotas and entered into collective bargaining contracts with management, their role was ill defined and the contracts were formal instruments the purpose of which was not clearly understood.[96]

---

[95] Juan Triana Cordovi, "La Economía Cubana en el 2001, una perpectiva global," in *La Economía Cubana en el 2001* (Havana: CEEC, 2002), p.p. 6-7.

[96] See, Memorias, XVII Congreso de la CTC, April 27-30, 1996 (Havana: Editorial de Ciencias Sociales: 1998) p. 53.

Perhaps the most important pillar in the program of economic reforms has been the decentralization of the state-owned enterprise. Dismantling the obsolete structures and patterns of relationships dictated by the centralized economic system erected in the 1970s necessitated redesigning the organization of the state enterprises, both those involved in export and those supplying the domestic market. This required both the expansion of managerial autonomy and the withdrawal of state subsidies. It also meant introducing changes that will strengthen, if not alter conceptually, the role of the workers and their unions and their relationship to management. Although the elimination of state subsidies in all but the most essential industries began as early as 1993, the necessary reforms to make the state enterprises more efficient did not come until later and have not yet been fully implemented.

Since 1994, all the key Cuban export and foreign trade industries have been reorganized leading to the creation of independent Cuban owned corporations which are registered as *sociedades anónimas*,[97] each with its own shareholders. In general, each has a board of shareholders and a board of directors as well as a management council comprised of the manager and the directors of the various departments. These corporations are registered on the Commercial Register of the Ministry of Justice. No longer supplied with funds from the state budget, they function with their initial capital and earnings. Under the 1994 tax law, they pay a 35% tax on their net profits. The remaining profits may be used to retire debts, particularly for start up capital and assets acquired from the predecessor companies, or they may be reinvested, distributed in the form of bonuses, used to improve conditions for workers, or distributed to the shareholders.

The state enterprise is in a process of considerable reform as well, although the design and implementation of the reforms have taken longer to evolve. In August 1998, based on experiments in new forms of enterprise organization and management in various areas of the economy, primarily enterprises directed by the military, the Council of State approved a plan to restructure the state enterprises.[98] The reforms are to be introduced gradually as enterprises achieve the requisite level of preparation to assimilate such changes. The "General Bases for the Perfection of Enterprises," an-

---

[97] For example, in 1994 HABANOS, S.A. was created to undertake the export of Cuban cigars which had previously been the responsibility of Cubatabaco, a state enterprise belonging to the Ministry of Foreign Commerce. Similarly, the production of export quality rum, previously produced by a state entity which produced many beverages, was entrusted to the new Cuban corporation Cuba Ron, S.A. The Cuban airlines, Cubana, is now run and operated by
Cubana, S.A., etc.

[98] Decreto-Ley No. 187 Anexo (Bases Generales del Perfeccionamiento Empresarial), *Gaceta Oficial*, September 14, 1998.

nexed to Decree Law 187 establishing the new system, lays out the steps necessary for a state enterprise to enter into the new system.[99]

To obtain approval, an enterprise must demonstrate capacity in a variety of areas. Since the prior system lacked efficient accounting systems, making it impossible to determine profitability or to control the theft of resources and materials, one of the critical factors is the implementation of a solid, modern accounting system..[100] In addition, the enterprise must undertake a market study, demonstrate the marketability of its goods or services and develop a marketing plan. Finally, it must demonstrate its financial capability in terms of assets and facilities.

The process of implementation has been deliberately gradual. Of the slightly more than 3,000 state enterprises, about a third are currently in various phases of preparation. As of June 2002, only 321 had satisfied the requisites for full implementation; approximately 684 were in the final stages of approval.[101]

Unlike the export enterprises that have been reorganized as independent corporations, the state enterprises approved for the introduction of these reforms remain enterprises created and supervised by the various ministries. However, their management has been given substantial flexibility in establishing internal organization and production plans as well as reinvestment and development plans. Management is now responsible for marketing and profitability as state subsidies have been withdrawn.[102] In this new context, the negotiation and fulfillment of contractual obligations bears no relationship to the prior system of "planned" contracts. Thus, management personnel must acquire new skills and aptitudes to fulfill their new role.

The introduction of this new system will transform labor/management relations as well. Although the labor unions have always had a role in dis-

---

[99] For an interesting assessment of the new system, see Philip Peters, "State Enterprise Reform in Cuba: An Early Snapshot," a report of the Lexington Institute, July 2001.

[100] At the end of June 1999, the National Office of Audits found that 72% of state enterprises were either deficient or very poor in terms of internal controls and accounting. As expected advancement in this area is slow, but the pace is slower than what is needed. "Importancia del Control Interno," *Juventud Rebelde*, July 23, 1999, p. 1.

[101] "Suman 321 las entidades en Perfeccionamiento Empresarial," *Granma*, July 18, 2002, p. 3. See, also, "Biggest Change in Cuban Economy," *Granma Internacional*, March 18, 2001, p. 7 (115 enterprises approved for implementation); Report of the Minister of the Economy and Planning to the National Assembly, December 1999, reprinted in *Granma*, December 29, 1999, pp. 4-5; "Hemos Aprendido," *Opciones*, January 7, 1999, pp. 8-9 (An interview with Jose Luis Rodriguez, Minister of the Economy and Planning).

[102] The process of eliminating subsidies to state enterprises began in 1993. At the end of 1999, less than 30% of state enterprises continued to receive such subsidies mostly in the sectors of sugar and food production. Presentation of the Proposed Budget for 2000 by the Minister of Finance and Prices to the National Assembly in December, 1999, reprinted in *Granma*, December 30, 1999, pp. 4-5.

cussing and approving production plans under the centralized economic system, this role was fairly formal since the plan itself was approved at the national level. There was little incentive for the unions or workers to participate actively in discussion and implementation of efficiency measures. In addition, salaries were fixed by statute. The contract between the union and management was rarely negotiated or relied upon as the instrument which controlled labor/management relations.[103]

Under the new system the interests of management and labor, despite their mutual interest in profitability, have points of divergence that did not exist before.[104] Implementation of these reforms sets a new stage in labor/management relations in Cuba, with labor taking a stronger role. A union representative sits on the management board of each enterprise, and management must provide the workers with monthly reports on production, costs and profits. Because it is a radical departure from past practices, both sides need considerable preparation to confront it. Once the requisites are established, the enterprise must begin the process of preparing both management and labor to function under the new system of self-management and self-financing. This preparation has not been an easy task as there is very little prior experience, and old bureaucratic patterns of thinking and management are difficult to uproot.[105]

In the current situation, the CTC argues, the collective contract must become the primary "instrument" to govern relations between the union and workers and the management whether it be in a state enterprise, a joint venture with a foreign partner or any other kind of enterprise.[106] A comparison with the areas of negotiation under the former system illustrates the dramatic expansion of the nature of the collective bargaining agreement. The most important subjects are related to size, distribution and evaluation of the workforce, work rules, occupational health and safety issues, working conditions and bonuses. Although salary ranges for each job are still predetermined, the application of limited differentials and bonuses are also subjects

---

[103] For a description of collective bargaining in Cuba today, see Evenson, Workers in Cuba, pp. 53-61.

[104] As noted in the Thesis of the 1996 Congress of the CTC, "[i]n previous periods, for reasons that are well known, there was practically no possibility that contradictions or litigations of great importance would emerge between the management and the workers." *Memorias, XVII Congreso de la CTC, April 27-30, 1996* (Havana: Editorial de Ciencias Sociales: 1998) p. 53.

[105] The CTC has undertaken the development of training courses for workers and union leaders to enable them to understand the new dynamics of the role of the unions in the new system. A guide entitled "The Perfection of the Enterprise and the Union Movement" published in March 1999 explains the main aspects of the system and sets out a plan of the points which the union should negotiate with management in the collective agreement.

[106] Ibid.

of the agreement. On issues where the law does not grant unions participation in the decision making responsibility with management, the union can bargain for a role in the elaboration of plans and decisions.

Cuban labor regulations apply to all enterprises: those with foreign investment, those applying the new management systems and those that are not. The difference, perhaps, is that the new state enterprise system more clearly defines the aspects of the collective bargaining agreement. Moreover, the same system for resolution of labor disputes, including both claims of violations on part of management as well as disciplinary measures imposed by management on workers, applies to all enterprises.[107]

The system also requires the development of a managerial culture, one that is guided by economics, not politics, but which at the same time respects and promotes worker participation. Bookstores increasingly carry books on enterprise management techniques. The ministries have developed and imparted courses for management as part of a continual process of improving management know how. In general, enterprises applying the new system registered significant gains in productivity and profitability.[108] Yet, implementation is not entirely smooth and the vast majority of the enterprises still demonstrate difficulties in areas such as cost control.

The potential of the new reforms to create the basis for sustainable development will depend in substantial measure on Cuba's ability to create an effective legal framework. As structural transformations take place in the enterprise system, decentralizing decision making, imposing accountability and changing labor/management relations, the legal framework remains in a state of evolution. Work on drafting a new Labor Code began in 2000, but it is not expected to be completed before the end of 2002. As noted previously, new laws are being developed in many areas of commercial law such as contract, enterprise organization and bankruptcy law.

V. SELF EMPLOYMENT AND FAMILY BUSINESSES

In order to mitigate the growing unemployment produced by the economic crisis that closed many state owned enterprises and forced the government to streamline the state bureaucracy, the Council of State expanded

---

[107] Decreto Ley 176 (Sistema de Justicia Laboral), *Gaceta Oficial,* No.28, August 15, 1997. Adopted in October 1997, the new system took effect on January 1, 1998.

[108] "Suman 321 las entidades en Perfeccionamient Empresarial," *Granma*, July 18, 2002; for brief descriptions of specific enterprise experiences, see Peters, pp. 5-7.

the areas of permissible self-employment in 1993.[109] An additional objective of the measure was to alleviate the decline of services needed by the population. The action was mistakenly perceived by many in the foreign press as the beginnings of capitalism in Cuba. It was never conceived as such, and since the measure was adopted, it has undergone several modifications designed to maintain self-employment within clearly defined boundaries.

It was expected that approximately 200,000 Cubans would engage in service activities like repair of domestic appliances, carpentry, plumbing, hair cutting, etc. In 1996, the self- employed, known as *cuentapropistas*,[110] in fact numbered 198,000.[111] A year later the numbers had shrunk to 166,000 and subsequently increased to its current level of approximately 180,000 persons licensed,[112] with perhaps an equal number operating illegally without registering. The fluctuation is attributed to the imposition of taxes, greater control over materials used as well as competition and the recovery of attractive positions in the workforce. Permissible advertising is limited to signs and handbills, but the most common promotion is word of mouth from satisfied customers.

To engage in self-employment, a person must obtain a license from the Ministry of Labor and Social Security. Today, the only workers who may not engage in such activities are professionals who may not sell services in their areas of professional training. Thus, a medical doctor may not legally provide private medical services. Self-employment may develop into a family business, but no one outside the family may be employed without special permission that is sparingly given.[113] The market for the services of those who are self-employed, with the exception of family owned and run restaurants, is limited by regulations that prohibit state and non-state enterprises from contracting for their services. Thus, they can only provide services to individuals, whether Cubans or foreigners.

While the re-opening of the farmers markets in 1994 cut deeply into the black market, there was concern that the expansion of self-employment would increase thefts of materials from state enterprises that would be di-

---

[109] Decreto-Ley No. 141 (Trabajo por Cuenta Propia), *Gaceta Oficial*, September 8, 1993. Regulations specifying the areas of self-employment and other regulations were issued in subsequent resolutions by the Ministry of Labor and Social Security and the Ministry of Finance and Prices.

[110] The term in Spanish for those who are self-employed in Cuba is "trabajador por propia cuenta," thus *cuentapropista*.

[111] "Las cuentas del cuentapropismo," *Juventud Rebelde*, June 21, 1998, p. 4.

[112] Ibid.

[113] One exception is a small bamboo furniture cooperative organized by retired lawyer Orlando Mena
"Entrepreneurs, Big Hopes, Big Pains," *BusinessWeek*, March 17, 1997, p. 38.

verted to supply these independent workers. To control the use of stolen materials, the law requires that upon request independent workers show receipts of purchases of the materials used. Such materials must be purchased from state operated outlets, generally at retail prices and in hard currency.

One type of private enterprise is the family owned and operated restaurants, known as *paladars*.[114] By law, these restaurants may only seat 12 persons at a time, thus limiting their size and growth. All ingredients used in the food served, as well as beverages, must be purchased from retail stores, the farmers markets, the local urban gardens or be produced by the restaurant owner herself. Certain foods are prohibited from sale such as beef and shell fish, even if purchased in hard currency from the appropriate retail outlets. In addition to these restaurants which frequently occupy the living room of an individual's home, many Cubans have opened refreshment stands outside their homes where they sell homemade pizzas, sandwiches, beverages, and pastries.

After a brief initial boom, many of the in-home restaurants closed. Some were victims of competition from other *paladars* or improved state run restaurants. A number lost their licenses to operate because of infractions, most frequently the sale of prohibited items or use of illegally obtained supplies. A large number continue to operate although the price of a meal has stabilized at prices above those initially charged. A main course in 2002 cost about $6-8 and often more, as opposed to the $3-5 charged at the average Havana *paladar* in the late 1990s. From the beginning, these restaurants have primarily served foreigners visiting or living in Cuba as well as the small number of Cubans who have sufficient income to afford them.

Another category of independent worker includes artists, musicians and authors. These workers are governed by different regulations than those applied to the *cuentapropistas*. Artists and artisans may freely sell their works at prices they establish; composers and writers may freely license or sell the copyrights to their works; and performers may contract to perform in Cuba or abroad. They, must, however, pay taxes on their earnings after discounting the costs and expenses incurred related to their artistic activities. Also, some 11,000 Cubans work as independent transport providers using their own vehicles as taxis, moving vans, haulers, etc. In addition, another source of private income is that derived from renting rooms, garages and other space which was made subject to new regulations in 1997.[115] Each such ac-

---

114 The term *paladar* for small restaurants was adopted from a popular soap opera which featured a restaurant by that name.

115 Decreto Ley No. 171 (Sobre Arendamientos de Viviendas, Habitaciones o Eespacios), *Gaceta Oficial Ext.*, No. 3, May 15, 1997, Resolución No. 255-97 of the Housing Institute, May 20, 1997 and Resolución No. 20-97 of the Ministry of Finance and Prices, May 22,

tivity is licensed and taxed whether the income is derived in Cuban pesos or in hard currency although the tax rates may differ.

Although some activities are taxed on the basis of income, such as artists, most are required to pay a flat tax regardless of income although local municipal officials have discretion to moderate the flat tax in cases they find appropriate. In some cases, such as the rental of rooms in areas considered to be "special" or suitable for tourism, the tax is $200 a month per room rented. If the lessor is able to keep a steady stream of renters, then the payment of the tax is affordable.[116]

These areas of private business have given a small sector of the Cuban population access to income levels not obtainable by most workers, with the exception of those who work in the tourism area and receive income through tips. While many argue that Cuba must expand small business activities if the economy is to thrive, officials worry about the consequences of wealth differentials created by such measures and insist that the current regulations governing such activities are necessary to keep differentials limited. Thus, the proposal to expand the area of private business to include small and medium size service or manufacturing operations has been firmly rejected. Rather than permit the development of a small capitalist class, it is hoped that the new system of management of the state owned enterprises will fill this area of commercial enterprise. At the same time, however, the government insists that it has no intention of eliminating the small private sector made up of the self-employed.

VI. BANKING AND FISCAL REFORM

Equal in importance to the restructuring of economic activity have been the bold measures taken in the area of fiscal management. In some ways, the management of monetary affairs has been far more complex. Cuba had to both confront enormous public debt and severe shortages in hard currency in the context of excessive liquidity. Cuba also remains blocked from access to international financial institutions. Like some of the decisions made in other spheres, measures to solve fiscal problems have proved both successful and problematic.

1997. These regulations provide for the registration of such rentals and the taxes to be applied.

116 Today, the going rate for most rooms rented to foreign visitors in Havana is $25 a night.

"Dollarization"

In 1993, the government permitted Cuban nationals for the first time to possess and use the U.S. dollar as currency in Cuba.[117] Prior to that all purchases and savings accounts had to be in Cuban pesos. When Cubans entered the country with U.S. dollars or received remittances from relatives abroad, they were required to exchange those dollars for Cuban pesos at the rate of one to one. At the time the use of the dollar was legalized, many consumer goods and food items were sold only in hard currency at special dollar shops. Not unexpectedly, the measure has resulted in an economic divide. Although the range of the differential between those who have access and those who do not is quite modest compared to the enormous differentials in wealth almost everywhere else in the world, acceptance of such inequalities has not been easy.[118] Yet, Cuban officials argue that the measure was necessary for many reasons, not the least of which is that most of the goods must be imported and paid for in hard currency and the sales help subsidize food purchases and other essential goods distributed to the population as a whole.[119]

At the same time, other measures were taken to reduce liquidity, reduce the national debt and stabilize the Cuban peso. These included raising prices on non-essential goods like tobacco and alcohol, increasing some license fees and instituting for the first time a tax on income.[120] These measures have been highly successful in both reducing the deficit and excess liquidity. The peso which was exchanged on the black market in 1994 at the rate of 150/1 stabilized after 1997 through state run exchange houses at a rate of 20/1 and in 2002 fluctuated between 25 and 26/1. Production has increased and become more efficient supporting stable prices which, in some instances, have fallen, thus improving the purchase power of the peso. Moreover, the state is now able to offer a much greater range of goods in national currency. Although the objective is to make the Cuban peso convertible, thus returning to use of a single, national currency, that goal is not yet attainable.

[117] Decreto Ley No. 140, *Gaceta Oficial Ext.*, No. 4, August 13, 1993. This decree law revokes provisions of the Criminal Code which made illegal the possession of hard currency.
[118] In 1999, it was estimated that more than 60% of the population has access to dollars from some source, but that still leaves a substantial portion without such buying power.
[119] "No Hay Otro Camino," *Trabajadores*, October 13, 1997.
[120] Ley No. 73 (1994).

Banking System

A fundamental step in decentralizing the economic system and shifting from centralized production management to fiscal management has been the restructuring of the banking system. For almost four decades, the National Bank of Cuba performed both the central as well as commercial banking functions. In 1997, however, these functions were divided. The Central Bank of Cuba was established to assume all of the central banking functions: to control currency; to regulate the money supply and credit; to establish interest rates and internal exchange rates; to supervise all financial institutions and to represent the government of Cuba before all international financial institutions and negotiate the foreign debt.[121] The National Bank of Cuba became a commercial bank which functions along with the five other government controlled banks currently operating in Cuba in addition to a number of finance companies established since 1995.[122] The largest of the commercial banks, the Banco Popular de Ahorro (500 offices) and the Banco de Crédito y Comercio (221 Offices), mainly operate in Cuban pesos; a few banks such as Banco Internacional de Comercio, S.A. (BICSA) and Banco Financiero Internacional, S.A. operate exclusively in hard currency.

The commercial banking system has also been modernized and some banks now offer citizens checking accounts, bank cards, interest bearing deposits and automatic teller machine access. These banks also offer limited credit to individuals for personal use as well as credit in hard currency to enterprises for investments. Thus, as part of the decentralization process and the elimination of state subsidies, the central control of credits and loans previously carried out by the central planning institutions has now passed to the banking system.

Like other developments that have taken place, these reforms require substantial modifications in current law as well as the introduction of new legal concepts. Thus, not only must the banking laws and regulations be amended, but new legislation must be drafted concerning commercial instruments, secured loans, mortgages and bankruptcy.

---

[121] Decreto Ley No. 172 (1997).
[122] Decreto Ley No. 173 (1997).

Tax Laws

Adopted in August 1994, the Law on Taxes introduced a wide variety of income taxes on individuals and enterprises.[123] Although included in the law, no taxes have yet been imposed on wages earned by Cuban workers as contributions to social security.[124] Painters, sculptors and artisans who sell their works as well as musicians and other performing artists who earn money in addition to their state salaries must pay taxes as must those who are self-employed in other service of production capacities. Money received as family remittances as well as gifts are not taxed.[125]

Implementation of these levies, particularly on individuals, took several years to develop, but in spring 1996 the National Tax Office (OTAN) began receiving sworn tax reports together with the obligatory contributions. Tax reports and payments are due in March, and those who do not file on time are subject to penalties as well as arrest in cases of deliberate evasion or fraud.[126] For the year 2000, OTAN issued revised forms to be used in a new automated system. The implementation of the new tax law was accompanied by intensive efforts to institute sound accounting procedures in the state enterprises, but the process of improving these systems has been slow.

VII. CONCLUSION

While maintaining its fundamental socialist character, the Cuban economy has undergone important structural changes since 1990. A measured process of reform, which is still on going, is aimed at decentralizing and modernizing the Cuban economy to confront the extraordinary challenges of the past decade and to lay the basis for the future. In terms of legal reform, many important modifications have been adopted; yet, there is much to be done to establish the regulatory framework for a decentralized and mixed economy. Cuban lawyers and academics are well aware of the challenges

---

[123] Ley No. 73 (1994).

[124] Ibid., Art. 56 (establishes a social security contribution on the part of workers, but states that implementation of this tax will be by special legislation.) The unions objected to the implementation of this provision since salaries are still not adequate to enable workers to make such payments. As a result, implementation was suspended.

[125] Ibid., Art. 19(a).

[126] In March 1999, there were over 170,000 individuals registered as tax payers. More than 95% had filed their tax returns within the time prescribed by law. "Presentó el 95,39 por ciento de los contribuyentes su Declaración Jurada en tiempo", *Granma*, March 5, 1999, p. 2.

and are hard at work developing their expertise and preparing the legal framework for the implementation of reforms. Over the past decade they have shown both perseverance and creativity in formulating the necessary regulations.

In 1989, outside observers waited impatiently for Cuba to commence its transition to capitalism in the face of the collapse of socialism in Eastern Europe. What has occurred has disappointed many and inspired others: Cuba has embarked on a transition to a new socialist system capable of surviving in a capitalist world. Setting aside theoretical questions concerning the viability of this model, the vicissitudes of the international economy and the continued denial of access to Cuba's most natural market, make the task that much more difficult. While recognizing the limitations to wealth creation presented by this project, Cuban leaders hope to demonstrate that such a system can lift all Cubans out of poverty and satisfy the collective needs and aspirations of the population.

INDEX

www.ingramcontent.com/pod-product-compliance
Lightning Source LLC
Chambersburg PA
CBHW071241230926
51849CB00001B/186